D1452928

THE ORIENTAL

By the same author

A Hundred Years of Ceylon Tea
Chatto & Windus, 1967

1 The Smoking Room, 'Alice' serving

THE ORIENTAL

Life Story of a West End Club

DENYS FORREST

With a Foreword by
Sir Percival Griffiths, K.B.E., C.I.E.

B. T. BATSFORD LTD London

First published 1968
Second edition, with supplement 1979

Printed and bound at William Clowes & Sons Limited,
Beccles and London
for the Publishers B. T. Batsford Ltd
4 Fitzhardinge Street, London W1H 0AH

ISBN 0 7134 2149 5

Foreword

One of the many advantages of the traditional illogicality of the British people is that it enables them to combine gregariousness with the love of privacy. They will, whenever possible, surround themselves with a high wall, but inside the enclosure there must be a few chosen spirits. A club is thus a typically British institution and the only serious problem it presents to its sponsors is that of deciding who is to be admitted into the charmed circle. No such problem perplexed Sir John Malcolm and other distinguished servants of the East India Company when, in February 1824, they met in the rooms of the Royal Asiatic Society to found a club. Like their successors today, they did not fit in easily to English society. Their interests and affections were focused on India, where they had governed vast provinces or commanded great armies. What had they in common with stay-at-home Englishmen whose thoughts were bounded by Brighton or Hampstead! The Oriental Club was therefore to be composed of individuals who had served His Majesty or the East India Company in the East—but an access of liberalism led at once to the enlargement of the magic circle to include persons who had resided or travelled in the East. Fortunately for the future of the Club, a number of leading British businessmen were thus recruited at an early date.

Liberalism, however, is heady wine, and the same breadth of view which had thus been displayed in 1824 soon began to work wonders. In 1843, after a long and anxious debate, guests were allowed to dine in the Club; 40 years later, ladies were admitted between the genteel hours of 4 p.m. and 6 p.m.; and in 1897 the Committee took the daring step of proposing that ladies should be admitted to luncheon. The Committee's progressive ardour was soon checked, and the monstrous proposal was turned down.

In the twentieth century the pattern changed altogether and the Club today owes its prosperity in no small degree to the new life injected into it by the numerous professional and business men, not connected with the East, who have joined it in the last decade or so. Symptomatic of the Club's new attitude is the fact that as Associate Members, ladies now have their own rights in the Club and the considerable use that they make of its facilities has brought new brightness and prosperity to the Club.

The Oriental Club today is in many respects unique and it is indeed fortunate that the task of recounting its history should have been taken up by Denys Forrest. Club histories can be—and usually are—incredibly boring, but this book is fascinating from cover to cover. Forrest possesses the rare gift of combining lightness of touch with depth of research and he allows a delightful sense of humour to play around the whole subject. He has produced not only a Club history, but a vignette of British upper-middle-class social life in the nineteenth and twentieth centuries which should be of considerable interest to the historian. As for Club members present and future, Forrest has placed them under a great obligation.

P. J. Griffiths

Note to Second Edition

With the original edition of *The Oriental* exhausted, and with a continued demand from the general public and in particular from the steady flow of newly-elected members of the Club, it has become necessary to embark on a re-issue.

It was felt by the Committee that the opportunity should be taken to bring the story up to date and that this could best be done by producing a facsimile of the text as it stood, with a few verbal alterations, and asking the author, Denys Forrest, to provide a Supplement which would cover the events of the past decade. It will be found between pages 234 and 249.

It is hoped that in this way *The Oriental* will continue to interest and entertain readers for many years to come.

J. Morris Gifford
Chairman, 1978–79

Contents

Illustrations

Note The portraits are from the Oriental Club's collection. Modern Stratford House interiors by Stewart L. Galloway. Plate 6 reproduced by courtesy of Mr. Geoffrey Fletcher; Plates 7, 10 and 24, Greater London Council; Plates 15, 16 and 18, the British Museum; Plate 17, The Records Office, Guildhall; Plate 20, The Royal Institute of British Architects

Figures in the text

Preface

My first acknowledgment must be to the two men who, in their very different ways, tackled the same job as myself—Alexander Baillie, author of *The Oriental Club and Hanover Square* (1901) and Stephen Wheeler, editor of *Annals of the Oriental Club, 1824–1858* (1925). Their aims and achievements will be described later, and while I shall also have to hint at their limitations, it would be churlish not to record that I wrote the present book with theirs always at my elbow.

Baillie remarks that though he entered upon the work of examining the Club's records with a light heart he soon found he had undertaken 'a serious and not very edifying labour'. By 'not edifying' he evidently meant 'unrewarding' rather than that he was shocked, so at first it was rather depressing to discover that the fact that he had ploughed through some 77 years of documentation was not going to absolve me from doing the same—with another 67 years added. However, the task proved far from boring. The archive consists of the Minutes of the General Committee, preserved in their entirety from 1824 onwards; membership lists from the same period, though with one or two gaps; House Committee Minutes for that body's rather intermittent spells of existence; and various scrap-books and minor documents. Access to them was rendered easy and pleasant through the good-humoured patience of the Secretary to the Club, Mr. R. N. Rapson, M.V.O., who gave me the freedom of his office and helped in a hundred other ways.

To supplement my information, I went outside to the following, among many other bodies, and was always helpfully received: The East India and Sports Club (Mr. J. Gledhill, Secretary) and the United Service Club (Mr. J. C. Allan, Secretary, and Mr. A. Buck, Assistant Secretary); the British Museum (Mr. E. F. Croft-Murray,

C.B.E., Keeper of Prints and Drawings); the National Portrait Gallery (Miss A. M. Wrinch, Assistant Keeper); the India Office Library (Mrs. Archer); The Corporation of London Record Office (Mr. P. E. Jones, Deputy Keeper of the Records); The Royal Institute of British Architects (Mrs. Margaret Richardson, Drawings Collection); the Greater London Council (Mr. B. A. Barker and Mr. Quiney, Historic Buildings Section); the Royal Asiatic Society (Miss Diana Crawford, Secretary); Sir John Soane's Museum (Sir John Summerson, C.B.E., and Miss Dorothy Stroud); the Royal Academy of Music (Mr. W. H. Stack); the St. Marylebone and Westminster Public Libraries; and the London Library. I also received help on architectural or historical points from Mr. Howard Colvin, C.B.E., Sir Francis Dashwood, Bt., Mr. John Cornforth, Mr. Daydon Griffiths (Architect to the Club), from the Oriental's old neighbours in Hanover Square, Messrs. Knight, Frank and Rutley, and from Messrs. Phillips, Sons and Neale.

The long and picturesque history of Stratford House brought me into friendly and fruitful contact with many of the families or organisations which have occupied it in the past. These included: among the descendants or collaterals of the Hon. Edward Stratford (builder of the house), Dr. Esmé Wingfield-Stratford, Sir Edward Verner, Bt., Miss R. W. Verner and Commander Geoffrey Marescaux de Saubruit; for the Leslie ownership, Mr. Seymour Leslie and Sir Shane Leslie, Bt.; for the Colebrookes, the Hon. Lady Packe, daughter of Lord Colebrooke; for Christies' tenancy during World War II, a first-hand narrative from Sir Alec Martin, K.B.E.; for 'Hutchinson House', Miss Katherine Webb; and for Messrs. Birfields' ownership, Mr. H. Hill. The Earl of Derby and the late Randolph Churchill kindly let me quote from the latter's biography of the 17th Earl of Derby, and Mrs. Alix Strachey and Mr. Michael Holroyd from *Lytton Strachey* (vol. II, *The Years of Achievement*). Out of all the above I recall with special relish the animated correspondence of Dr. Wingfield-Stratford and Mr. Seymour Leslie.

For the end of this brief note I have reserved my most warm thanks to my fellow-members of the Oriental Club and to the Club servants. It would be impossible to mention individually all those who gave me information or (even more welcome!) encouragement, but I cannot withhold the names of the Publications Sub-Committee, Messrs. Geoffrey Bozman, C.S.I., C.I.E. (Chairman), Denis Campbell, and Fergus Innes, C.I.E., C.B.E., the last-named being also most helpful in his capacity as Honorary Librarian. My only criticism of the Sub-Committee is that I felt all along that they were being too indulgent to me, and I hope they will not regret their kindness!

D.M.F.

Note

The initials H.E.I.C. have been used from time to time to designate the Honourable East India Company. The symbol (e. . . . .) after the names of some of the more prominent past members indicates their year of election, and *O.C.L.* after the title of a book means that it is in the Library of the Oriental Club. The almost inevitable apology is offered for any inconsistencies in the transliteration of Indian names.

I

HANOVER SQUARE

PROLOGUE

A Club on the Move

On 30 November 1961 the premises of the Oriental Club at 18 Hanover Square were in use for the last time. A member arriving at about 9 p.m. in expectation of some sort of a 'wake', asked the hall porter:

'Many people in the Club?'
'Five gentlemen, I think, sir.'

The member went upstairs, and sure enough there were three gentlemen reading at one end of the great Drawing Room, and two at the other. Perfect silence reigned.

This little scene, besides telling something about the Oriental Club as it used to be, marked an important stage in a story which had begun in 1824, in the London of George IV. Throughout its entire existence (after four tentative years) the Club had inhabited its own freehold building at the north-west corner of Hanover Square. Now it was being expelled by forces which it did not feel well equipped to resist. Yet the moment of departure, though sad, was not tragic. Remarkably enough, the Club discovered at the last moment how to 'roll with the punch' and make the triumphant new beginning which has been the occasion of this book.

Later chapters will show why No. 18 Hanover Square had become untenable. But the main problem of course was economic. As the deficits mounted up, and on a parallel graph property values in the West End rose even more steeply, the most tenaciously conservative member began to ask himself, 'How much longer are we going to sit helpless on this gold mine?'

The thought was not a new one. More than half a century earlier, one of the Club's recurrent financial crises was being discussed in an

Extraordinary General Meeting (31 March 1903). One member pointed out that a hospital building in 'an inferior position in Hanover Square' had just been sold for £40,000, whereas the Clubhouse was still being carried on the books at an 1881 valuation of £36,000. Yes, agreed the Chairman, it was probably worth more like £100,000; in fact a few years before it had been revalued at £78,000, 'but' (he added ingenuously) 'we were recommended not to say anything about it as the tax assessments would go up double'. Even so, there was as yet little support for the idea of selling out and moving, and indeed at many a later time of stress the whole idea was rejected with horror.

Yet the possibility was always there, and in the Club's records one finds a curious recurrence of 'offers' from estate agents which suggest that feelers had been put out. In the late 1920s, in particular, a whole array of alternative premises loom up and disappear—Winchester House, St. James's Square . . . half the site of Grosvenor House . . . 16–17 Bruton Street . . . Brook House, Park Lane . . . and (here we prick up our ears) 'a plan for the site of 17–19 Stratford Place', submitted by Messrs. Knight, Frank and Rutley in January 1929.

All were turned down. Wars and depressions came and went, and the ponderous old structure in which the members felt so happily at home continued to sprawl over its gold-plated site. To the few outsiders who were even aware of its existence, the Oriental seemed more and more of an anachronism in an area which had long since been given over to commerce and which had never been in 'clubland' proper (but there were good reasons for that). It certainly lacked visual charm. 'That the Oriental?', said a taxi-driver. 'It looks so damn dreary I thought it must be the Ministry of Education!'.

By the mid-1950s it was clear that not the Clubhouse but the piece of ground on which it stood—'this blessed plot', as a later chairman lyrically called it—was the members' most precious possession. As in earlier crises, every possible way of 'cashing in' was canvassed round the newly instituted bar[1] below the Grand Staircase. One

[1] The subject of much vain propaganda over the years. When Mr. H. W. Sparkes complained at the 1918 Annual General Meeting that this was the only club in London where you could not get a vermouth and claret on the ground floor, many members sympathised with his views—if not with his choice of tipple.

irreverent spirit would declare—'Why not simply sell the place and divvy up—one could always use the money to get in somewhere else!' More moderate men thought that amalgamation was the ticket, and were not sparing of suggestions for partners. But always the undercurrent was towards keeping the old Club alive and independent, at whatever cost.

This meant one of two alternatives. The first, which has since achieved quite a vogue in the club world, was to get planning permission for an office block to be put on the site, while reserving two or three floors as club premises. A tentative proposal of this kind was actually considered by the 1957–8 Committee under the chairmanship of Sir Robert Hutchings. It had not matured, however, by the time the 1958–9 Committee took over. The new Chairman was Sir Arthur Bruce, who had previously held office in 1954. He and his colleagues were now undertaking what turned out to be a four years' stint, almost entirely concerned with the second solution—to clear right out of Hanover Square and to find (and somehow to finance) alternative shelter elsewhere.

This meant nothing less, of course, than a sortie into the jungle (maybe 'a voyage through the shark-infested seas' would be the more appropriate cliché) of the West End property market, then at its speculative height. One wonders how the Committee would have fared but for the appearance of an expert pilot in the person of Mr. (shortly afterwards Sir) Aynsley Bridgland[1], with whom the Chairman was put into touch by a mutual friend. Sir Aynsley was a property magnate, some of whose earlier ventures were familiar enough to City members of the Club—for example Plantation House and Bucklersbury House, famous respectively for tea auctions and the Temple of Mithras. As one of those concerned in the Oriental deal remarked, neither in his exterior nor his manner of address was Sir Aynsley 'noticeably in the style of a fairy godmother'—but that in fact he became to the Oriental Club.

The task of finding a new home was far from easy. Compared with any period before World War II, this was an inauspicious time to pick up what the Oriental instinctively knew it needed—an

[1] Born 1893. Spent his early life in Australia and was severely wounded while serving with the Anzacs in Gallipoli. Knighted 1959, died 1966.

eighteenth- or early nineteenth-century mansion with dignity and style, yet capable of serving a modern way of life. Such were once plentiful in what Henry James used to call the 'Quadrilateral', bounded by Piccadilly, Park Lane, Oxford Street and Regent Street, but by now commerce had preempted whatever the bombs and bulldozers had left standing. There were slightly better prospects southward in St. James's and northward in Marylebone, and the latter in fact gave the Club its first opening.

It became known during the later part of 1958 that Lord Kemsley might be interested in disposing of Chandos House, the beautiful Adam mansion which he held on long lease from the Howard de Walden Estate. Built in 1769–70 for the 3rd Duke of Chandos, it was occupied in the early nineteenth century by the Austrian Ambassador, Prince Esterhazy, of whom we shall hear more. Chandos House had much to offer the Oriental Club—fine entertaining rooms (carefully restored by Lord and Lady Kemsley), a rear wing which could be adapted to provide extra bedrooms, and a location, in the angle between Cavendish Square and Portland Place, only slightly less convenient for the members than Hanover Square.

The negotiations were arduous, but they went far enough to justify a closer look at how best to realise the value of the old site. Sir Aynsley and the Committee were now convinced that simply to sell to a third party would be throwing money away, and that if any other structure were to go up the Oriental itself should build it and retain the freehold. It was estimated that this, together with the purchase and conversion of Chandos House, would cost about £800,000. An interesting operation for an old-fashioned club with less than 1,300 members, a total annual budget of £37,000, a deficit in 1957 of £4,000 and a bank overdraft of £14,000! It is true that a hard drive for efficiency had brought the revenue account back to a narrow surplus in 1959, but this was no more than a holding operation until the full financial miracle could be achieved.

This did not in fact happen until negotiations over Chandos House had broken down in July 1959—a simple matter of one side not being prepared to give as much as the other thought their property was worth! The search was resumed, and in March 1960 the news came in that the firm of Messrs. Birfield Ltd. wished to dispose of their freehold property, Stratford House. This seemed to have everything. It was little behind Chandos House in architectural panache and well ahead of it historically; there was just as much scope for bedroom-building; the location, at the end of a cul-de-sac opposite Bond Street tube station, combined a measure of privacy with excellent communications, especially to the City. The cost of the total transaction had now gone up to over a million pounds!

Yet the money was found. After the Club's bankers, the Westminster, had granted temporary cover, the Legal and General Assurance Society agreed to take a head lease of the building which the Club was planning to put up in Hanover Square, the *quid pro quo* being enough cash to finance the whole operation, plus a substantial ground rent. The lease was to be for a period finally agreed at 120 years, and the exact amount of the cash settlement was to depend on whether the Club could find a single sub-tenant to occupy the whole building and thereby to ease the management problem of the head lessees.

Anxious times—the spectre of a new office block remaining empty for months, even years, on end was only too familiar! But the Club was lucky enough to be caught up in one of those great tidal waves of change which pass over the commercial face of London from time to time—in this case the drift of the textile trades from the neighbourhood of St. Paul's Churchyard to that of Oxford Circus. British Celanese were already established on the south-west corner of Hanover Square, but the head office of the Courtauld group to which it belonged was still marooned at St. Martin's-le-Grand. It was in January 1961, with the Club already committed to Stratford House and the dust rising from the demolition of 18 Hanover Square, that the first hint came that Courtaulds might be on the move, and more than a year longer before the deal was clinched whereby they became sole occupants of the Oriental Club's new Hanover Square block.

Considering their commitments, the members showed laudable phlegm—and the Committee laudable wisdom in keeping them in touch and avoiding the formation of hostile cabals! There were two crucial Extraordinary General Meetings, one in January 1960, in the 'dead' period between Chandos House and Stratford House, and the other in November 1960, when the full package deal had to be approved. Each time the Committee received sweeping votes of confidence; on the second occasion, when proxy votes were allowed, the verdict was 844 For, 5 Against. Only a few purists doubted. It was at this second meeting, I think, that a member arose and delivered a stern attack on 'speculative finance'. One of those present whispered to his neighbour,

> 'Who is that man who looks and talks like Gladstone?'
> 'Gladstone.'

And in fact the spokesman for orthodoxy was Sir Albert Gladstone, Bt. (e. 1920) a grandson of the G.O.M. and a faithful member of the Club until his death in 1967.

So far as the old Clubhouse was concerned, there was not even the muted protest which usually arises when any familiar London building is under sentence. The then L.C.C. had it is true struck a faint blow for the residential character (long since vanished) of Hanover Square by insisting that no building on the site should have a floor area of more than five times in excess of the ground plot, and that not less than 30 per cent of the space should be used for some residential purpose. However, this was got over by an ingenious 'swop'; Stratford House already carried a commercial 'user' and the L.C.C. agreed that this should be transferred to Hanover Square, provided that Stratford House became and should remain wholly residential.

Poor No. 18. Too late architecturally to arouse the protective instincts of the Georgian Society, too early to benefit from the recently generated interest in Victoriana, it was indeed a poor relation to its supplanter Stratford House, which gloried in a comprehensive Protection Order. No. 18 perished in a carve-up in which there were no losers—least of all the members of the Oriental Club, who could make a fresh start, free from mortgage or overdraft, with a steady income assured and (if clubs, squares, freeholds, property itself, London itself, still exist 120 years hence) the prospect of eventually having at their disposal the unencumbered freeholds of two fine West End buildings.

Very justly, they made Sir Aynsley Bridgland an Honorary Life

Member; presented their unwearying Secretary, Brigadier R. G. W. Callaghan, with a gold watch; and, when they moved into Stratford Place, hung on the staircase a portrait of the 1958–62 Chairman, Sir Arthur Bruce[1], and a plaque with the names of his Committee colleagues (Appendix III).

They had not only saved the Oriental, but had set in motion the vast task of giving it fresh life in a new and beautiful setting. They deserve a salutation from every reader of the tale which follows.

[1] Sir Arthur was also made an Honorary Life Member.

1 Servants of the Company

> I suppose with our tradition of Wellington it may be said we were born when Mars was in the ascendant, and it could equally be said, looking at the grey hairs of some of us, we are living when Venus is in the descendant!
>
> *Sir Henry Wheeler, at the Annual General Meeting, 1940*

The founders of clubs do not as a rule keep one eye cocked towards posterity. They are too busy bringing their brain-child to birth to speculate how long it will live, whether one day someone may wish to compile its history, and what future generations will think about themselves and their motives. So they have seldom left much documentation behind. A prospectus, perhaps, membership lists, committee minutes which from Day One are concerned with the minutiae of amateur house-keeping rather than with statements of principle—that is the most one can hope for. In some instances, indeed, it is impossible now to determine what brought the original members together; their impulse to form a club seems to have been as vague as Dr. Johnson's definition of one—'An assembly of good fellows meeting under certain conditions'.

The Oriental at least fulfilled a distinctive need. The condition of the expatriate returning to these shores has always been uneasy, but particularly for those who have spent their working lives in the East. This is perceptible today, in spite of air travel, more frequent leaves and business flights home, and the spread of what may be called an 'air-conditioned' way of life into the far corners of the globe. Even when his pension or investments are secure (not always the case!), the middle-aged official, businessman or planter near the end of his time is more often than not a worried man—he just cannot envisage where he and his family are going to find a niche at home, or how they are going to fit into it.

In one direction, the contrast between East and West may be thought to have sharpened. This is in the matter of domestic service, or as more vaguely phrased nowadays, 'help in the house'. Even in the East it is less lavishly available than of old, but it exists there all the same, whereas in their mental picture of an austere Britain, the homeward-coming family usually seems to give the most prominent place to 'washing up'.

Yet the curious fact remains that it was the supposed contrast between the luxury of Eastern living and the hardships to be expected in the Britain of 1824 which weighed most with those who brought the Oriental into being. The 'nabob' with his country estate, troop of servants and ostentatious equipage, was a minority figure! I owe to my predecessor, Alexander Baillie, a very relevant quotation from the *East India Military Calendar* for that year. This implies that it was only the prospect offered them by the Oriental Club of being able to live in London with 'that respectability and those comforts which their station in society renders so essential', that saved many 'Indians'[1] from prolonging their residence in the East and thereby shortening their lives!

It is worth while to look at the background of these men more closely. By far the greater number of them were servants of the East India Company, whether civil or military, but with the latter predominating. Brief biographies of about a third of the Club's 'Original Members' (see page 27) are included in *Annals of the Oriental Club* by my other predecessor, Stephen Wheeler, and, according to a rough analysis I have made, 66 of them were military officers, 32 were Civil Servants, 11 were merchants and 12 come into the 'miscellaneous' column. A further analysis shows that of the soldiers, the majority were 'Company's' officers, i.e. they were employed by the East India Company and not directly by the Crown. These men had strong feelings of inferiority *vis-à-vis* the 'King's officer', especially after they had come home—their military rank

[1] The term 'Indian' for the British resident in the East was common during the eighteenth and early nineteenth centuries. Later it was superseded by 'Anglo-Indian', which in our own time has become attached to what used to be called the 'Eurasian' community, and no convenient substitute has emerged.

gained them no precedence, they were excluded from the higher reaches of the Honours List, and their services, however illustrious, were unlikely to be crowned with the Governorships and other posts of distinction which the times afforded.

Club life would naturally appeal to such men, yet they could not even be sure of finding a congenial home among the limited number of clubs available. Left over, so to speak, from the eighteenth century were the great political and gaming clubs such as Brooks' and White's, and to these few East India Company servants could aspire. Of more recent growth, and a good deal more accessible, were the Union (founded c. 1799), the Alfred (1808) and the Travellers' (1819), but for naval and military officers as such there were only the Guards (1810) and the United Service (1815).

It has sometimes been suggested that the founding of the Oriental was directly due to Company officers not being eligible for the United Service—'The Senior', as it is known today. That is not so. This 'general military club' was launched at a meeting at the Thatched House Tavern on 31 May 1815, and the third and fourth clauses of the resolution then passed specifically stated that 'general and field officers of the East India Company's Service' should be eligible and that one or more officers of that Service should be asked to join the Committee. Within a month, Major-General Alexander Dyce, Colonel Sir John Malcolm and Colonel A. Allen had accepted invitations, and Lieut.-General Orr was co-opted soon afterwards. The question remains whether this high-level representation protected less eminent Company officers when it came to the ballot, or prevented some 'cold-shouldering' afterwards; there is at least no evidence that they were 'blackballed wholesale', as is said to have happened at the Junior United Service (founded 1827)[1]. But it is significant that a word-of-mouth tradition exists in the Oriental that the Duke of Wellington gave its originators two pieces of advice: 'Have a club of your own' and 'Buy the freehold'.

[1] Cf. *Asiatic Journal*, July 1831, quoting a 'London paper':
'Six officers of the East India Company's Service have been blackballed at the Junior United Service Club. The regular army appears to view them only in the light of militia or yeomanry officers.'
The *Asiatic Journal* adds: 'We can scarcely credit the statement as regards the principle of exclusion.'

Typical of the great man's terse common sense. Yet it might never have been translated into action, had not Sir John Malcolm, one of his old comrades of Indian days, been becalmed, so to speak, in England during the 1820s.

John Malcolm came of a potent and prolific tribe. He was the fourth of 10 sons of George Malcolm of Burnfoot, Dumfries, by his wife Margaret, sister of Admiral Sir Robert Pasley, Bt. There were also seven daughters. Most of the boys entered the public service and rose high in it. Three if not four, were founder-members of the Oriental Club—Admiral Sir Pulteney Malcolm (1768–1838), the third son; Sir John, the fourth; Vice-Admiral Sir Charles Malcolm (1782–1851), the tenth; and possibly David, the eighth, who died in India in 1826 and who may have been the 'David Malcolm Esq.', whose subscriptions are recorded for the years 1824 and 1825.

The portrait by Samuel Lane which now hangs on the Stratford House staircase and is reproduced in Pl. 3 does not, especially in its truncated state, give a complete impression of Sir John Malcolm's personality, as it has come down to us[1]. He was one of those men to whom the fine word 'exuberant' aptly applies. He was tall, he was corpulent, he talked a lot, laughed a lot, ate and drank a lot. But he also had the knack of getting along happily with colleagues and superiors—and the latter included at various periods General (later Field-Marshal) Sir Alured Clarke, Commander-in-Chief, Madras, whom he happened to meet on a voyage to India; the Marquess Wellesley, Governor-General; and the latter's brother, the future Duke of Wellington.

Yet in spite of services which included two famous missions to Persia (1799 and 1810) and warlike feats at the capture of Seringapatam (1799) and in the third and fourth Mahratta Wars, Malcolm was again and again disappointed of the high office which he felt had become his due. His membership of the original Committee of the Senior only lasted a year, as he had to go abroad again, though his brother Sir Pulteney took his place and was in fact Chairman in 1826. By 1822, John Malcolm was settled in England, apparently for

[1] The principal authority, among many, is John William Kaye, *The Life and Correspondence of Major-General Sir John Malcolm G.C.B.* (London, Smith Elder, 1861) (O.C.L.).

good, occupying first a cottage at Frant near Tonbridge and later Hyde Hall in Hertfordshire. It was at this stage when, for all his social gifts and bubbling zest for life, he was obviously sharing the disillusionment which we have already noted as the lot of the returned 'Indian', that he took a leading part in providing a remedy—or at least an alleviation—by the foundation of the Oriental Club.

Alexander Baillie's account of this event as given in Chapter II of *The Oriental Club and Hanover Square* is useful, but not quite explicit. He says the Club was probably conceived 'in the rooms of the Royal Asiatic Society'. Here a meeting was held on 24 February 1824, under the presidency of Sir John Malcolm, and a resolution was carried:

> That it appears to this meeting to be desirable to form a society on the plan set forth in the following prospectus, to be called the *Oriental Club*, to issue a prospectus and to nominate a committee.

It was announced that His Grace the Duke of Wellington was prepared to accept the Presidency of the Club, Sir John Malcolm was elected Chairman, and a numerous and impressive Committee was formed.

This Committee, however, was only an enlargement of one which had already come into being at a meeting on 17 February. A Sub-Committee then appointed to draw up the Prospectus was full of interesting names. Apart from Sir John Malcolm himself, it included Major James Rivett Carnac, future Governor of Bombay; Major-General Robert Haldane, an old comrade-in-arms of Malcolm's; Sir George Staunton, Bt., eminent authority on China and co-founder of the Royal Asiatic Society; Thomas Snodgrass (*Pl. 4*), hero of an immortal feud with the East India Company over his pension[1]; and 'Andrew Macklew Esq.'. The latter interests us in a negative sort of way since he seems to have had no ascertainable

[1] Mr. Snodgrass was Collector at Ganjam, in the Madras Presidency, between 1790 and 1800. Suspected of having lined his pockets too well, he was asked to produce his accounts to the Court of the H.E.I.C. He set off by water from Rhamba, where he was then living, but alleged that all his books were lost by the upsetting of the boat on Chilka Lake. As the lake is nowhere more than six feet deep, this did not create a favourable impression and Mr. Snodgrass was struck off the List, without pension. The subsequent scene of comedy, when the still opulent ex-Collector set up as a crossing-sweeper in front of East India House, thereby shaming the Court into restoring his pension, has often been described.

Indian connections (except perhaps as a holder of East India Company stock), yet the next few committee meetings were held at his house[1], and whenever money was to be raised or debentures to be issued, he was always to the fore.

The signatories of the document produced by this group are listed in Appendix I. The Prospectus is very much of its time. 'The British Empire in the East', it announces, 'is now so extensive, and the persons connected with it so numerous, that the establishment of an institution where they may meet on a footing of social intercourse seems particularly desirable.' The members of the Club, it is hoped, would not only be in touch with old friends and 'keep up their knowledge of the actual state of our Eastern Empire', but would have the opportunity of 'forming acquaintances and connections in their own country'. There was a third, rather vague, rather pious aspiration, that of acting as a sort of Asiatic Information Bureau for people wanting to study conditions in the East, especially those 'officially connected with our Governments abroad'. I suspect that this gesture, which was not at all what a club is about, was merely an attempt to keep on level terms with the Royal Asiatic Society.

For the rest, the Prospectus was a commonsensical production. Its first clause deals with the finding of a suitable house; the second promises economy and sets out the fees; the third adumbrates a reading room and library; the fourth returns to economy, this time in the management of the Coffee Room; the fifth promises 'occasional' House dinners; the sixth introduces the question of qualifications for membership. But here there was a manifest muddle. Comparing this sixth clause with one near the foot of the Prospectus, it would almost seem that alternative drafts found their way into the same document—not the only time that such a thing has happened! According to the first, the qualifications are:

> Having been resident or employed in the public service of His Majesty, or the East India Company, in any part of the East; belonging to the Royal Asiatic Society, being officially connected with the administration of our Eastern Governments abroad or at home.

[1] In the subscription lists Mr. Macklew's address is given as 'No. IN Albany', which confirms one's impression of him as a well-off, unattached bachelor. But perhaps he had a 'house' as well?

The second offers much wider scope. In addition to the Royal Asiatic Society, mention is made of Bengal, Bombay, India and China Club members[1] being invited to join the Oriental and goes on, ungrammatically, but quite clearly:

> That all persons who have resided or travelled or whose official situations connect them with that quarter of the globe, be considered eligible to become members.

The entrance fee was fixed at £15 and the annual subscription at £6, but within a year it was realised that funds were going to be inadequate, and a general meeting on 14 February 1825, agreed an increase to £20 and £8 respectively. The new scale held good for 57 years.

Eighteen months were allowed for gentlemen residing in the East to become Original Members on the old terms, and it was provided that they (or anyone else if stationed abroad on the public service), should be reckoned as 'supernumeraries', paying the entrance fee but no subscription until they came home and began to use the Club. This led to an entertaining feature of the Oriental's first half-century of history—the extraordinary vagueness on all hands as to who were members and who were not. 'Gentlemen residing in the East' would apply for admission. Sooner or later the news would seep through to them that they had or had not been elected. If successful, they would tell Captain Grindlay or some other agent to pay the entrance fee and then (provided they did not die of cholera or retire permanently to Ootacamund) would eventually come home, with their membership of the Oriental Club glowing on the horizon.

The results of all this can be imagined. It took Captain Roe until May 1830 to discover that his application to become an Original Member, transmitted through Messrs. Remington & Co. in 1825, had miscarried. In August 1849 Mr. Bannerman (Madras C.S.) walked confidently into the Club, only to be told that his application for membership had been withdrawn in 1837, without his knowledge. Ten years later Sir Charles Grey, an Original Member, came home for the first time since the Club was founded, and was quite

[1] These so-called clubs were really associations of interested people, maintaining an office and perhaps a reading room in London.

shocked to find that his name had been removed from the books 18 years before.

Contrariwise, the absent-minded Mr. E. H. C. Monckton, when dunned for his subscription, replied that he had never entered No. 18, for the reason that 'subsequent to becoming a member he discovered that he never intended to join, but had done so under the belief that it was the same as the East India Service Club'. He asked to have his entrance money and subscription returned, but this was refused. Sir Colin Campbell (a future Governor of Ceylon), similarly dunned, was quite sure he was not a member at all, and we hear of one of India's many Arbuthnots dining with a friend in the Strangers' Room and '*accidentally discovering*' that somehow, sometime, he had been elected.

Perhaps the most extreme case was that of Lieut.-Colonel James Alexander of the Bengal Horse Artillery. He mounted the steps of 18 Hanover Square one Tuesday morning in 1854 and (no doubt offended at not being recognised) told the Hall Porter firmly that he was a member of the Club, though it did happen that he had been absent from England since 1831. This veteran of the Afghanistan and First Sikh Wars was in fact elected in 1829, and his name had been taken off the supplementary list by mistake in the meanwhile[1].

One cause of muddle was the arrangement whereby the Committee had been empowered to elect Original Members up to a maximum of 400 without recourse to ballot, and to send the Prospectus to a certain number of specified high officials of the East India Company, in some cases with, in others without, an invitation to join. Mr. James Erskine, thwarted in an attempt to make use of the Clubhouse in 1842, declared that he had been nominated by Sir Mountstuart Elphinstone four years before, and in any case Sir John Malcolm himself had given him the impression that, as a Servant of the H.E.I.C., he was automatically entitled to Oriental Club membership. Mr. Erskine in fact was very cross indeed—

[1] At least one non-existent gentleman managed to get himself proposed, seconded and elected. He bore the convincing name of John Power Eyre, and the Committee was quite upset when a letter asking for his subscription was returned 'not known'. Eventually, however, his proposer, Mr. Boyd, revealed that the friend he had put up was John Power Esq. of the Bengal Civil Service—'"Esqre" in Mr. Boyd's letter being mistaken for "Eyre" which it greatly resembled.' (Minute of 5 September 1859).

threatened to tell his friends in India about 'the mode in which affairs are conducted at the Club', etc., etc. He was never elected.

Delicate questions of eligibility arose, and time has blurred the logic of some of the decisions. Why for example, was a Writer who had never been in India accepted in June 1825, whereas a pensioner of East India House had been turned down only two months before? The pressure of sheer numbers to be dealt with probably had something to do with it. 'Upwards of 300' applications had been sufficient to give the Committee their go-ahead in March 1824; this had swollen to 540 at the first General Meeting on 7 June, and a year later the nominal maximum membership of 600 had been exceeded by 144. To cope with this influx, as well as to carry on the day-to-day management of the Club, the Committee had in April 1824 appointed as its first secretary Mr. Thomas Cornish. He was a harassed man, and not over-remunerated with a salary of £200, in return for which he was to 'give up the whole of his time to the service of the Club, and not to hold any other situation'.

Mr. Cornish had a high-powered—and by tradition an irascible—set of members to deal with. Many of their names are to be found in the list of the original Committee men in Appendix I; others were exalted back-benchers. At the head stood His Grace the Duke of Wellington, K.G., not only the greatest soldier but also the most inveterate clubman of his day. Established clubs delighted to lure him in; new clubs deemed his sponsorship essential. I have traced him at the Athenaeum, Army and Navy, Carlton, City of London (not his milieu, one would think), Crockfords (where he gambled, but with Wellingtonian caution), Oxford and Cambridge, Union, United Service and United Universities—and no doubt the list is incomplete. Yet so far as the Oriental is concerned, he was no honorary figurehead. He paid his annual subscription regularly—in fact one year he paid it twice, and claimed a refund. He continued on the books until that day in September 1852 when

The Committee, trusting to the general concurrence of the members of the Club, have given directions that the blinds of the public rooms of the Club be lowered during the funeral ceremony of His Grace the Duke of Wellington.

The Club never had another President, nor any Vice-President except Sir John Malcolm, who accepted that office in March 1824. A list of names quickly becomes monotonous, but a few Original Members cannot be passed over. For example, the Rt. Hon. Lord William Bentinck, a past governor of Madras and future Governor-General of India at the time when he joined the first Committee; Vice-Admiral Sir Henry Blackwood, that same heroic Captain to whom Nelson murmured on the *Victory*'s quarter-deck 'God bless you, Blackwood, I shall never speak to you again'; two more of Nelson's band of brothers, Sir Philip Durham and Viscount Exmouth (P. B. Pellew when elected); General Viscount Beresford, the victor of Albuera; two future Field-Marshals, Sir Alured Clarke and Sir George Nugent; Sir Stamford Raffles, founder of Singapore—but he resigned after a year. And so the roll-call goes.

A celebrity to whom Alexander Baillie devotes a lot of space is Sir Hudson Lowe. When the Club was founded he was Second-in-Command of the forces in Ceylon. He is not recorded by Wheeler as an Original Member, but the Subscription Book for 1826 clearly dates his election from 5 July 1824. Baillie imagines a scene in the Club Library in the early thirties, where he brings together two Malcolms (Sir John and Sir Pulteney), Sir Hudson Lowe and Major Basil Jackson:

> Sir John . . . is seated at a table writing one of his political essays on the government of India, and at another opposite to him Sir Hudson Lowe is employed, as usual, in memorializing the British Government with regard to his claims for pension and compensation. Between the two, up and down the long room, stalks the tall broad figure of Sir Pulteney as though he were tramping the quarter-deck of his flag-ship, and every now and then he halts to reply to some query addressed to him by Lowe, relative to incidents that occurred when years ago the two were employed in maintaining strict guard in and around the island of St. Helena over the mighty but fallen conqueror, the Great Napoleon; or perhaps he turns to a younger man who is standing at the window looking down into Tenterden Street, Major Basil Jackson, of the Royal Staff Corps, who probably had more frequent communication with the Emperor than either of his superior officers[1].

[1] Sir Pulteney was Commander-in-Chief on the St. Helena station 1816–17 and Sir Hudson was Governor of the island 1815–21. Major Jackson, who was in the Quartermaster-General's department and was constantly on duty at Longwood,

A picturesque confrontation, indeed; one is tempted to cap it with another and perhaps less fanciful conversation piece of the same period, bringing together three Malcolms—Sir John, Sir Pulteney and their brother Sir Charles—and Lord William Bentinck. The subject? Steam navigation and the route to India! It is a fact that the so-called Overland Route (via Egypt) got its greatest impetus from a unique 'chain of command' round about 1830 when Sir John was Governor of Bombay, Sir Charles Superintendent of the Indian Navy and Sir Pulteney C-in-C Mediterranean. As for Lord William, he was an enthusiastic 'overlander' throughout his term as Governor-General (1827–35)[1].

Yet in leafing through the old subscription books, one's eye is caught and imagination wakened not so much by the scattered names of Governors-General and Commanders-in-Chief, as by the continuing dynasties which have kept the Club in touch with the Eastern world for nearly a century and a half. The Stracheys for example—seven listed by Wheeler and others unrecorded by him, and all descendants or collaterals of Sir Richard Strachey, the 1st Baronet, who was the confidential secretary of Clive.

We meet Henry, the judge and 2nd Baronet; Edward his brother, another Judge; Edward's sons—Henry the traveller, John and Richard members of Council, and the less conspicuous William. The family link is unbroken to this day, because although the last full member was Mr. Oliver Strachey (d. 1957), his daughter Mrs. Halpern remains an Associate Member. Nearly half a century ago, however, the connection took a somewhat off-beat turn with the election of the writer Lytton Strachey. He had started his London club life at the Savile in 1911, and it is most interesting psychologically that in moving to the Oriental in February 1922 he should have thus deserted his intellectual for his ancestral milieu. A characteristic letter to Virginia Woolf (6 February 1922) marks the occasion:

A vast hideous building... filled with vast hideous Anglo-Indians,

had a family connection with Lowe—his daughter married one of Lowe's sons. To Baillie it was a haunting memory that he had 'frequently conversed with a man who had stood in the presence of the great Napoleon'.

[1] See H. L. Hoskins, *British Routes to India* (Longmans Green, 1928, reprinted by Frank Cass, 1966).

very old and very rich. One becomes 65 [*he was then 42*] with an income of 5,000 a year directly one enters it. One is so stout that one can hardly walk, and one's brain works with extraordinary slowness. Just the place for me, you see, in my present condition. I pass almost unnoticed with my glazed eyes and white hair, as I sink into a leather chair heavily, with a copy of the *Field* in hand. Excellent claret too—one of the best cellars in London, by Jove![1]

Vintage Strachey, yet the Oriental seems to have suited him perfectly; he used it all the rest of his life, presented the Library with copies of his books as they came out, and left a kindly memory among the Club servants.

Almost as prevalent as Stracheys have been Colvins, mainly representing the merchant interest[2], from 'David Colvin Esq.' on the original Committee, through his brothers and nephews, but with at least one great civil servant in the family tree. This was John Colvin, Lieut.-Governor of the North-West Province at the time of the Mutiny, which to all intents and purposes killed him. Other mercantile names of the time are those of James Pattle of Calcutta (father of that galaxy of beauty and brains, the Pattle sisters), Sir Charles Forbes, Bt., of Bombay, and William Binny of Madras, a Colvin connection by marriage, who was nominated along with two other merchants by 'Mr. Arbuthnot' in December of the same year. The Arbuthnots themselves provide a bewildering tangle of relationships. At least 11 joined in the first 30 years, three of them as Original Members, the 'common denominator' being George Arbuthnot of Elderslie (1772–1843), founder of the historic house of Arbuthnot & Co., Madras.

As clubmen, these bearers of great names slip in and out of the records just like the generality of mankind—Arbuthnots complaining and suggesting, Colvins untiring on the Committee, two Stracheys (Sir Henry and Richard) falling victims to a 'blitz' in

[1] Michael Holroyd, *Lytton Strachey*, vol. II, *The Years of Achievement* (London, Heinemann, 1968) (O.C.L.).

[2] The Calcutta firm of Colvin, Ainslie and Cowie was founded by Alexander Colvin, a Stirlingshire man, in about 1778. David was one of his seven brothers. Other early Oriental Club Colvins included Bazett, Binny and the famous John, all sons of another brother, James, and two sons of a fourth brother, Thomas. The Colvin connection with the Club continued unbroken until 1965.

1831, when 35 subscription defaulters were swept off the books at one stroke (most of them were reinstated later on paying up).

It should never be forgotten that between the time of Clive to the Mutiny, the East India Company steadily attracted into its service the intellectuals and men of action of a great epoch, and from them the bulk of the Original Members were drawn. The gossip writers' conventionalised image of them, even in their retirement, must have been in large part a caricature. Maybe the Oriental Club *was* a 'nabobery'. But it was certainly something much more than what the *New Monthly Magazine* called it in 1834:

> A hospital in which a smell of curry powder pervades the wards—wards filled with venerable patients dressed in nankeen shirts, yellow stockings and gaiters, and faces to match . . . the region of calico shirts, returned Writers, and guinea-pigs grown into bores.

However, we are getting a little ahead of ourselves chronologically; we have not yet provided the 'hospital' with four walls.

2 *Grosvenor Street to Hanover Square*

The house is remarkable for nothing but the smallness of its windows. The tender plants within could not bear much of the London atmosphere being blown in upon them.

New Monthly Magazine, 1835

The architect of today is, or is supposed to be, a reticent professional gentlemen who, if he finds it desirable to canvass for business at all, does so only by discreet 'won't-you-have-lunch-with-me-one-day' telephone calls to old friends. Not so in 1824. As we have seen, the Oriental Club prospectus was only issued at the end of February. By 22 March the Committee had received communications from five gentlemen 'requesting to be appointed architects to the Club'—Mr. Basevi, Mr. Thomson, Mr. Vulliamy, Mr. Wyatt and Mr. Poynter. Four out of the five were to have distinguished futures. Apart from Basevi and Wyatt—'of whom presently', as the genealogists say—Lewis Vulliamy (1791–1871) was an eclectic designer whose most massive, though not his most enduring monument was old Dorchester House, Park Lane. Ambrose Poynter (1796–1886) favoured the Gothic, with results which may still be seen in the St. Katherine Hospital building, Regent's Park. Only Mr. Thomson remains in the shadows—perhaps he was the J. W. Thomson to whom Mr. Colvin's *Biographical Dictionary*[1] fleetingly refers.

No more is heard of these three in Oriental Club annals, but Basevi and Wyatt pervade the early phases.

George Basevi (1794–1845) was a pupil of Sir John Soane, architect of the Bank of England and of the Dulwich Art Gallery and

[1] H. M. Colvin, *A Biographical Dictionary of English Architects 1660–1840* (London, John Murray, 1956).

Mausoleum, and inherited much of his mentor's classical theory. His own surviving masterpiece is the Fitzwilliam Museum at Cambridge, left unfinished when he was killed by a fall while surveying the lantern of Ely Cathedral in company with the young Gilbert Scott. Some have felt that the wrong architect was spared . . .

The 'Wyatt' in the case was Benjamin Deane (?1775–1850), eldest son of that controversial genius James Wyatt, creator of Fonthill and Ashridge and merciless 'scraper' of Salisbury Cathedral. Benjamin's early life is of much significance to us. Educated at Westminster and Christ Church, he was in debt when he came down from Oxford. Perhaps for that reason, his father used his influence with Queen Charlotte to get him a Writership with the East India Company and in 1798 he set off to Calcutta in the company of his brother Charles[1]. Very soon he found a niche in the large and brilliant private office of the Governor-General, the Marquess Wellesley[2]. He could not possibly have been Private Secretary, as has been stated, since this highly important post was occupied at that time by Wellesley's brother Henry (Lord Cowley to be) and was taken over in 1801 by Captain John Malcolm, the future Sir John and founder of the Oriental Club!

On leave in England in 1802, Benjamin managed to produce a medical certificate to the effect that a return to India would be injurious to his health. Instead, he got himself a job, this time as full-blown Private Secretary, with Wellesley's brother Sir Arthur, then working his way patiently up the ladder, at the top of which he would later stand as the greatest subject of the Crown, Field-Marshal The Duke of Wellington. He was soon to proceed to Ireland as Chief Secretary, but it must be remembered that when Wyatt was serving under Lord Wellesley, Sir Arthur—no less than his brother Henry and John Malcolm—was part of the formidable 'in-group' round the Governor-General, the humblest member of which had the chance of cultivating enough 'interest' to last him a lifetime.

Sir Arthur Wellesley's Irish appointment lasted till 1809 and how

[1] Not the accomplished creator of Government House, Calcutta—that Charles Wyatt was a cousin.

[2] Lord Mornington until 1799.

Benjamin Wyatt passed the few years after that we do not know. But eventually the family profession called, and with as little architectural training as Sir John Vanbrugh, he obtained a hardly less conspicuous first commission than Castle Howard. In 1811 he sent in a competition design for Drury Lane Theatre, and won it. Nor was this a matter of paternal influence; James Wyatt passionately wanted the job for another of his sons, Philip.

It will be seen that George Basevi had powerful forces to contend with when he competed against Benjamin Wyatt for the favours of the Oriental Club. However, it was he who made the running. Both men were acting, quite frankly, as house agents as well as architects *in potentia*. On 9 April 1824 Basevi delivered to the Committee plans 'relative to No. 6 Grafton Street'; also proposals on behalf of Messrs. Seddons, of Aldersgate[1], for letting their premises at 16 Lower Grosvenor Street furnished to the Club for one or two years.

The other propositions were tabled at the same time. One was from a somewhat prophetic quarter—Mr. Blake of the Brunswick Hotel, Hanover Square, offered to let his establishment to the Club for as long as they liked. The other involved a lien on a site at the corner of Margaret Street. But on 17 April it was decided that it was 'not desirable to build at present', and negotiations were begun with Seddons to lease the upper portion of their premises at £1,200 for one year or £2,300 for two. Final agreement was reported at a General Meeting on 7 June, but members were warned that it would be impossible to open until July because of constructing a new staircase and other works.

Anyone wishing to see the exterior of the Club's very first home can still do so by walking down Bond Street and turning right into Grosvenor Street. No. 16 (there is no 'Lower' Grosvenor Street now) remains the solid red-brick building 'having all the appearance of a barrack' which Baillie describes.

But it has now lost by reconstruction of the ground floor the particular feature on which he expatiates, and for which the Club was responsible. This was a pair of identical porticoes closely adjoining

[1] Fashionable upholsterers of the period. The firm, which changed its title on several occasions, derived from George Seddons, a contemporary of Chippendale.

at the east end. In Baillie's day the house was occupied by the piano-forte manufacturers, Collard & Collard, and he says that the then Mr. Collard had always been puzzled by the duplication of doors. The explanation was that, when the Club took over the upper part of the building, Seddons insisted that they must construct a separate entrance, and the additional staircase referred to above.

It is significant, perhaps, that Messrs. Seddons already enjoyed a snug connection with both actual and imaginary nabobs. William Hickey[1] lamented having to dispose of an excellent billiard table 'made by the famous Seddons', when he left Calcutta in January 1808; while Jos Sedley[2], retired from Boggley Wollah, adorned his house in Gillespie Street with Seddons 'carpets, costly mirrors and handsome and appropriately planned furniture'.

We know comparatively little about the Club's daily life in its Grosvenor Street phase, which was eventually extended until mid-1828. Most of the Committee's energies were devoted to the admission of members, the collection of a staff, and the search for a permanent home. Candidates continued to flock in, and a few of the names are still resonant. Lieut. James Brooke (e. 1826) . . . yes, that is the future founder of the famous Sarawak dynasty, but as yet only a Bengal Infantry subaltern; Lieut.-Colonel George de Lacy Evans (e. 1825) . . . veteran of the Peninsula and Waterloo, will die General Sir George after the Crimea; Captain George Everest, Bengal Artillery (e. 1827) . . . as Surveyor-General of India will be Sir George also, but it is his surname that will over-top the world; Lieut.-Colonel James Lushington (e. 1825) . . . triply distinguished as cavalryman, East India Company Chairman and M.P., the first of his great clan to join the Oriental. And many others, destined to future fame and then to the obscurity which has fallen upon all except the greatest of those who served Britain in the East.

In the previous chapter I recorded the appointment of the Club's first Secretary. He was immediately faced by the job of advertising for and vetting a complete staff. By 12 July 1824, the House Committee could report to the General Committee that the establishment

[1] *Memoirs of William Hickey*, ed. Alfred Spencer (London, Hurst and Blackett, 1919) (O.C.L.)
[2] *Vanity Fair*, Chapter LX.

was as follows: Steward (£200 a year), Butler (£100), Cook (£130), five Waiters (£25 each), Hall Porter (£25), Housekeeper (£50), Stillroom Woman (£20), Woman Cook (£40), Kitchen Maid (£15), Scullery Woman (£12), two Housemaids (£14 each), Girl in the Bar (£10).

Out of this inaugural team we only know two by name. The Steward was Mr. Pottanco, mentioned variously as 'for many years in the employment of Sir John Malcolm' and as 'chef to a line of Indian Governors'. That he was Malcolm's nominee there is no doubt, for when Sir John went back to India as Governor of Bombay in 1827 he took the Steward with him. Pottanco left with a high testimonial to his 'integrity and ability' and is supposed to have bequeathed to the Club a rich hoard of curry and other oriental recipes. The Cook (not yet grandly nominated *chef*) was M. Jerome Dutôt. He gave satisfaction, and got a rise to £150 within six months of his appointment.

In spite of this strong leadership in the commissariat department, criticism was clearly anticipated, and the Secretary sought to forestall it by putting up a notice in the Coffee Room:

The prices in the Bill of Fare are, as far as circumstances will permit, regulated by those of the Union Club.

Evidently the Union (founded c. 1799) had already established its long-held reputation for good food at reasonable prices[1]. Complaints soon came, however, and it happens that the first I have to record superbly sets the tone for everything that was to follow in this strange sector of club life:

Colonel Gilbert and Captain Fleming having complained that a charge of 6d. each had been made in their Coffee Room bill for July 13th for Bread, when they had not used any, the sum of 1s. was ordered to be returned to them.

How many Committee members must have since relinquished office, with Minutes of this sort written on their hearts!

But the chief immediate business was house-hunting. While nego-

[1] The Union originally occupied the fine building by Smirke at the eastern end of Cockspur Street which has now been inflated into Canada House. It moved later to Carlton House Terrace and thence to St. James's Street, but closed down in 1964.

tiations over Grosvenor Street were still going on (26 April 1824), Basevi came forward with another contractor's offer to build a clubhouse, and once the Club was settled in, the search began again. In October the name of the eventual man of destiny looms up: 'Mr. Trant to consult Mr. Wyatt, the architect, as to the value and suitability of the Marquess of Anglesey's House in Burlington Street'. Propositions pour in: Mr. Rainey offers the Duke of Portland's house in St. James's Square for £28,000; Mr. Bearley says he knows someone who will put up a building at the top of St. James's Street and rent it to the Club for £1,600–£1,800; another plot in King Street, St. James's, is also turned down, as is Lady Carhampton's house in Bruton Street. Meanwhile (13 December 1824), the Club finally committed itself to Benjamin Wyatt as its agent, on the basis that he was to receive one half per cent of purchase price if he found a freehold house, or the equivalent on the calculated value of a leasehold house.

This put the Committee on an uncomfortable footing with Mr. Basevi, who was still representing Seddons over Grosvenor Street and making various other offers. He hung around until March 1826, when the Chairman rashly decided to dispose of him by the dispatch of a £50 note in recognition of his 'zeal and activity' in trying to find the Club a home. Basevi acknowledged the letter but re-enclosed the note! He had, he said, been

> actuated by an ambition not unnatural to obtain the distinction of being appointed architect to the Club (which honour I had been given to understand could only be obtained by such services) and not by motives of pecuniary emolument, but if I had thought of such acknowledgment I should not have considered the services and the expenses involved (little as I am disposed to value the former) . . . to be at all remunerated by the note sent me . . .

The Committee seem to have pocketed their £50 as well as the rather cumbrous reproof, and, except on Seddons' business, Mr. Basevi is heard of no more[1].

Months go by and Benjamin Wyatt continues to produce one suggestion after another. Lord Carnarvon offers two houses—one in

[1] He later consoled himself with some excellent Club commissions, including the Conservative and the Carlton.

Grosvenor Square for which he wants £12,000, but it is 'fit only to be pulled down', and the other in the ever-interesting territory of Tenterden Street, but it is let for five years to the Royal Academy of Music; Captain Tyler's house close by at No. 20 Hanover Square is rejected without reason given; Sir Claude Scott's in Grosvenor Square would not be suitable without great alteration; and some well-placed premises at the corner of Bond Street and Vigo Lane also fall into the 'fit only to be pulled down' category and would provide inadequate ground space.

One trend is clear. When the Oriental finally takes root it will not be in 'clubland'—Pall Mall and St. James's. The reason for this unfashionable decision, which has influenced the Club's history (not always for the worse) from that day to this, was that the great stronghold of the East India Company's retired servants was the area just north and south of Oxford Street centred on Cavendish and Hanover Squares, and particularly the Harley Street complex now garrisoned by doctors. The 'Indians' wanted their Club to be what a later writer called 'an easy drop down' from their residential quarter, and that they achieved at last.

The decisive date was 2 March 1826, when a special Committee Meeting was held with Sir John Malcolm in the Chair. It was then decided to offer £14,000 to Mr. J. D. Alexander for his house at 18 Hanover Square, plus £200 for *not* taking the furniture. Mr. Alexander asked for more and a Committee member, Mr. Trant, was authorised to negotiate. There was also a stable yard held under lease from the City of London.

And who was Mr. Alexander? None other than Josias du Pré, a director of the East India Company and well within the magic circle! Josias' father Robert was a brother of James Alexander who, springing from a family of Ulster linen merchants, went out to India in the eighteenth century and became one of the most opulent of nabobs. On his return he bought great estates in Ireland, entered Parliament, and received the full benefit of the peerages then being showered on supporters of the Union (Baron 1790, Viscount 1797, Earl of Caledon 1800).

Born in 1771, Josias joined the firm of Gardiner Alexander & Co. in Calcutta, and on his return in about 1820 became M.P. for the famous Rotten Borough of Old Sarum. He was an original member of the Oriental Club[1], and, after selling it No. 18, he moved a short way away to No. 16. He died in 1839.

By 20 March the little haggle over furniture was completed (in the Club's favour) and on 21 August possession was obtained. But this was not quite the end of the 'repeated failures and disappointments' to which the Committee feelingly referred in one of their reports. Benjamin Wyatt, secure of this handsome commission, was adamant that the alterations and additions necessary to turn No. 18 into an acceptable clubhouse would cost as much as building a new one 'and would leave the Club at last in but a patched, disfigured and inconvenient residence'. So once again it was a case of a mansion 'fit only to be pulled down'—did Benjamin inherit a destructive strain from his cathedral-wrecking father? The point was bitterly contested, but pulling down was finally agreed upon by eight Committee votes to five, and Sir Simon Clarke next door was warned that demolition would begin at any moment.

Wyatt now produced his drawings and estimates—the former are lost to us, but the latter totalled £32,300—£14,300 to Mr. Alexander, £14,000 for the building (after getting back £3,000 for the old materials[2]) and £4,000 for furniture. To meet this imminent liability the Committee was relying heavily on a plan going back to November 1825, when 100 members[3] undertook to take up five-per-cent debentures of £160 each on the security of 'any house which the Club could satisfactorily buy'. But when the moment of truth approached, more and more of the 100 said they wanted to withdraw. The Committee saw they must take the offensive and on 29 May they told the Secretary to send the following uncommonly sharp memorandum to the defaulters:

I have the direction of the Committee of Management once more to call upon you for your subscription of £160 for providing a new Club

[1] Other Alexanders to be elected were Josias' cousin Robert, the latter's son Robert J. (Bengal Civil Service), and James (also Bengal Civil Service), a son of Josias' brother Henry. A present-day member of the family (though not of the Oriental) is Field-Marshal Earl Alexander of Tunis.

[2] Typical architect's optimism. They only fetched £1,028 12s. 6d.

[3] The original list of subscribers is on view in the Smoking Room to this day. It includes the signatures of Snodgrass, Carnac, Lord William Bentinck, Lord Powis, Sir Richard King, divers Stracheys and Colvins—the founding fathers, in fact.

House, and to observe that the means hitherto taken to procure a suitable House for the Club were adopted on the faith of gentlemen's punctuality [in] meeting the engagements into which they had voluntarily entered; and the Committee do not feel themselves authorised to proceed while any doubt exists as to the payments being made good. I am further to request that you will pay the sum of £160 on or before the 10th June.

This ultimatum must have succeeded, since the work went forward without delay.

While the demolishers were still busy, however, a controversy arose over the lay-out which had its amusing side. Mr. Alexander's front door faced Hanover Square in the conventional manner, and the Committee took it for granted that the Club's would do the same. But, so Baillie tells us, Mr. X, the owner of No. 16, had other ideas[1]. Himself a member of the Club, he was the father of several fair young daughters. He strongly objected to members being able to lounge on the Clubhouse steps and stare directly across at them—as he declared was the case, though in fact his house was a knight's move away on the north side of the Square. No, the entrance must be round the corner in Tenterden Street. A palliative only! Standing today on the site of the old Club's front door, it is still (and always must have been) possible to leer across at the windows of No. 16—one of the few houses in the Square which retains something of its original character—though admittedly the range is longer than from the Square frontage and the protruding bulk of No. 17 comes partially in the line of fire.

Whether Mr. X's protest would have been effective, or whether the Committee would have told him (with circumlocution) to Lock Up his Daughters we can only guess, but Wyatt settled the matter by saying that *he* must have the entrance in Tenterden Street, otherwise it would be impossible to provide a Coffee Room of adequate size. He carried the day and the Club got a Coffee Room with a frontage of 60 feet to the Square and 30 feet to Tenterden Street, and a Drawing Room of similar dimensions above.

The rest of the two-storey block consisted of an entrance hall with

[1] There is nothing of this affair in the Club Minutes, and Baillie does not name the objector. The owner (though not necessarily the occupant) of the house at the time was Mr. Neil Malcolm, never as far as I know a member of the Oriental. It is possible that the tale relates to Mr. Alexander himself, after he had moved across the way.

Billiard Room and Small Dining Room on the right, and Library, Card Room and Secretary's Office above them, the upper floor being reached from the inner hall by one of those monumental staircases which were an essential feature of all early nineteenth-century clubs. A mystery here! Such staircases were of course imitated from the country houses and London *palazzi* of the day, where they formed part of the machinery of social life; up them, on festive evenings, the guests were slowly marshalled, to be received by the hostess at the top; down them flowed the return procession to the supper room. But if the early clubs had one tenet in common it was the rigid exclusion of all guests whatever! The sole users of the great staircases were the members themselves. Hence one of the archetypal images of the Clubman—a spidery decrepit figure with a stick, pausing for breath at the half-way landing of some vast cataract of marble and red carpet. I would add that the Oriental's own staircase (*Pl. 7*) was a good deal less ostentatious than most, its 47 steps being dictated by the lofty ceilings on the ground floor.

The Kitchens were placed at semi-basement level at the west end of the building—i.e. as far away as possible from the Coffee Room. This again was an almost universal practice of the time and it is hardly worth commenting on its effect upon the service!

The verdict of architectural taste has been hard on Benjamin Wyatt's buildings generally and on his Oriental Club in particular. Wyatt built Crockford's (later the Devonshire) at the top of St. James's Street at about the same time as the Oriental, and Sir John Summerson dealt with the two together in *Georgian London*[1]. They were, he says, very like each other:

> Both were ponderous in scale (like his earlier Drury Lane Theatre) with great slabs of Corinthian pilaster surmounted by an entablature of coarse Greek profile ... The Oriental has a poor site, facing north ... Here Wyatt pilastered the ends and slightly recessed the centre (again like Drury Lane). The Oriental is a dull building, rendered ugly now by towering increments in its skyline ...

The great difference between the two clubs was that Crockford's, 'a gambling hell of the most lavish and patrician character', as Sir

[1] London, Pleiades Press, 1946.

John calls it, had a beautiful Louis XIV interior[1], whereas the Oriental had to make do with a stolid version of the still-current Regency style.

Mr. Colvin is another who sums up Benjamin Wyatt with such phrases as 'great competence but small invention' and 'ponderous in scale and uninteresting in detail'. We can all test this verdict against two of his most conspicuous legacies to the London scene—the Duke of York's Column in Waterloo Place, and the façade of Apsley House, refaced by Wyatt for his faithful patron the Duke of Wellington in 1828. Neither quite lives up to its splendid site.

However, the Oriental Club members fitted comfortably enough into the setting provided for them, and their Clubhouse became a sober ornament of Hanover Square.

The West End of London, in 1828 as in 1968, was a stimulating mixture of the respectable and the raffish. Hanover Square itself came into the first category. It originated with the great wave of building which followed the Treaty of Utrecht (1713) and which engraved the names of three great family estates, Burlington, Grosvenor and Cavendish, so enduringly upon the map of London. The Hanover Square speculation belonged to none of these, but was based upon a number of small properties. Who took the initiative we do not know. Sir John Summerson draws our attention to the strong military and Whiggish element among the early occupants, who included no fewer than five of Queen Anne's generals. And as Whig loyalties were transferred to George I when he succeeded Anne in 1714, this would reasonably account for the Square being christened in honour of the House of Hanover.

By the early nineteenth century, Hanover Square was still recognised as a thoroughly 'good' if not tip-top fashionable address. Alexander Baillie justifies the title of his book *The Oriental Club and Hanover Square* by devoting a pleasant first chapter to gossip about 'Our Square'—its origins, famous inhabitants, romances and scandals. Since the Square is 'ours' no longer, I must not follow him, except into the north-west segment where the Oriental came to rest.

[1]Benjamin Wyatt has never been credited with this, but recent research by Mr. John Cornforth into the history of Stafford (now Lancaster) House shows that he was in fact responsible for the even grander Louis XIV interiors there. Evidence has also emerged that Benjamin was inclined to take his clients for a ride!

To members looking out of the Drawing Room windows (and avoiding those of No. 16) on their first day of occupation, the most conspicuous object in view would have been Harewood House. This mansion occupied the whole eastern side of what is still called Harewood Place, that overtaxed artery through which the buses are now extruded from the Square into Oxford Street, but which was then defended at the upper end by a pair of iron gates, only opened when the Earl of Harewood was in town. Designed by Robert Adam, the house had a majestic bow-window commanding Harewood Place, and an array of pilasters on which Baillie supposes (without much justification) that Benjamin Wyatt modelled his Oriental Club façade.

Westwards from Harewood Place, the first house of interest was No. 15, famous as the residence of Admiral John Jervis, Earl St. Vincent. Next of course came No. 16, about which we need only add that before being occupied by Mr. X it housed the Royal College of Chemistry (Hanover Square always had its sprinkling of 'institutions') and much later was a sort of boarding house, where Club members roosted from time to time.

Baillie devotes a lot of space to No. 17, which formed the angle of the Square and Tenterden Street. Its first owner seems to have been that energetic Anglo-Dutch tycoon, Sir Theodore Janssen, who lost a fortune in the South Sea Bubble of 1720. By about 1785 it was occupied by Sir Richard Ford and here lived for several years as his mistress the great actress Mrs. Jordan. But in 1790, Mrs. Jordan became the mistress—and perhaps the morganatic wife—of the Duke of Clarence (William IV). She stayed on at No. 17 for many years and her eldest son by the Duke, George Fitzclarence, Earl of Munster, was born there in 1794. It is pleasant to record that 30 years later, after much military service in India, he was enrolled as an Original Member of the Oriental Club.

Baillie, visiting No. 17 in 1896, when it had been recently vacated by the Arts Club, tells of a long, narrow and mysterious extension, stretching back to Oxford Street, which in his view could only have been a studio or practice stage on which Mrs. Jordan rehearsed her parts.

Maybe yes, maybe no, but Baillie is on firm ground in associating this corner of the Square with Eastern traders, long before the Oriental caravan halted there. No. 17, together with No. 2 Tenterden Street next door, had been for many years the property of the Dashwood family, whose founder was an opulent seventeenth-century 'Turkey merchant' and Alderman of the City of London.

What is more, the Dashwoods became possessed of the actual site of the Club. This arose through the dispersal early in the eighteenth century of the Pollen family's estate, which included No. 18 and the houses next to it now occupied by Messrs. Knight, Frank & Rutley. The Pollens sold No. 18 to John Fane, later Earl of Westmorland, and when he died in 1762 the property, along with his subsidiary title of Lord Le Despencer[1], passed to the 'Wicked' Sir Francis Dashwood of West Wycombe Park and the Hell Fire Club; it was his cousin, also Lord Le Despencer, who sold it to Mr. Alexander. The latter, in fact, warned the Oriental Committee that he had given the Dashwoods the first refusal, but the option was evidently not taken up.

On to Tenterden Street. We do not seem to know much about No. 2 just opposite the Club's entrance, but its neighbours have a lively interest for us. Baillie describes No. 3 as a fine family mansion, though with enigmatic and even sinister associations. It had an extra-massive front door and some peculiar features within which he vaguely relates to (*a*) The detention of Hannah Lightfoot, 'the fair Quakeress' with whom George III is supposed to have been in love at the age of 16[2]; (*b*) The use of the house as a lunatic asylum; (*c*) Its occupancy by William Knighton, apothecary and accoucheur, who is said to have been given it 'in acknowledgement of the services he rendered in a delicate case'. Not long afterwards he clambered into the position of Private Secretary to the Prince Regent, and died a baronet in Stratford Place.

No. 3 Tenterden Street, like No. 16 Hanover Square, was eventually divided into 'chambers' and among many notable Oriental Club members lodged there was the centenarian Mr. Macauley, whom we shall meet later on. It was only demolished in 1959.

[1] The title actually went into abeyance for a time, but the complicated succession does not concern us.

[2] No support for this Tenterden Street connection in any published version of the Hannah Lightfoot legend.

As for No. 4, its first claim to notice was that it brought a tumultuous levy into this quiet corner. This was at the time of the Gordon Riots, when its owner, Henry Herbert, Lord Porchester, was one of the mob's *bêtes noires*. He made a show of strength by dexterously switching his defending force of three guardsmen from room to room, and the attack was not pressed home. In 1793 Lord Porchester was upgraded to the Earldom of Carnarvon and it was his son who 30 years later leased No. 4 to the newly formed Royal Academy of Music. Another Hanover Square dignitary was the Academy's virtual founder Lord Burghersh, collateral descendant of that Lord Westmorland who once owned the Club site.

In spite of its grand title, the R.A.M. was at first more like a small co-educational school, consisting of only 10 boys and an equal number of girls. To preserve the proprieties, the garden at the back was divided by a wall, over which precocious and animated courtships were nevertheless pursued; one young man, the future bass singer Edward Seguin, actually used a battering ram—'a log of wood tied to a string'—to bash his way through to the lady of his choice. This youth has his own niche in the Oriental story as the ringleader in various frolics at the expense of its members, natural victims for teenage high spirits. A favourite ploy was to fling candles across the street—only stopped after one had been successfully lobbed through the Oriental skylight[1]. Another was to get up 'Dutch concerts' of all the loudest instruments played in ingenious discord, and to answer protests with a plaintive 'Surely we are allowed to practise?'

There must have been many occasions, too, like the day in 1850 when one of the professors, calling to apologise for a ball having shattered the Club's Billiard Room window, was brusquely handled by the Steward; the Committee had to patch things up with the Principal and civilly returned the money he sent to pay for the damage. The Academy gradually spread along Tenterden Street but did not absorb the next door but one, 5a, judging by the fact that the Club took temporary rooms there quite late in the nineteenth century.

[1] See Frederick Corder, *A History of the Royal Academy of Music* (London F. Corder, 1922).

It was at the far end of the little street that the Club came into contact with the grimier side of West End life. It will be recalled that as well as buying Mr. Alexander's freehold house, the Committee took over his stable yard on lease from the City of London. It seems an oddity, until we observe that this patch of ground bore the name of 'Conduit Yard'. It was in fact an outpost of the Corporation's City Mead Estate which, for reasons fully explained in the Prologue to Part II of this book, links the new Clubhouse with the old in a fascinating manner. The yard was overlooked by No. 1 Tenterden Street. This house, just to fox the topographers, was situated as far as physically possible from No. 2[1]—it occupied in fact the corner masked today by a shiny black wall inscribed GOR-RAY. From here swung away at right angles what is now called Dering Street, but was Shepherd Street when the Oriental first moved in. This thoroughfare, along with No. 1 Tenterden Street, had a thoroughly bad reputation. It was, in truth, simply a row of brothels. Hence arose a serio-comic succession of manœuvres by which a body called 'The Committee for Preventing Nuisances in the Neighbourhood of Hanover Square' kept trying to get the ladies out of Shepherd Street and legal expenses out of the Oriental Club.

On 8 July 1844, Messrs. Arrowsmith, solicitors to the C.P.N.N.H.S., wrote that the disreputable tenants had agreed to quit or to give security for good behaviour. The Committee voted £10 towards the costs—only to be told a week later that the nuisance had not been quite abated after all. Nine years passed, and now another set of solicitors acting for Lord Carnarvon (the acknowledged Squire of Tenterden Street) suggested that a subscription should be got up to prosecute the keepers of these same disorderly houses; the Club agreed, provided other residents would join in. Short pause, then on 20 March Messrs. Arrowsmith suddenly surface with an exactly similar suggestion. This time the Club has 'no funds available'. In December comes the only too familiar communication: the removal of brothels has 'succeeded to a very great extent', but more money is required. Two fresh proposals are also made—that the name of the street should be changed from notorious Shepherd to aristo-

[1] This was not originally so—until a renumbering in the early nineteenth century, No. 17 Hanover Square was No. 1 Tenterden Street.

cratic Talbot, and that Lord Carnarvon should be persuaded to remove the bar which (like the Harewood Place gates) closed the end of the street. This, it was supposed—goodness knows why—would 'prevent the re-establishment of the nuisance'.

The Committee gloomily stumped up £10 as before, but preferring the nuisance to the traffic, made their support conditional on the bar remaining. It did. Whether the tenacious tenantry stayed on too, no further Minute informs us. They have certainly gone now, yet Shepherd Street's successor Dering Street[1] retains a faintly raffish air to this day.

Planted at the angle of the serene Square and its turbid tributary, the Oriental quickly became identified with the former. To one man, indeed, the identification was so complete that for him the Square and the Club were synonyms. William Makepeace Thackeray was never a member of the Oriental—the Reform, the Garrick and the Athenaeum were his haunts—but his ties with the world which it represented and with many of the actual inmates were exceedingly close. Thackeray himself was the son of Richmond and grandson of William Thackeray, both servants of the East India Company; it has been suggested that he may have had some Indian blood through his mother, one of the Calcutta Bechers. His uncle Charles, a Bengal barrister and contributor to the *Englishman*, joined the Club as early as 1825.

Thackeray's father died in 1816, and the following year he was sent home to live with an aunt, Mrs. Ritchie, almost all of whose close relatives had served in the East. Thus, as Gordon Ray puts it[2], the boy 'passed his early days as part of a self-contained Anglo-Indian group' and felt to the full that general hostility or indifference to returned 'Indians' which actually brought the Oriental into being.

In 1818 Thackeray's mother married Major Henry Carmichael-Smyth, Bengal Engineers. He was the second of eight sons of Dr. James Carmichael-Smyth, head of the ancient family of Carmichael of Balmedie; three of his brothers and several nephews were Oriental Club members, though their erratic use of the surnames

[1] Renamed in 1878. The 'Talbot Street' suggestion was not taken up.
[2] *Thackeray, The Uses of Adversity* (Oxford University Press, 1955).

Carmichael and Smyth, independently or together, does not help in pinning them down. The eighth brother George (Original Member) has his place—an unhappy one—in Indian history; he commanded the 3rd Light Cavalry at Meerut in 1857 and ordered the crucial firing parade which ushered in the Mutiny.

The most generally quoted of Thackeray's references to the Oriental is certainly that in Chapter II of *Vanity Fair*. Jos Sedley, as lonely in London as in Boggley-Wallah, drove in the Park, frequented the theatre and 'dined at the fashionable taverns (for the Oriental Club was not as yet invented)'. This was 'while the present century was in its teens'. Seven or eight hundred pages later we are in the year 1827; Jos is on leave again and

> His very first point, of course, was to become a member of the Oriental Club; where he spent the mornings in the company of his brother Indians, where he dined, or whence he brought home men to dine.

Vanity Fair has always had more readers than *The Newcomes*, in which Thackeray's love affair with the Oriental reaches full flower. The first glimpse is in Chapter XIII, where a posse of Members (three of them 'Scotchmen') turn up at one of Colonel Newcome's parties. Thereafter they are simply referred to as 'the gentlemen from Hanover Square' and later in the book Thackeray introduces 'correct East India gentlemen from Hanover Square' without further explanation. In Chapter XV, the Colonel's visit to poor old Mrs. Mason, the family nurse, at Newcome is cut short:

> On Thursday he must be up in London, he has important business in London—in fact Tom Hamilton of his regiment comes up for election at the Oriental on that day, and on such an occasion could Thomas Newcome be absent?

But my favourite 'Oriental' passage in the whole enormous novel is in Chapter XXII and relates to Clive Newcome's historical painting 'The Battle of Assaye':

> So large was this picture that it could only be got out of the great window by means of artifice and coaxing, and its transport caused a shout of triumph among the little boys of Charlotte Street. Will it be believed that the Royal Academicians rejected the 'Battle of Assaye'. The masterpiece was so big that Fitzroy Square could not hold it; and the Colonel had thoughts of presenting it to the Oriental Club . . .

Thoughts shared, one suspects, by more than one actual donor —hence some of the surgical operations to be described on page 109!

Finally, there is the 'real-life' connection of Colonel Newcome himself with the Club. Several originals have been suggested for Thackeray's pious old hero. His own step-father Henry Carmichael-Smyth was one, but Baillie is among those who plump for Major-General Charles Montauban Carmichael, the fourth brother. Here are the parallels:

COLONEL NEWCOME	CHARLES CARMICHAEL
Charterhouse boy	Charterhouse 1801–5
'Wore the grey uniform of the Bengal Cavalry'	Bengal Army
C.B.	C.B.—a rare honour for a Company's Officer
Returned from the East in 1852 and joined Oriental Club	'Colonel Carmichael has arrived from India and joined the Club' (Committee Minute, 3 February 1851)

Baillie adds the quaint corroborative detail—Colonel Newcome was proud of his moustachios, then out of fashion; Charles Carmichael was the only member who wore them in the 1850s. Another candidate for the honour, by the way, was Thackeray's second cousin, Captain John Dowdeswell Shakespear (e. 1849), but Thackeray himself admitted to David Freemantle Carmichael (e. 1855) that, sure enough, the originals were uncles Charles and Henry, though he added significantly, 'I had to *angelicise* the old boys a bit'.

Since the Club's aboriginal rule against admitting strangers had been relaxed by the time Thackeray became a London diner-out, he must often have been the guest there of his numerous relatives, though unfortunately none of the early lists of 'strangers' survives. We, on the other hand, have the full freedom of the House, and it is high time that we should exercise it, and go inside.

3 *Above and Below Stairs at No 18*

. . . the traditional moroseness of the retired nabob.

Sir John Kaye

If a man cannot be morose in his own club without having to listen to boisterous laughter, then the club is not the sanctuary it was.

Thomas Girtin, The Abominable Clubman

The members who took possession of their new building in 1828 could be classified as late Georgians, since the reign of George IV had still two more years to run. But my impression is that, like their Clubhouse, they looked forward in spirit to bourgeois William and even to Victoria, rather than back to the Regency. The contretemps with Mr. X irresistibly calls up a picture of a group of dandies and swaggerers lounging on the steps dressed, like Jos Sedley, in 'buckskins and Hessian boots, with several immense neckcloths that rose almost to his nose, with a red-striped waistcoat and an apple-green coat with steel buttons almost as large as crown pieces'. True to type in St. James's, perhaps, but *not* the prevalent style in the north-west corner of Hanover Square.

The Oriental Club ethos was altogether quieter. The proportion of members who had come home from the East in indifferent health and with by no means the legendary nabob's fortune, must have tended towards a sobriety of tone. There is a remark attributed to Thackeray that the Oriental prided itself on being the dullest club in London (sometimes repeated with the sly footnote that it had always done its best to maintain the tradition . . .). This chimed with the accepted view already quoted from the 1842 *New Monthly Magazine*. A year later the same satirical pen, pleased with its handiwork, returned to the theme of 'gentlemen who have passed the bloom of life in the money-making regions of Bundlecund and Ferruckabad and who, like Rosina's morning, "return in saffron dressed" . . . They feed chiefly on curry and drink madeira.'

Yellow faces . . . curry and madeira . . . such was the oft-repeated stereotype. Well, the old members' complexions have passed beyond our scrutiny, but I doubt whether they were much affected by curry-eating in Hanover Square. Apart from Mr. Pottanco's alleged bequest of recipes, there is strikingly little about this dish in the early annals of the Club! All news from the Coffee Room relates to strictly conventional English fare—chops and steaks, game and fish, with oysters and the like as trimmings. The very word *curry* does not appear in the Committee minutes until 12 August 1839, when Mr. Williamson (Bombay Civil Service) suggests that 'a native Indian cook' might attend the kitchen to give instruction to the chef, but this is turned down as 'the curries now made by the cook give general satisfaction'. However, the public image of the Oriental as an assemblage of curry-gourmets was sufficiently strong for Messrs. Crosse & Blackwell to value an endorsement for

CAPTAIN WHITE'S
Fish and Chicken Curry and Mulligatawny Paste
EXCLUSIVELY USED AT THE ORIENTAL CLUB

The label on a small stone jar which has miraculously survived bears, along with a tribute from the Reform Club's famous Alexandre Soyer, the following testimonial, which happens to echo the Committee's phrase:

Kitchen Department, Oriental Club,
July 8th, 1851

I have for four years exclusively used your CURRY PASTE AND POWDER and I have invariably found that they have given general satisfaction.

G. Fidle[1]

No doubt this label continued to be used for many a decade, but, alas, Captain White's concoction must have ceased to give such universal pleasure by 1859, as in October of that year it was decided

[1] G. Fidle was presumably the chef of the time, though no record of him seems to be extant.

to change to a Madras variety from Payne's, Leicester Square, and also to obtain a consignment from Parry & Co. in Madras itself.

Complaints are always a good guide as to the pre-occupations of the members. If they had been, so to speak, strongly curry-conscious, the Committee would have heard plenty about it, as they did about the stewed beef with old potatoes 'made into marbles' which upset Mr. Eldridge, or the mean little steak which Mr. Deans Campbell, encouraged by the Committee's imprudent habit of meeting at 1.30 p.m., caused to be carried straight upstairs and 'laid before them' as though it were a Resolution—a precedent joyfully followed. The Committee believed in the soft answer. When Colonel Campbell rebelled at being charged 1s. for an apple dumpling their patient enquiries showed that a dumpling of extraordinary size had been prepared, and they confirmed the price. They had a quiet retort, too, for Mr. Persse's squeamish plaint that the woodcock served to him was 'fetid'—had he not actually chosen it himself at the poulterer's? (A curiously domestic touch.) And no doubt when Colonel Burton fumed that his fish was 'bleeding raw' they swallowed the epithet in its literal rather than in its cockney significance.

On the other hand, it does seem that the pettiness of many complaints must be blamed on a certain boarding-house mentality ('cruet 6d.') in the Committee itself. Mr. Rutherford may have objected unreasonably to paying 3d. for sugar served with a glass of brandy, but the Committee went one further in a subsequent ruling (March 1841) that 'if two gentlemen order spirits, one with sugar, and they then split the sugar between them, two portions are to be charged for'. The table charge was naturally the focus of much niggling. Surely, exclaimed Mr. R. C. Nichol, one shilling was more than sufficient to cover one pickled walnut! A system of petty extortion! The Committee for once stood on their dignity—complaints, they said, should be in language such as one gentleman may with propriety address to another, and a General Meeting would be called unless Mr. Nichol retracted. Mr. Nichol did.

But the favourite gambit when there was trouble in the Coffee Room was a promise to reprimand the cook. This was done either directly or through the Steward. Usually, in that age of outward subordination, such rebukes were meekly received, but one day in May 1855, when there were no carrots with the beef, tempers boiled over: 'You're a puppy!' shouted the Steward. 'I'll stick you! I'll put you on the fire! I'll make mutton of you!', the Cook yelled back. Victory on points.

Most of the early cooks were temperamental. The first, M. Dutôt, actually lasted four years, but when his successor proved unsatisfactory[1] and he was recalled (9 November 1829), he put on prima donna airs, was late arriving from Paris, tried to charge £18 6s. 8d. travelling expenses (given £10 only) and eight months later was discharged.

Club servants below M. Dutôt's exalted level led a life not easy to evaluate today. Obviously, the pay was low by modern standards and the little evidence we have (coupled with the records of other clubs) suggests that the hours simply consisted of working all day and a good deal of the night, about thirteen days out of fourteen. Much later than the period we are discussing—in April 1874 in fact—it was noted that Richard Stamp, head billiard-marker, was leaving through failing health from overwork; he and the other two markers were on duty every day of the week[2] from 2 p.m. till 2 a.m. all the year round. (Rather than lose Stamp's services it was decided to take on a boy at £12 per annum.)

Even the Steward had a roster of duties which began with a 6 a.m. inspection and continued until service in the Coffee Room was finished at about 11 p.m. The Clubhouse was supposed to close at 2 a.m. (in 1834 this was brought forward to 1 a.m.), but the members tended to linger on and to expect service. It must have been a tired as well as exasperated Drawing Room Waiter who 'answered impertinently' when Colonel Daly requested him to cut the leaves of a book ('Cut the —— leaves yourself', is what one irresistibly reads into this), and got a reprimand in set terms.

Long hours were encouraged by the fact that almost everyone

[1] The Committee, according to their rather terrifying custom, had dined together to judge the Cook's abilities. The test meal was a failure and, though the newcomer pleaded that he had not yet got the measure of his assistants, he had to go.

[2] This *may* not have included Sundays. The rules about Sunday games in the Club are erratically documented.

slept in; 'lodging out' allowances of £5 a year were only granted most reluctantly. The menservants seem to have slept in the attics, with the maidservants dangerously adjacent; upper servants slept more or less on the job—the Butler in the Pantry (he was refused one of the new bedrooms constructed in 1853), the House Porter in a cubby hole off the Hall, and so on.

Dirt as well as disorder reigned in these unvisited regions. As early as 1832 there was a question of spending £114 on new bedsteads and bedding for the staff, but as it had been found possible to 'clear the rooms of bugs' by fumigation, £4 was devoted to stopping and colour-washing the walls instead. However, infestation (as in Shepherd Street) remained, and two years later a 'complete and thorough change' of beds and bedding had to be made.

Two things mitigated the rigours of life in livery—a faint but real social conscience among the Club members, and a marked degree of easy-going indiscipline. To the former the staff owed a system of free medical attention which lasted right up to the coming of the National Health Service. Already by October 1826 the Club was subscribing £5 a year on the servants' behalf to the dispensary of St. George's and St. James's parishes, and later there was a regular 'medical attendant to the establishment' getting first £10 and then £20 a year. The only pity was that the first holder of this post, Dr. Clarke, tried to take advantage of his opportunities:

> The Under-Stillroom Maid, Elizabeth Ball[1], complained that Dr. Clarke treated her in a very improper and indecent manner, that he put his legs round her waist, and tried to get her to sit on his knee. He also kissed other members of the female staff... Ordered: That the Club solicitor should take out a summons. (Minute of 12 December 1853).

Dr. Clarke lost his job and was succeeded by Dr. French of Marlborough Street. For the rest, the Club rented a pew for the servants in St. George's Church at £5 a year; followed Union and United Service Club precedent in giving them £4 for a 'feast' at Christmas, and that was about that.

In Club service, as in the domestic and industrial underworld of Victorian England, it was alcohol and absenteeism which provided the safety-valve. It was fairly common for servants to disappear for

[1] Was she still in the same job in October 1854? Compare p. 94, note 2!

a day or two on a drinking bout, though not all of them produced such an ingenious excuse as Charles Willis, Bathman, who explained his lost week-end by saying his beer had been drugged while he was playing skittles. Inside the Club walls things were much the same. Members put in routine complaints of being served in the Coffee Room by intoxicated waiters; one afternoon a servant called George Powell was found drinking in the Entrance Hall with two men he had brought into the Club, while the Hall Porter lay on a bed in the adjoining room 'apparently drunk'; and in 1831 there was a round robin by the staff against the alleged drunkenness and high living of the Steward at the expense of their own rations, though this was partly malicious.

Once, hard drinking ended in a near-riot. On 21 May 1827 the Committee had before them a report of a 'disgraceful disturbance in the Clubhouse at half-past one of the clock on Saturday morning last, occasioned by a quarrel between the Butler and five of the waiters . . . during which the Housekeeper had sent for the Watchmen (predecessors of the police) who came into the House to quell the disturbance'.

The servants were examined separately. It seemed that the Butler had been out till 1.15 a.m., came back to find the five men drinking in the Servants' Hall, and struck three of them. The Housekeeper then called in the Watchmen to arrest the Butler. The Committee found the Housekeeper's action 'exceedingly blameable'; but they warned the Butler that if he ever again struck a servant or used abusive language he would be dismissed, as would the other servants if 'another instance arose of their carousing to a late hour'.

So much for the bottle. Women certainly, and for all I know song, added their mitigations. There is the usual rather melancholy procession of kitchen-maids and so forth 'sent away' for obvious reasons. But maybe the Committee did not take too seriously the horror of Dr. Frere, when he caught two Coffee-Room Waiters, J. Boyce and Jas. Bridges, 'romping with some women' on the very front doorstep of the Club.

Where does all this lead us? To get an idea of how the life of the members and their servants really interacted, perhaps we should start with a page or two about a drama above-stairs, one of the very few preserved in the archives. It concerned Captain Trelawney and his hat.

The affair began at the end of October 1831, when the Committee put up a notice expressing their 'mortification' at having to remind members of the rule against removing publications and stationery from the Club—seven periodicals and a quire of paper were missing. On 7 November James Dawes, the Drawing-Room Waiter, reported that writing paper had disappeared on 1, 2 and 5 November. Each time it was in position in the portfolios before Captain Jonathan Trelawney entered the room alone, and had disappeared when he quitted it. At a special Committee meeting on the 9th Dawes told an even more dramatic tale about events the previous day.

Being determined to solve the mystery, he had enlisted another waiter called Samuel Scott as co-investigator. Together they had removed overnight the globe[1] which stood before the keyhole of the door leading from the Card Room to the Library. Captain Trelawney came upstairs and after having been in the water closet went into the Library. Dawes, looking through the keyhole, saw him take paper from one portfolio, put it in his hat and leave the room. Samuel Scott corroborated.

There followed an agitated exchange between the Committee and the Captain—all he did, he said, was to take two newspapers, the *National Omnibus* and *Paris in London* out of his hat and put them back; he would produce the actual papers; he was unpopular with the staff because he had been overheard saying that the Drawing Room Waiter 'should never have been promoted from the knife-board'; he would have sunk under the affair if he did not possess *mens sibi conscia recti.*

There was nothing for it but an Extraordinary General Meeting. This was fixed for 5 December, but meanwhile a pro-Trelawney posse, headed by Colonels Baker, Becher and Tod, announced that they would move that the accusation was entirely unfounded and

[1] This was a terrestial globe given to the Club by Mr. Snodgrass. According to Baillie, it was so large that nobody could understand how it got into the room ('formerly a Card Room but later a Private Dining Room') where it stood for so long. When it was eventually moved elsewhere, the globe (like 'the Battle of Assaye') had to be taken out through a window. But where is it now?

that the two Club servants who resorted to peeping through the keyhole should be dismissed. Came the day, and Sir John Malcolm happening to be home on leave, he was unanimously voted into the Chair.

Not much of the prolonged discussion is on record, but we may note the argument of Mr. Bracken, who remarked that, while both the main witnesses had deposed to observing the deed, he did not understand how two people could look through the same keyhole at the same time. A good point, though Samuel Scott, shaky in penmanship but firm in recollection, met it vigorously enough in his written statement: 'I saw Captain Trelawney walk in from the Reading Room and take the paper . . . then I take my head from the keyhole and let Dawes see, then I look againe, then let James Dawes look againe . . .'

The feeling of the meeting was wholly with Trelawney, and on a motion that there was no proof of a breach of the Rules, there voted *For* 69, *For a contrary opinion* 9. However, with a final fling at 'a system of obtaining evidence which strikes at the root of all morality and social system', Captain Trelawney resigned.

Perhaps because the vivid little picture of those two liveried figures crouching down by the great globe and taking turns at the keyhole lingers in the mind, the name of James Dawes catches one's eye whenever it appears in the Minutes. Follow him along, and a dusty ray of light falls on much that would otherwise be lost in the shadows.

Like a persistent minority of the staff from then until now, James Dawes gave the Club a lifetime's service. He had only been with it a year or two when the *affaire Trelawney* loomed up. It certainly did him no harm, and within 18 months, 'his conduct having met the approbation of the Committee', his pay was increased to £25. Further small rises in 1834 and 1837 brought him to £30 in all. In March 1839 he survived an awkward business of three sovereigns missing from Mr. Charles Hope's purse, left lying about in the Drawing Room (the actual malefactor was identified, and leniently treated).

On 29 May 1843, Dawes was chosen for the responsible post of

Clerk of the Kitchen at £45 per annum, when Mr. Sturt, the incumbent, became Secretary to the Club. A week later he was given an extra £5 for clothes, but alas he was out of his depth as Clerk, and in June reverted to his old post as Drawing Room Waiter, keeping the higher salary.

In July 1847, this steady fellow attains the dignity of Deputy President of the Servants' Hall. Just two years later he gets a rise to £47 5s. od. and in April 1853 petitions for another, pointing out that he has been in the Club service 22 years (20 in the Drawing Room) and 'has pride in saying that he has never been called before the Committee for any misbehaviour or neglect of duty'. Upped to £52 10s. od.

Our penultimate news of James Dawes is that in December 1853 he is appointed deputy to the Steward during the latter's absences, with £5 per annum extra.

Then on 9 April 1855 comes the abrupt entry 'James Dawes died on Saturday morning'. And with it the fact, so shocking at first and yet almost a commonplace of Victorian Club records, that he left a wife and seven children, five of them unable to earn anything. So it is, time after time, with Steward[1], Waiter or Cook; after whatever decades of 'living in', death reveals a widow and a helpless young family. Where did they lodge? How rarely did they see their husband and father? What hope did they nurse for the future?

Of course, there was no money, not a penny. The Committee quickly agreed that a 'paper inviting subscriptions' should be placed on the Drawing Room table, and when the undertaker and the landlord began to press, the Secretary was told to pay something out at once. The use of the rest of the money could be decided as soon as Mrs. Dawes had 'determined as to her future way of getting a living.'

Whatever Mrs. Dawes determined did not greatly matter. In May she was allotted 10s. a week out of the members' fund, but on 10 September the Secretary reported: 'During his absence from Town the widow of James Dawes the Drawing Room Waiter died sud-

[1] 12 May 1834: The Steward, Mr. Hilton, is in 'such precarious health that it is doubtful whether he will live through the day.' He dies, a wife and *eight* children unprovided for. Subscription authorised.

denly and her five children were on the same day removed to the workhouse.' On the application of her friends, Captain Gordon (the only member of the Committee who happened to be in the Clubhouse) had ordered the Steward to pay a sum not exceeding £5 for her funeral expenses. The actual cost was £4 10s. 0d.

I suppose that somehow the pieces were picked up. Later the same year £6 was given to provide the eldest girl with clothes so that she could go to a situation which the Steward had promised to find her, plus £1 a month towards the support of the youngest child. By then about £30 was left in the kitty from whatever the members had raised, and presumably this was paid out bit by bit. But one wishes that the very last heard of the Dawes family (April 1857) had not been a request by Colonel Bradford to be reimbursed 17s., owed for medicine by one of the Dawes boys who had left his service. The Committee refused.

Apart from the Trelawney incident, there were other occasional rumpuses in the early days, but it would be a mistake to overemphasise them. I have noted three as 'Lewis-Lutyens', 'Wyllie' and 'Osbaldeston v. Simpson and others'.

'Lewis-Lutyens' (September 1835) comes straight out of Pinero or Henry Arthur Jones. A quarrel in the Card Room ... 'extreme violence of conduct and language' ... a demand for satisfaction in the usual manner ... satisfaction refused. The evidence of bystanders, however, suggests a certain loss of dignity. 'You are an impudent fellow!', cried Mr. Lewis, and when Mr. Lutyens threatened to knock him down, he seized a bottle and declared he would use it if his antagonist struck him. The outcome was equivocal—Mr. Lutyens resigned, and when Mr. Lewis apologised to the Committee, the latter decided to leave the affair where it was.

'Wyllie' was the oddest of the three. One day in November 1841, according to his story, Dr. Bucke was placidly dining when Dr. Wyllie, to whom he had never spoken in his life[1], came up and threw a glass of water in his face saying 'Take that! You have insulted me deliberately.' Dr. Bucke added that this was not the first episode of

[1] Yet the fact that both Dr. George Bucke (e. 1839) and Dr. John Wyllie (e. 1830) belonged to the Indian Medical Service, Madras, could be more than a coincidence. Was there some sort of professional clash in the background?

the kind. Reporting to the Committee, the Secretary said he had told Dr. Wyllie that he had taken measures to secure to the members 'that quiet and protection from personal violence which they have a right to expect', to which the alleged aggressor retorted that he himself had been insulted—'premeditatedly, without provocation, insulted'. And we never hear another word.

'Osbaldeston v. Simpson and Others' was the title of an action heard in the Vice-Chancellor's Court on 12 November 1840. Baillie mentions this case, but does not seem to have realised that the plaintiff was the famous George Osbaldeston, 'the Squire of England'—M.F.H., amateur jockey and universal athlete. It was a much more serious affair than the others. Though the report in the next day's *Times* does not tell the story in full, we know that some sinister business took place on the Club's premises in which a member, from whom Osbaldeston had won £2,000 at cards, tried to blackmail him out of £10,000 by an allegation of cheating. Mr. E. D. Cumings has some sensible reflections on the case in his edition of Osbaldeston's *Autobiography*[1]; he is convinced of the Squire's probity, but thinks he lost his head in this tight corner.

An Extraordinary General Meeting expelled the peccant member, unanimously and without debate.

Though no doubt less yellow-faced and invalidish than alleged, the vast majority of members were not, of course, the sort to hurl insults and glasses of water at each other. Their routine seems to have been simple and not unpleasant, within the limited resources of the Clubhouse. Its great rooms, reckoned 'gloomy' by some, even in their final, electric-lit phase, must have been inconceivably dim by the flicker of lamps and candles. Gas was introduced as early as March 1828—at first in the form of 18 burners in the basement, which Mr. Edge of the Gas Light Office, Great Peter Street, Westminster, promised would save the Committee £70 per annum. Thereafter the new illuminant spread slowly through the Clubhouse, but with many setbacks.

Members never liked the heat and stink produced by the primitive flares of that time, and a curiosity of our story is the perpetual

[1] *Squire Osbaldeston: His Autobiography*, ed. E. D. Cumings (London, John Lane, The Bodley Head, 1926).

fiddling with the lighting arrangements—candles (gone up to 6d. per lb.) displaced by oil lamps which had been removed the year before (October 1834); candles instead of oil at the request of the 'gentlemen in the Card Room' (1838); gas in the Billiard Room (1839); candles instead of oil in the Coffee Room (1840); lamps to replace candles on the Drawing Room sideboard (1842); gas for oil in the Coffee and Strangers' Rooms (1851); wax-candles for hand-lamps in the Library (1855); and—a triumph of reaction!—gas replaced by oil lamps in the Drawing Room as late as October 1864.

A major operation was the lighting of the Grand Staircase by gas (1839). It was accomplished by placing 'two series of burners, one over the other on the same suspending rod or pipe' at a cost of £64 2s. 6d. A hideous arrangement, one would guess, but of macabre splendour when in full flare.

With these varied aids, the members pursued their round. They enjoyed billiards and cards, but did not play very deep—most of the allegations of reckless late sittings belong to a later date. They read the newspapers to which, by a happy coincidence, *Punch* and *The Illustrated London News* were added in the same year, 1843[1], and perused the play-bills hung in frames on the upper landing.

The Library, growing fairly fast thanks to a medley of gifts and purchases, was well used, and its silence jealously guarded by readers or sleepers; there will be more about its contents in a later chapter, as also about the Club's pictures, most of which date from the period 1825–40.

Nobody smoked at first, but the decision—under pressure—to convert Dressing Room No. 3 into a poky little Smoking Room in May 1841 was the presage of many a controversy to come.

One of the seldom-recorded problems of mid-nineteenth-century England—where and how a gentleman could get a bath—was solved four years later, when the Steward was ordered to entertain[2] a servant for the baths (the skittle-playing George Willis?) and to pay him £20 per annum. The members responded with the volup-

[1] In this year also we get a curiously up-to-date complaint—someone has walked off with the *Sunday Times Supplement*.

[2] A favourite word of the then Secretary. Sometimes it reads quaintly: 'The boy just entertained was found too small for the duty of billiard marker. The Steward to be instructed to entertain another.' (Minute of 11 January 1847).

tuousness of Roman soldiers after a long campaign—they kept wanting to have 'bowls of soup, etc.' served to them while stewing, and the Committee had to prescribe a limited menu of sandwiches, tea, coffee, wines and spirits.

These were solitary pleasures. For conviviality, there were the periodical 'house dinners', of which notice had to be given in advance by 'not less than six or more than twelve persons' and for which the stiffish price of 12s. (later reduced to 10s.) was charged. Wine was of course a great preoccupation. A Committee memorandum of 1844 on how it should be served at house dinners provides a 'period' note:

> Neither madeira nor hock to be placed on the table as a matter of course. Port to be handed round with the cheese but not put on the table. Sherry at dinner to be put into pint decanters and after the cloth is removed what is left to be re-decantered into quart decanters and one at each end of the table to be put down, which, with claret, the only wines to be put on the table after dinner. Champagne to be handed round.

From mid-century onwards, the system of obtaining wine was that a select group of merchants were encouraged to keep stocks in the Club cellars at their own expense, to be drawn upon as required, but the members themselves were not averse to doing a deal with the Committee. The Hon. Andrew Ramsay was one who sent 'samples' in 1835. A still more commercial approach came from Captain Robert Melville Grindlay, who the previous year had offered the Club a hogshead of Hodgson's Ale, bottled in Bombay, at 18s. a dozen. He was asked to send a sample dozen, but we are not told the verdict.

The Club's other dealings with this famous member deserve to be put on record. They may be summarised as follows:

15 March 1830. Captain Grindlay announces establishment of a 'House of Agency' for passages to India, and offers to supply the Club with an occasional report of arrivals from and departures for the East. Committee agree, provided the expense is not too great. Two months' trial to be given.

27 December 1830. Grindlay sends prospectus as 'East India Army Agent', together with a book for names of subscribers.

7 May 1832. Grindlay writes that the cost of collecting and forwarding information, and of sending a messenger to take the India letters to the City, amounts to between 8s. and 10s. a week. Committee doubt whether the Club should bear so great an expense!

14 May 1832. After prolonged discussion the Committee decide that £10 a year is as much as they can afford for the Grindlay service. Captain Grindlay replies rather huffily that he will send his reports free of charge, since the amount offered 'falls so far short of his actual expenses'. Committee stand firm.

16 June 1834. Grindlay reports that he has now established an office in the West End of town, and can furnish reports and forward letters to India for the sum originally proposed by the Club. Committee decide that as his reports are held 'in much estimation' by the members, they will pay £10 a year.

15 March 1841. Grindlay sends in a four years' account. Committee agree to pay it, but in view of 'new arrangements for the transmission of letters to India' and the prompt supply of information by the Press, they will cease to take the service.

My impression is that the Committee never felt quite at ease in these transactions with the energetic Captain. Grindlay himself, with his 'House of Agency', and later his Bank, expanding so rapidly, was always in a bit of a muddle; he was an Original Member of the Club but his membership seems to have lapsed, as he was readmitted in April 1849, and there was further confusion over his subscription in 1851. But how many members, then and since, have had cause to bless his name!

In addition to the House Dinners referred to above, there were rare occasions on which, as the result of a round-robin to the Committee, it was resolved to dine some especially distinguished member or even non-member of the Club. The first to be honoured was Sir Charles Metcalfe (later Lord Metcalfe), acting Governor-General of India, 1835. He was entertained twice—the first time in 1839, when he returned home and was able to take up active membership of the Oriental, which he had joined on its inception; the second was just before he sailed for Canada as Governor-General in 1843.

On his return, a dying man, two years later, there was a moving occasion at the Club. A great gathering of 'Civil and Military Servants of the East India Company and others personally connected with India' signed their last tribute to Charles Metcalfe. He was too ill to attend, but when the scroll of signatories was unrolled in his room, it covered the floor. He died on 5 September 1846.

This was the year in which a dinner was given to His Highness Ibrahim Pasha, son of Mehemet Ali, Viceroy of Egypt[1], who was on a visit to England and had been made an Honorary Member. It was a grand affair—no other meals were served to members on the chosen day (10 July), since the kitchen and coffee rooms staffs were wholly engaged in preparations. An enjoyable time was had, especially by the guest of honour who, according to Baillie, 'departed from the strict rules of the Prophet and became so elated that he had to be carried to the Drawing Room after dinner on the members' shoulders'.

Less boisterous, one imagines, was the entertainment given to Viscount Gough (a non-member) in 1850, in recognition of his 'signal services in China and India especially'.

Honorary Membership was hardly less sparingly conferred. The first recipient seems to have been one of Ibrahim Pasha's countrymen, Oman Effendi (1831). Others I have noted are M. Rio, 'a French gentleman of high literary attainments', proposed by Sir John Malcolm in 1833; another Frenchman, M. de Barbier, and Count Wachmeister of the Swedish Horse Artillery, in the same year; Sir William Nott and Sir Robert Sale, the heroes of Afghanistan, elected by the Committee on 29 July 1844, as an 'extraordinary tribute of respect and anticipating the unanimous sentiment of the Club'; and a sprinkling of Indian gentlemen—the Prince of Oudh (January 1839) and 'Baboo Durkanath Tagore[2]' and Mohun Lal (June 1842).

The latter is one of the most interesting figures on the Club's books. He gained fame as *munshi* or secretary to Sir Alexander

[1] See also page 110. It is symptomatic of the Club's quickly developing mercantile bias that it made particular 'pets' of Mehemet Ali and his family. Even when the British Government was most fiercely at odds with the Viceroys of Egypt, the commercial route to the East was kept open, and in 1842 a City of London Committee recognised Mehemet Ali's co-operation by presenting him with a gold medal and a laudatory address.

[2] Dwarka Nath Tagore, Calcutta merchant and philanthropist and the first Indian J.P. Visited London, 1841 and 1845. There are interesting sidelights on him in Gerald Ritchie, *The Ritchies in India* (London, John Murray, 1920) (O.C.L.).

Burnes (e. 1833) through all his wanderings in Afghanistan and adjacent regions until Burnes's murder at Kabul in November 1841[1]. He came to Britain in 1844–5, and there is a charming account of his reception in his *Journal of a Tour through the Panjab, Afghanistan etc.* (London, W. H. Allen, 1846). Several London clubs besides the Oriental honoured Mohun Lal, but he attended at least one of its important functions, since he mentions meeting Sir James Lushington at a Club dinner to Sir Henry Pottinger. The Library still possesses a specially bound copy of Mohun Lal's book, presented by the author to Sir Henry Hardinge (Governor-General, 1844–7), as well as an earlier version of the *Journal*, printed in Calcutta in 1834.

An Indian Honorary Member who took the rather unusual course of asking to be transformed into a subscriber was H.H. Maharajah Duleep Singh, son of the famous Ranjit Singh, ruler of the Punjab. Duleep Singh had been placed on the throne in 1843, at the age of six, but abdicated after the Second Sikh War and came to England in 1854. It was then that the Club conferred Honorary Membership upon the boy, now 17. However, in 1858 came a slightly ornate letter from Mr. Edward Thomas, I.C.S. retired (e. 1839). It announced that the Maharajah,

> . . . having now come of age, is desirous of taking advantage of the compliment paid him by our Club in 1854, of electing him as an Honorary Member. But with a highly laudable feeling he is anxious that he should appear within our walls on precisely the same footing as ourselves with regard to money contributions. He therefore asks to be allowed to pay the usual entrance donation and subscription.

H.H. was accordingly admitted (without ballot), paid his dues and before long was exercising that other privilege of membership —filing complaints about the wine. A hint that the Club might like

[1] Two other celebrated members whose frontier service led them to their deaths may be mentioned here:

Captain Arthur Conolly (e. 1827) went to Bokhara to attempt the rescue of Colonel Stoddart, imprisoned there by the Emir. He himself was incarcerated and both were murdered, after many barbarities, in 1842. His *Journey to the North of India*, presented by himself, is still in the Library.

Lieut.-Colonel Frederick Mackeson (e. 1850), who has been described as 'perhaps the greatest Frontier officer of all time', was murdered by a fanatic in Peshawar in 1853.

to try his own vintner was, however, gently diverted by the Committee, who had already far too many suppliers on their books. Duleep Singh retired from the Club in 1874 and died in Paris 19 years later.

Apart from this sprinkling of Honorary Members, the outside world was kept at a distance. Colonel Hughes might endorse the appeal for rebuilding the Convent of Mount Carmel after its destruction by the Pasha of Acre (July 1836), but he was firmly discouraged from collecting contributions; and a cold eye was turned on some admiring non-members who asked to be allowed to subscribe to Sir James Carnac's portrait (December, 1838). The only public event regularly acknowledged was the Sovereign's birthday, when the Clubhouse was loyally but frugally illuminated:

> The person employed to illuminate the Clubhouse having stated that a small device could be used that would reduce the cost from £10 to £5, resolved to spend only £5 in future. (Minute of 9 May 1831.)

An enigmatic statement about which one would like to know more. £5 was again specified the following year as the maximum to be spent 'in case anything like a general illumination takes place on the passing of the Reform Bill'—this was, one suspects, less an expression of the members' political sympathies than a precaution against having their windows broken by the mob. In 1838 the Committee plunged £22 10s. 0d. on an 'apparatus' for illuminating the Clubhouse by gas.

The Oriental was now launched upon the first decade of its long Victorian heyday, but was not destined to reach the end of it without a series of disagreeable upsets, as the following chapter will show.

4 *Crises and Recoveries*

> Not for many, many years did club committees acquire a comprehension of the fact that by allowing the stranger within their gates they increased their profits and attracted new members.
>
> *Alexander Baillie*

The Committee Minutes for 19 September 1842 appear in Mr. Thomas Cornish's writing—the same thin but regular script which has been so familiar since the year 1824. Never again. On 10 October a more sprawling, agitated hand records that a meeting had been called at Mr. Cornish's request; that he was not present; that the Steward had been sent to his lodgings in Marlborough Street, but had got no news there. The Committee dispersed in perplexity. They only had to wait two days to know the worst. When they met again they had a letter from Mr. Cornish to the Chairman in front of them:

> Pecuniary embarrassments have of late pressed so heavily upon me that I have been unable to stand up against them. Each hope I entertained, and I had many well-founded ones, has failed me, and I am in the position of having failed in the trust reposed in me by the Club. To meet yourself, Sir, and the other gentlemen of the Club with my present feelings is impossible, and I have quitted London . . .

In short, the Club's first secretary had absconded. He left behind him a deficiency which gradually revealed itself as £2,635 11s. 7d. As this crisis unluckily coincided with a falling off in subscriptions and coffee room receipts, the Committee were faced with total liabilities by the end of the year of £4,400—assets £889 10s. 0d.

It would not be worth while to reproduce all the details of this sorry story, even if they were recoverable, but there is room for a word about the *why* and the *how* of Mr. Cornish's proceedings. Part of the trouble at least seems to have been that though he had engaged to devote all his time to the affairs of the Club, he was in partnership with a Mr. Laver in a print-selling business which did not pay. He started to use the Club's money, squaring his books at the end of the calendar year by paying tradesmen out of the subscriptions coming in for the following twelve months and then staving off all other bills until after the Annual General Meeting in May. Eventually of course this system caught up with him.

The Committee went anxiously to work. Each meeting brought its quota of bad news. On 24 October Mr. Laver demands the return of prints and other articles owned jointly with Mr. Cornish—refused for the moment. On 14 November, the Club's solicitor attends with grim legal advice. The Committee keep an intrepid countenance and move to thank Dr. Moore for a gift of mangoe pickles. 14 November is the blackest day of all. It is revealed that the late secretary had forged a bill in a member's name for £300, that he owes £6,000 in addition to the Club's claim, and that he has now left for America!

It was sensibly decided not to waste time over a prosecution, but to start raising money, and quickly. At a General Meeting called for 12 December two devices were adopted: 40 gentlemen were allowed to compound for their subscriptions for life by paying £100 down, thereby wiping off the Club's immediate deficit; to make up the consequent annual shortfall of £320, members were asked to pay a voluntary levy of £8 per head. There was a rapid response. By Christmas, 160 members had paid up, by 23 January 1843, 260, and by May, 392. Other members did their bit by withdrawing notices of resignation sent in before the debacle. However, as always in Club life, the more petulant side of human nature could not be repressed. The Committee must have sighed when they received (March 1843), a letter from Captain St. Leger announcing that having paid £8 towards the 'disgraceful losses of the Club' he did not intend to enter its doors again.

However, the Committee now felt they had reached more or less firm ground again, and looked round for future savings. Predictably, in that age, the Club servants were the first sufferers. Wages were reduced, starting with the Steward (down from £150 to £100),

James Dawes and his fellow waiters lost £2 a year, and a triumphant £6 10s. 0d. was saved by providing the Steward's room boy with two undress suits a year instead of two dress and two undress. Moreover, just when spiritual comfort might well have been welcome, the staff pew in St. George's Church was given up.

The Club members lost free snuff.

There was another, and probably ill-advised economy. The Committee decided that, whereas Mr. Cornish had worked himself up to £300 per annum, his replacement must revert to £200. For this sum they obtained the services of a Mr. Abrahams, who was appointed on 14 November 1842, but who within a few months had proved inadequate for his task. Since they nearly always concern the writer's departure, the few surviving letters from Secretaries to Chairmen form a plaintive little anthology. On 3 April 1843, poor Mr. Abrahams writes:

> This expression of disapprobation I have heard with great surprise and deep concern. I have attended 12 hours daily since my appointment to the office, with one or two exceptions only . . . and I can conscientiously aver that I could not have done more if my life had depended on the result. Yes, instead of going to Church I have devoted each Sunday to the interests of the Club . . .

Softened, perhaps, the Committee voted Mr. Abrahams three months salary in lieu of notice—and proceeded to promote Edward Sturt, Clerk of the Kitchen, to be Secretary at the lowest salary yet —£150. He served them for eight years, and at his death in March 1851 his brother wrote of the Committee's 'greatest kindness' to him while his health was failing. There is the usual melancholy sequel—a petition from members that as Sturt's family had been 'reduced to near destitution', a fund should be opened for them. The modest sum of £61 13s. 0d. was handed over to the widow in due course.

As sometimes happens, a time of financial crisis was followed by a quick recovery. Over 100 new members were recruited in the first few months of 1843, and with a Treasurer in charge of their finances for the first time, and three auditors keeping an eye on the books, the Committee were able to show a substantial surplus. At the Annual General Meeting it was decided to return their 'composition money' to 27 of the Life Subscribers (presumably the Committee had reserved the right to do this), and it was even possible to start reducing the Club's loan indebtedness. This had long stood at over £20,000, but by May 1845 it had been trimmed to £17,800. Nor, one is thankful to say, were the servants forgotten. The Steward got back £25 of his forfeited £50 on 1 January 1844 (with the promise of more to come) and there were other partial reinstatements at the same time and in subsequent years.

It was no doubt a sign of financial pressure that 1843 had seen the first timid step towards a more welcoming attitude to strangers. Clubs of a conservative temper only set their doors ajar when they are short of money. The sequence of events was characteristically tortuous. As far back as May 1840 Mr. J. A. Anstruther had begun collecting signatures to requisition an Extraordinary General Meeting 'to determine on a proposition for admitting strangers to dine at the Club under certain conditions'. No meeting was held and all went on as usual, with Major Willock, for example, receiving the inevitable reprimand for daring to bring his nephew into the Club (November 1841). He explained that elsewhere—e.g. at the Navy Club—the casual introduction of near relatives was overlooked, and added a significant growl about the effects of the 'exclusive mode adopted by the Oriental Club'—older members retiring from it and newer members being deterred from joining.

Rebellion stirred again in March 1842. The attention of the Committee was called to 'a very generally expressed desire . . . that some regulation should be made for the admission of visitors to dine at the Clubhouse'. The Committee thought this *might* have some advantages and authorised a paper to be put on the drawing room table for signatures, For and Against. On 25 April it was recorded that the approval column had been very numerously signed and there had been no disapprovals!

The Committee jinked. Deciding on their own account that there was 'a strong feeling in the Club hostile to the admission of strangers', they suddenly produced, as a diversion, the problem of sick officers on furlough. They pointed out that, of 165 military officers on sick leave from India in 1841, only two had joined the Club and at the Annual General Meeting on 2 May 1842 they proposed that 'Officers of Her Majesty and the Honourable East India Company's service visiting England on sick leave from the Government be admissible to the Club as visitors for the period of their leave on payment of an annual subscription of £8'. This was carried by 44 votes to 18. A motion by Sir Thomas Colebrooke (see page 188) that every member be entitled to introduce one visitor to dine daily was defeated.

However, 1843 provided the 'break-through' though it was only a tiny crack—Sir Thomas got his fellow members to agree that guests should be admitted to house dinners, at a cost of 15s. against the members' own 12s.

The next move was quaintly expressive. Ralph Nevill in his *London Clubs*[1] comments that in the older clubs it was usual to treat strangers like the members' dogs—left in the hall under proper restraint. That was the Oriental's attitude too, but now it was decided to provide a doghole:

> July 24th, 1843: Ordered that the small room adjoining the entrance hall, at present used for urinary purposes, be converted into a waiting room for strangers.

In this ill-begotten apartment many generations of visitors were destined to drum their fingers while their friends were—or somewhat frequently were not—informed by the pageboys of their presence.

The liberalising party continued to nibble away. At the following year's Annual General Meeting a proposition of a rather charming, Newcomeish cast was brought forward:

> That members of the Club who may have with them in London, temporarily, sons or nephews or other young gentlemen (being minors) to whom they may stand in the place of parents, shall be allowed to bring them to breakfast, lunch or dinner.

The hard-hearted majority said no[2].

A month later, however, there was a sudden 'give'. At an Extra-

[1] London, Chatto and Windus, 1911.

[2] An obstacle to all reforms, it may be noted here, was the archaic rule whereby resolutions brought forward at the A.G.M. had to be voted upon at a second meeting held a fortnight later. In the meantime, one third of the Committee (including sometimes the Chairman) had been replaced. The second meeting was not abolished until 1903.

ordinary General Meeting, held on a requisition by 40 members, it was decided that henceforth each member should be *allowed to invite one or more guests to dinner daily*, provided that such dinners were not in the Coffee Room.

So the Strangers' Room was born. To provide the space the Billiard Room and another apartment on the ground floor were converted into a dining room with six tables and an ante-room. William Collins was appointed Head Waiter—little imagining, no doubt, that he would still be taking orders there in the year 1880. Table money was fixed at 1s. 2d., with a shilling surcharge on a bottle of wine. But it was made very clear that the alien faces were to show themselves *only* in the Ante-Room and Dining Room, and never before 5 p.m. Thus matters rested for the next six years.

Apart from the problem of making room for strangers, the continued rise in membership during the 1840s put an increasing strain on the Clubhouse. By May 1844 the figure reached was 542—489 Ordinary Members, 45 Visiting and eight Free; in 1845, 597. In each case this excluded the Supernumerary Members in the East, and if I admit to having no idea how many there were of *them*, the Committee were in the same boat—'difficult' they said, 'to obtain any accurate return'.

In 1847 the membership reached 633—and the pressure produced an explosion. On 1 November 1847 the Committee received a strongly supported protest against the ballot for new members due to take place that very day, on the grounds that 'there are already eighty or ninety members more than the printed Rules of the Club admit and neither the establishment nor the premises are calculated to accommodate such an extraordinary excess without manifest inconvenience to the other members of the Club'. The Committee called off the ballot and summoned an Extraordinary General Meeting. Despite the protests against overcrowding, the only resolution passed was that '600' in Rule I should be changed to '800'—the number, as the Committee put it, for which the Clubhouse was 'originally designed and intended'.

From that moment, perversely, membership seems to have declined again, the fall being accelerated by an important event in another famous West End square, St. James's. This was the opening on 1 January 1850, of the East India United Service Club. This club had actually been founded at a meeting at the British Hotel, Cockspur Street, in February of the previous year—not 1847, as Baillie states. The records of its origin are unfortunately scanty, but an anonymous article in the *East India Army Magazine* for July 1853 makes the somewhat surprising assertion that:

> The proposal for starting an 'Indian Service' Club in the great Metropolis originated at the Cape, amongst the 'Hindus', as the Indians on leave are there irreverently termed...

The need, continues the writer, was particularly felt by officers on furlough, who found that donations paid in one sum at other clubs were high. Just what the E.I.U.S. arrangements were with regard to 'donations', or entrance fees, is not clear, but there is an obvious hint that the Oriental's stiffness about doing anything to help officers on furlough (other than sick leave) left an opening which the new club intended to fill.

The main difference in qualification between the Oriental and the E.I.U.S. was of course that the latter was confined strictly to Company's servants, together with military officers who had served in India and one or two analogous categories—there was no room for the 'nabobs' or the eastern travellers of the Oriental. On this somewhat narrow basis the promoters of the new club set to work with energy. Recruiting committees were formed for India and for home—the latter sent out no less than 4,000 circulars to 'Indians' in England. These brought in a mere 80 members, whereas some 3,000 light-heartedly signed on in India.

The first Chairman of the East India United Service Club was a Mr. Boileau of the Madras Civil Service, but in November 1849 he was succeeded by another Madras man, Mr. Malcolm Lewin, who had retired from the Service the previous year at the age of 33. Lewin held office at the E.I.U.S. only until the club was formally inaugurated on 1 January 1850, but he interests us because he was destined to become Chairman of the Oriental a few months later, and to fill the post in several subsequent years.

When it opened at its beautiful and historic house in St. James's Square, the E.I.U.S. had only 133 members in England, plus 521 furlough members and 2,380 subscribers in India—a number which quickly dwindled to less than 1,200. On the other hand the home membership increased, and this must certainly have been to some degree at the expense of the Oriental. It is not true to say, as Baillie implies, that the military element migrated wholesale from Hanover Square to St. James's, but henceforth one senses a slow evolution of the Oriental from being a club for East India Company servants into one predominantly of merchants[1].

It was not long before the respective characters of the two clubs were brought closely under examination, though the first 'character' I have to record as under scrutiny is that of a cook! A certain A. F. Lloyd from the E.I.U.S. applied for a post in the Oriental kitchen and the secretaries exchanged grave correspondence.

The E.I.U.S. had not been a going concern for two years before the question of amalgamating the two clubs came up. It was on 20 October 1851 that the chairman of the Oriental received a letter from his 'opposite number' at the E.I.U.S. stating that at a meeting on 13 October they had resolved:

> That a suggestion be made to the Committee of the Oriental Club for a union, and that if favourably received, a deputation be proposed to be made by each club to discuss the terms on which the two clubs can unite . . .

By a majority the Oriental Club Committee agreed to appoint three delegates—Colonel Bagnold, Lieut.-Colonel Taylor and Mr. Viveash. A meeting was duly held in the Committee Room of the Oriental, but negotiations broke down, apparently on financial grounds, though details are lacking.

It was against this background of strong competition in its own field that the Oriental decided that an extension to the Clubhouse was essential. The immediate impetus came from those two peren-

[1] Those recruited since the brief list given on page 32 included the founders of three famous firms still in existence—F. W. M. Gillanders (e. 1833) (Gillanders, Arbuthnot & Co., Calcutta), E. D. Kilburn (e. 1852) (Kilburn & Co., Calcutta) and Alexander Guthrie (e. 1842) (Guthrie & Co., Singapore). Also as many as six Calcutta and Hong-Kong Lyalls, starting with Charles (e. 1845), and two Finlays—Robert (e. 1828) and Alexander (e. 1828), members of Ritchie, Finlay & Co., Bombay, and grandsons of the founder of James Finlay & Co.

nially discontented classes, the billiard players and the smokers. On 28 June 1852, a requisition from 30 members pointed out that:

> The lack of a good Smoking Divan and Smoking Billiard Room in the Club is a source of great inconvenience and discomfort to the members, and very injurious to the interests of the Club.

The matter was promptly referred to a sub-Committee and by 12 July a plan was produced, followed a week later by a financial estimate—£2,387 inclusive. Orders were given for a more fully developed design to be laid on the Club table and for a circular to go out to members.

Unfortunately neither these initial plans nor any of the others to which reference will be made in Part I of this book, have survived. It is most tantalising, and it might be questioned how far it is worth-while to discuss the successive metamorphosis of a building which no longer exists and the memory of whose interior, even in its most recent form, is already fading. Yet points of interest do emerge. In broad terms, the problem in 1852, and for ever afterwards, was whether to extend westwards or upwards—i.e. to make use of the vacant ground and the stables in Tenterden Street, or to add extra floors to the two-storeyed façade. It is fairly clear that the first plans favoured a westwards movement, including a partial rebuilding of the West Wing, which then housed the servants' bedrooms and (presumably) the Billiard Room displaced when the Strangers' Room was inaugurated.

One special attraction of the scheme was that it would 'remove the male servants from close proximity to the sleeping rooms of the females; this, as we can readily believe, was 'very desirable from the moral point of view'.

The Committee moved forward energetically, spurred by a significant hint about 'retaining those who might otherwise secede'. Four architects were invited to submit detailed plans—Messrs. Thompson, Elmslie, Railton and Decimus Burton. The last was of course the most eminent name on the list and he got the job. Son of a famous speculative builder, James Burton, who largely developed the Foundling and Bedford estates in Bloomsbury, Decimus Burton was born in 1800. As Sir John Summerson puts it, he was 'rocketed to success' by the influence of his father and his father's friend John Nash, but his talents stood the test:

> Before he was twenty he had designed his father's Regent's Park villa, 'The Holme' and when he was twenty-one Cornwall Terrace was being built from his designs. At twenty-five he was commissioned to design the two works by which he will always be remembered—the screen and arch at Hyde Park Corner.

The Athenaeum followed in 1827–30. Compared with these great undertakings Burton's architectural contribution to the Oriental Club was modest. Had they employed him in his dazzling youth, instead of Benjamin Wyatt, they might have found themselves possessed of a masterpiece which would have rendered the events in my Prologue impossible!

As it was, Burton proved himself a sensible adviser and practical man of building affairs. The first thing he did was to sweep aside the westwards proposition, partly for reasons of space, partly because building in that direction would darken rooms already subdued enough. No, the upwards solution was the right one, and Burton accordingly submitted plans for two billiard rooms over the Drawing Room and part of the Library, one of them to be a non-smoker. It was these rooms, facing Hanover Square, that long afterwards became a residential suite and the abiding place of 'Pickie'[1].

The members as a body acquiesced and to complete a high-powered team, the great contractor William Cubitt, creator of Belgravia, was engaged as builder. In February 1853, however, a few debenture-holders began to run scared—was their security, the Clubhouse, being endangered by the weight to be imposed on the walls? The Club's solicitor, William Ford of Gray's Inn, cared not a pin for such fears. Unless, as he caustically put it, it was alleged that there was 'a risk of the whole building falling in and becoming a heap of ruins', it would be a waste of money to spend a full £20 on taking further advice and enduring the delay '*inseparable from consulting Counsel of eminence*'. This evidently impressed the Trustees, those austere guardians of the Club's assets, of whom the

[1] Sir Alfred Pickford. See page 147.

members hear so little though they owe them so much, and the work went ahead on the basis that Cubitt was to start on 8 August and finish within three months.

The result was an undoubted improvement—in fact the only people left grumbling were the card-players. Originally they had occupied a fairly spacious first-floor room, overlooking Tenterden Street. When the Library was extended in about 1843 they were squeezed out of this and into the Secretary's little office next door. They had a legitimate grievance, since even the three tables which were all this hutch would accommodate returned an annual income to the club of £42. One member, Captain MacMullen (e. 1829), actually resigned on the ground that he could not 'go to the Club for a rubber of whist and to meet my friends in a small room where my health was likely to receive serious injury'. In February 1844 there was a round robin: considering the proportion of card players to all those using the Club, why should they be allotted the smallest room in the house?

As a compromise, it was permitted to erect three card tables in the Drawing Room and when the Decimus Burton alterations were brought forward, an integral part of them was to be an extension of the Card Room. Alas, this proved too expensive and again the card players lost out. Their mumbling and muttering fills the subsequent decades—'annoyance and discomfort are frequently insufferable . . . close, confined, unwholesome atmosphere . . . small room crowded to suffocation . . .'. The Committee blandly sympathised, but had no intention of returning the Back Library to this malcontent sect.

Whether it was because of the heavy expense of the alterations (intensified by the loss of revenue while they were in progress[1]), or because the new accommodation was not being fully employed, the Committee almost immediately turned their thoughts to amalgamation, and the East India United Services was the obvious first choice. This time the approach was from Hanover Square to St. James's, and, while we only have the Oriental's side of the story, it does seem that the older club was treated with unwarranted *hauteur*.

[1] On 14 November it was decided to make an obligatory levy of £2 on all the 550 members to meet a deficiency estimated at £1,060 for the full year.

To a letter of 30 October 1854 the E.I.U.S. replied that they would be very glad to see an amalgamation, but on the following terms:

1 Limitation of the admission of Oriental Club members to classes admissible under E.I.U.S. rules.

2 Non-liability of E.I.U.S. members for any Oriental Club debts.

3 The bringing into the common stock by the Oriental Club of realized or available property not less in extent than the sum which their collective donations, at the rate fixed by the E.I.U.S. club rules for members entering by ballot, would amount to.

The letter added that the E.I.U.S. would not be prepared to consider the house and furniture of the Club in Hanover Square as part of such available property, it being their opinion that it would not be desirable to have the amalgamated club in that district. In other words, the Oriental must sell up and migrate from its remote suburb to St. James's Square, cash in hand.

The Oriental reply was brief—the first condition alone involved a difficulty (the exclusion of some existing members) which could not be overcome. Mr. Bunbury Taylor, Secretary of the E.I.U.S., next suggested that the Oriental should put forward its own ideas on amalgamation, ignoring the obnoxious Clause I for the moment. But when the Committee proposed joint discussion, as before, between three delegates from each side, they were informed that if they sent a deputation it could submit its terms to the full Committee of the E.I.U.S. This was too much. Negotiations were broken off, as on the first occasion.

The final breach took place on 10 December. It was almost certainly influenced by the fact that, just 10 days earlier, the Committee of the Oriental had received a letter enquiring whether they would consider admitting 'a large body of the Alfred Club', and on what terms. This communication, we suspect, did not come out of the blue—indeed, the subsequent Extraordinary General Meeting was told that it had been ascertained that 'the Alfred Club was breaking up'.

Since there was not the slightest natural affinity between the two clubs, one can only assume a rather desperate marriage of convenience; the Alfred members needed somewhere to go, and the

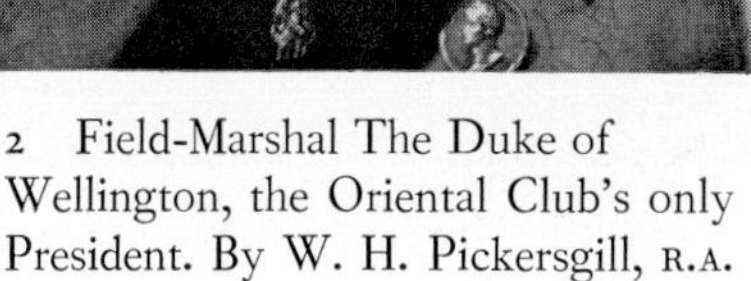

2 Field-Marshal The Duke of Wellington, the Oriental Club's only President. By W. H. Pickersgill, R.A.

3 Major-General Sir John Malcolm, Vice-President and first Chairman. By Samuel Lane

4 Thomas Snodgrass, active promoter and benefactor of the Club. Artist unknown

5, 6, 7 No. 18 Hanover Square: (*top left*) after Decimus Burton had added one floor to Benjamin Wyatt's two-storey building in 1853 (windows remodelled later); (*left*) in its final phase, from a drawing by Geoffrey Fletcher; (*above*) the Staircase

8 Sir Jamsetjee Jejeebhoy. By John Smart.
A portrait now reduced in size

9 Major-General Sir Thomas Munro. By R. R. Reinagle, R.A.
Also since cut down

10 The old Drawing Room, showing its fine ceiling

11 Dinner given by the Oriental Club to Major-General Sir Archdale Wilson on 1 June 1858 in its 'spacious banqueting hall, Hanover Square'. The dinner, we are told, was 'of the most sumptuous description', every effort being made to give *éclat* to the occasion. An *Illustrated London News* drawing

12 The Bar (former dining room) at Stratford House. Mather Brown's great picture of 'Earl Cornwallis receiving the Sons of Tippoo Sahib as Hostages' dominates the left-hand wall, and another portrait of Cornwallis by Samuel Lane is next to it. Barman Ramm in charge

13 Lord Lake. Bust after the Club's portrait by an unknown artist

Oriental needed their subscriptions. Established in Albemarle Street since 1808, the Alfred was a sort of secondary Athenaeum, with a lower I.Q. Being within a few hundred paces of Mr. Murray's publishing office, it suited Byron to belong for a time—'a decent resort on a rainy day'—but perhaps, like Lord Alvanley, he 'stood it as long as he could and only gave in when the seventeenth Bishop was elected'. Apart from this superfluity of gaiters, we have few clues to the Alfred's decline—one legend attributes the final collapse to a tussle *à outrance* on the subject of smoking[1].

In any case, the application to the Oriental was in urgent terms, and an answer was sought in time for a general meeting of the Alfred Club the following Wednesday. The two sides met within 24 hours. Negotiations went smoothly and, while the Alfred saved face by talking of an 'amalgamation', the Oriental Chairman was justified in his use of the term 'admission'. The formula reached was that Alfred members would be enrolled at the Oriental without ballot on payment of the annual subscription from 1 January 1855, plus the £2 levy. They were supposed to sign up within six months —a provision which caused trouble later, since the Alfred men, like the Orientals, tended to roam away into desert or jungle for years at a time; it was a grim homecoming to find their dear old club extinct and their right to join the Oriental exhausted[2].

The immediate result, however, was a large migration to Hanover Square. By 14 December there had been 170 'adhesions', 240 after the Alfred's last General Meeting on 21 December, and 272 by April 1855.

It was one of those events which go to the heart of club life. Committee Minutes of course give no glimpse of the feelings of the Oriental rank-and-file, who, after twice steeling themselves to joining up with their own kind at the E.I.U.S., were now confronted with

[1] Sir Henry Drummond-Wolff, *Rambling Recollections* (London, Macmillan, 1908), dates the decline of the Alfred from an incident in 1827. A dozen men at a house dinner were joined by a member who apologised for being in day clothes, but who quickly enchanted them with his conversation. As nobody recognised him enquiry was made and he turned out to be George Canning, the Prime Minister! Drummond-Wolff alleges that people thereafter refused to join a club so dim that among 12 members not one knew the Prime Minister by sight. A Gothic tale.

[2] In practice, the Oriental Committee took a lenient view when the traveller's case seemed genuine.

a flood of part-literary, part-clerical evacuees from Albemarle Street. Much grunting together in corners, one suspects, and more audible complaints about crowding and over-taxed service. Of this last, by the way, we have £18-worth of evidence, that being the tally of excess breakages (glass and china) recorded in March 1855 and blamed upon 'the unavoidable confusion attendant on the admission of the Alfred members'.

Not all the latter became permanencies. Some graduated to the Athenaeum, others just drifted away into the darkness, but perhaps a couple of hundred stayed on and were assimilated. A few survivors were still to be seen asleep in the Oriental armchairs as late as 1899[1].

As for the East India United Service Club, it went its individual way, attracting an ever-increasing number of famous soldiers and administrators. As soon as the custom of lodging came in (see page 86), the Oriental and the E.I.U.S. gladly played host to each other. There was no more talk of amalgamation, however, and when in 1939 the E.I.U.S. did join forces with another club its choice was the Sports, a hundred yards away on the north side of St. James's Square. A marriage of propinquity, one might assume, since on the face of it the new partners had as little in common as the Alfred and the Oriental. But they did share the characteristic of having very large numbers of members stationed in the East, and this was a main reason why they became so happily blended into the East India and Sports Club of today.

[1] One of them, Mr. C. E. Austen Leigh, survived, incredibly, until 1924. He had thus been a member of the Oriental for 70 years.

5 Late Victorians

> *Ordered*, that three hedgehogs be obtained for the kitchen, to kill the black beetles.
>
> *Committee Minute, 27 June 1859*

By the time the changes described in Chapter 4 were complete, two great public events were at hand—the Indian Mutiny (1857–8) and the dissolution of the Honourable East India Company (1859). Though the H.E.I.C., nursery of the Club, had long been in decline, the one event certainly hastened the other.

When the Mutiny broke out, the Club's military and civil service membership was still strong enough to provide an impressive link with Cawnpore, Lucknow and the Delhi Ridge. Of the great names concerned, John Lawrence (Lord Lawrence) had been elected in 1841 and his brother Henry in 1848, James Outram in 1843, Archdale Wilson[1] in 1846 and Colin Campbell (Lord Clyde) as far back as 1826.

Viewed purely as clubmen, Outram was certainly the most active among them. His densely whiskered visage was constantly seen in Hanover Square both before and after the Mutiny and he kept up a mildly eccentric commerce with the Committee, sending them specimens of military caps in 1852, and of German beer in 1856; they rather vaguely thanked him for the former, and said they would not trouble him for further supplies of the latter.

It is characteristic of Club records that though almost every member must have followed the course of the Mutiny with an acute and even agonised sense of personal involvement, the references to it in the annals are of the slightest. Once or twice, the confusion of the times was used as an excuse for not paying subscriptions, but the

[1] The Club dined him in June 1858 (*Pl. 11*).

Committee, aware of the special financing arranged by India House for its servants, took a sceptical view. Otherwise, we only find recorded the opening of a subscription book in aid of the Lord Mayor's Fund for sufferers from 'the present insurrection', and a further whip-round three years later for the Memorial Church, Cawnpore.

On the other hand, it may or may not be quite a coincidence that from this terrible time onwards the Club took a far more generous view of appeals for help from the outside world. The Indian Famine Relief Fund (1861), the Distressed Lancashire Operatives' Fund (1862)[1], the 'Bombay' and 'Racehorse' appeals (1865)[2], another Indian Famine Fund (1877) and the Strangers' House for Asiatics (1884) were among the causes which touched the Committee's (and subsequently the members') hearts. Only one appeal seems to have 'flopped'; a collecting-box in support of the 'Sufferers by the landslip at Naini Tal', authorised on 26 October 1880, was removed three weeks later—'no subscribers'.

It is noticeable too, that the admission of distinguished Honorary Members took a fresh impetus for a short period after 1857. Among the more interesting names are those of Sir Cursetjee Jamsetjee Jejeebhoy (the 2nd Baronet), elected in May 1860, H.E. Nazim Bey, Prime Minister of Turkey (May 1862), M. de Vabason, former French Consul-General in Calcutta (June 1862) and H.H. Nawab Nazim of Bengal (April 1869).

In the seventies the impulse died down, to be revived strongly during the full tide of late Victorian imperialism. At the 1886 A.G.M. it was agreed that properly sponsored visitors from India and the Colonies should enjoy honorary membership during the run of the Colonial and Indian Exhibition; over 40, headed by Mr. John

[1] No Eastern connection—the distress was caused by the American Civil War disrupting cotton supplies.

[2] Lloyd's of London have kindly supplied the following notes:

4th November, 1864: H.M.S. Racehorse wrecked in the China seas about five leagues south-east of Chefoo Cape. The ship's company were sent aft, and told that if they held on till daylight there was every hope of all hands being saved. But the poor fellows dropped off one by one from the effect of the cold and the force of the sea. Only nine were saved.

14th December, 1864: H.M.S. Bombay, burnt off Flores Island, near Montevideo; 91 lives lost.

Shand of the well-known Ceylon planting family[1], were elected in this way. The same courtesy was offered to delegates to the Imperial Conference (1887), to the International Geographical Congress (1895), and to Diamond Jubilee visitors (1897); the odd men out were (in spite of their name) the Orientalists, whose 1890 Congress did not inspire the Club's hospitality.

Meanwhile, another aspect of 'involvement'—the gruelling campaign to get non-members admitted into the Clubhouse—pursued a parallel course. In my previous chapter we saw them allotted their strictly segregated Strangers' Room. Not until 1851 were they allowed to penetrate as far as the Smoking Room after dinner, but then the pace quickened. The following year they could be asked to luncheon and in 1853 to breakfast—the easiest way, argued Lieut.-Colonel Tait, of meeting one's friends 'in this large city'.

Games-playing by strangers was long frowned on, with one exception. In 1855 it was laid down that members and friends dining together in the Strangers' Room might play cards there afterwards, 'but only at the table at which they had dined'—play not to commence before 9 p.m. or to finish after one o'clock in the morning. It is a curious scene—the white cloth, already removed for the dessert, replaced by green baize, the candlelight falling on cards and counters, instead of decanters and bowls of fruit....

Here and there, of course, there were abuses of the strangers' rules. The members had rather quaintly to be reminded that they were 'held to be inviting their friends to a meal of which they were themselves partaking', and for which they would be charged whether they ate it or not; and the Rev. Charles Padley was censured for sending up three youngsters by themselves to the Billiard Room, where they misbehaved in an offensive and annoying manner. But the tide was coming in, and when it was finally decided that strangers could ascend to the Drawing Room to be received before dinner (1885), it was only a matter of time until they would win the full access they enjoy today.

[1] Ceylon was rather thinly represented in the earlier days of the Club, but one notices the name of Captain Keith Jolly, first secretary of the Ceylon Planters' Association (elected before 1851). Sir Edward Barnes (Governor 1824–31) was an Original Member; Sir Colin Campbell (Governor 1839–47) insisted (p. 28) that he was not!.

Strangers yes, female strangers no—at least not for a long time. But when the barrier did fall down, it happened rather suddenly and with curiously little reverberation. It was in June 1885 that General Sir Henry Thuiller (e. 1844) first raised the question. The Committee decided that the matter was 'not within their competence', but at the Annual General Meeting held on 18 May 1886, the following notable resolution proposed by Sir Henry was carried by 35 votes to 10:

> That ladies may be admitted, when accompanied by a member, to the Strangers' Room for Tea, Coffee, or Light Refreshments, between the hours of 4 and 6 daily.

Infiltration had begun, but until the end of the century it was not extended beyond special arrangements for luncheon on Royal Wedding and Jubilee days; in fact when in the euphoria of the Diamond Jubilee the Committee resolved by 11 votes to three that 'ladies should be admitted to luncheon until further notice' there were petitions and letters of protest and the Committee had to back down.

A development which also tended to modify the extreme introversion of the members' routine was the custom of 'lodging'. How and when did it come in? During the Club's early days there seems to have been no question of an annual closure for redecoration and staff holidays. The first reference to anything of the kind in the Minutes is dated 11 July 1859, when an extensive programme of repairs, etc. forced the members to move out temporarily.

However, there may have been at least one earlier migration, since in offering the use of six rooms and three water-closets, Mr. Jarman of the Brunswick Hotel across the Square, says the charge will be nine guineas per week—'same as before'.

The members then sat tight for the next four years, and when, in 1864, it was again decided to find a transient home they moved rather dashingly to Claridge's, where Mr. Claridge agreed to take them in at 15 guineas per week. It is amusing that even on 'away' territory the members continued to back their bills as usual—it irritated Mr. W. Morris-Beaufort no end that during 'the whole time he was sitting at breakfast on the 8th inst. the waiter was seated at a side table writing a letter'. Mr. Claridge expressed regret.

Again there was a long pause, and it was in 1870 that the first suggestion came (from Mr. S. Lloyd Foster) for 'affiliating our members on some other Club' during August. The following year, having failed to stave off further pressure by arranging for entrées to be sent in from Verrey's while the Kitchen was closed, the Committee tried to negotiate an exchange with the East India United Service, but they were already 'booked' by the Army and Navy. From 1874 onwards, however, the system of lodging was in full swing. The E.I.U.S. was the usual opposite number, and it was unfortunate that when a move was made to the Naval & Military in 1885, an Oriental member chose that moment to do £8 5s. od. worth of damage to their furniture and was extremely recalcitrant about paying up.

As a matter of fact, Victorian Clubmen seem generally to have been hard on the furniture and fittings. We may perhaps ignore the case of old Mr. Wilton who 'partly destroyed' 14 chairs in 1833–4, since this was caused by his 'infirmities', whatever they may have been; the main culprits were those members who insisted on putting their feet up on sofas and ottomans. Time after time they were appealed to as gentlemen, were 'shown the relevant notice' by the waiters, were bribed with additional leg-rests, until, bored by all this governessy exhortation, Mr. Courtenay produced the memorable dictum:

'*What are sofas for except to put your feet on?*'

Stunned, the Committee never mentioned the subject again[1].

It is perhaps the regrettable truth that a man's club has always been the place where he feels entitled to behave a little worse than in society outside. This was of course one of the psychological barriers to the admission of ladies! However, even in the barbarous days before they got in, the standard of impropriety varied a good deal, as the following few examples of misconduct laid before the Committee will show:

Captain F.: Filing his nails during breakfast.
Mr. G. P.: Wearing the Club bath slippers in the Coffee Room.
Mr. C. F.: Reading aloud to himself in the Library.

[1] A Bye-law outlawing the practice was, however, in force until quite recently.

Mr. G.: Scraping toast on the Coffee Room floor.
Dr. W.: Drinking ale and using a fork in the Drawing Room[1].
Anon.: Entering the Strangers' Room in flannels and a cap.
Several members: Spitting, throat-clearing and the like in a variety of contexts.
Ditto: Snoring.

Removing the boots was a frequent source of scandal. At an earlier date it was one of several grievances against Prince Jameh-ud-Din (e. 1837). That the Club should have had a son of Tippoo Sahib in its midst at all was such a singular circumstance that one regrets all the more that neither his personal habits nor his treatment of the staff made him a very acceptable member.

A particularly disastrous case of boot-removing occurred in July 1875, and the letter apprising the Chairman of it is a fine composition:

Sir,

I would draw your attention to the fact that I saw one of the members, Mr. Payter, sitting in the Smoking Room of the Club with his boots off—an act I consider filthy and ungentlemanly. A member of the Conservative Club noticed it, and I fear that he left the Oriental Club with an erroneous impression of its character and tone.

I have the honour to be, sir,

E. A. Trevor
(Capt. R.A.)

The Committee concurred—to Mr. Payter's understandable distress, having regard to the ferocious adjectives of Captain Trevor.

Even the twin vices of drinking and gambling were seldom pursued to ruinous extremes. The former takes us straight into the cartoonists' world of intoxicated 'swells' propping up lamp-posts or each other. And, as in those old *Punch* drawings, hats were the principal sufferers. 'Oh it is your hat that Mr. Bright walked off with after trying on ten or twelve!', the Hall Porter exclaimed to Mr. Uvedale Price. And recalled, perhaps, the evening when a *large number* of members tottered out all wearing each other's hats, and acrimony ensued; or the misdemeanour of Mr. Bennie, who disappeared with Mr. Colvin's hat and Dr. Richardson's coat and could not be traced for several days.

[1] Where only small sandwiches and the like were allowed.

As mentioned earlier, the Oriental never had the character of a gambling club. Nevertheless, an epidemic of late card-playing in the sixties nearly led to a personal disaster. A 'school' had evidently been formed, not in the cramped little Card Room itself, but in the Smoking Room (or Smoking Billiard Room) on the top floor. The ringleader was a clergyman, the Rev. J. O. Oldham (e. 1857), and one can only trust that a session which is said to have lasted until '7 a.m. on December 26th 1862' really began on the 26th rather than on Christmas Day! After repeated warnings the Committee suspended card-playing in the Smoking Room, and Mr. Oldham apologised (though this did not inhibit him from criticising the Club's anchovy toast). The trouble went on for years—'final warning' given after an 8 a.m. session in July 1867, then play continuing till 3.30 a.m. on successive Saturday and Sunday mornings in August.

There was nothing for it—Mr. Oldham must be asked to resign. His reply had a touch of melodrama—

> ... Made a spectacle not only to the members of the Club, but to the menials of the same ... severed from the circle of my friends ... publicly disgraced and a stigma attached to my name.

This shook the Committee and the month being August, they rather ingeniously decided that 'a General Meeting could not be summoned at that season' and the whole thing was allowed to slide into oblivion....

Mr. Oldham, one feels, was a relic of an earlier age. Nobody who is even slightly acquainted with the life stories of the great Indian administrators and soldiers of the Mutiny period will be surprised to know that side by side with much that was mildly disreputable there was a strong strain of piety and even of religious fanaticism among the members of the Oriental Club.

The placing of tracts on the Drawing Room tables, for example, had constantly to be discouraged, and at least once a member's rigid tenets brought him into serious collision with the Committee.

Mr. James Farish (e. 1827) was a distinguished Bombay Civil Servant, having been a member of Council in 1836. But he was also an ardent proselytiser. This had led to a painful scene at the moment of his leaving India in 1841, when a meeting to found scholarships in his honour was virtually boycotted by the Indian community—Mr. Farish had 'wounded them in the tenderest part' by his missionary zeal[1]!

Alas, when he came home and joined the Club he soon wounded the more sporting members in *their* tenderest part—the holding of Race Lotteries.

The course of events was:

Move 1. (8 July 1844.) Mr. Farish points out to the Committee that lotteries are 'contrary to the spirit and strong wording of Rule XLIII'. The Committee temporises—says Mr. Farish can bring the matter before a General Meeting if he wishes.

Move 2. (25 November.) Mr. Farish submits an opinion (anti-lottery, of course) by the Solicitor-General. The Committee refuses to be impressed.

Move 3. (3 March 1845.) Mr. Farish writes again. Still no reaction.

Move 4. (24 March.) Mr. Farish resigns.

But our stubborn evangelical won in the end! On 21 July Colonel Limond drew the Committee's attention to the result of Allport v. Nutt in the Court of Common Pleas, in which the illegality of Race Lotteries was placed beyond doubt, and reminded them of their delicate responsibility *vis-à-vis* Mr. Farish.

The game was up. It was agreed to sanction no more Race Lotteries and ('having received a hint that this would be acceptable') to re-enroll Mr. Farish.

For a while we continue to catch glimpses of him, and always in a characteristic posture—attempting (June 1849) to get the *Church Missionary Intelligencer* taken by the Club, but being told that it was 'more suitable for private families', or (December 1850) making a gift to the Library of *Wilson's Sermons on the Sabbath.*

Then follows a long silence until, early in 1873, comes a concatenation of Minutes:

13 February: 'The death of Mr. Farish was reported'.
8 April: 'An annual sweep on the Derby was sanctioned.'

[1] *Asiatic Journal*, April 1841.

Cause and effect? Sheer chance? At any rate, a story with a symmetrical ending[1].

Mr. Farish, I feel sure, would have backed Mr. Carter and the Rev. W. H. Davies in another campaign which may recall for a few readers the long-forgotten past. It all related to 'intermediate sizes of black-edged paper'. When the correspondence started in December 1855, the Club only stocked two widths of black-edged, and though the Committee were prepared to widen the narrower border somewhat, they did not wish to increase the range. Mr. Carter was not satisfied and his next letter took a sardonic turn. He suggested that a medium size should be provided

> ... unless the Committee ensure that members should only lose wives or cousins. The deepest bordered black used in the Club is what is commonly used by widows or widowers.... It is deeper than that used by fathers and mothers for loss of sons or daughters, or vice-versa, and Mr. Carter appeals to the Committee whether the paper on which he is now writing is sufficiently deep-edged for the purpose.

The Committee refused to go beyond their previous decision, but when the Rev. W. H. Davies took up the running six months later, they yielded and an intermediate size was placed in the Writing Room.

Superior both in rank and in good works to either Mr. Oldham or Mr. Davies was Bishop Tozer[2]. Apart from the theological contributions to the Library which might be expected of him, he was one of the few late Victorian members who took a practical interest in the welfare of the staff. For example, in January 1883 he headed the second of two attempts to provide the Servants' Hall with a library. The first initiative had been in 1869, when recesses were fitted up with shelves, a subscription list was opened and Mr. Alfred Burton contributed a nucleus of 20 to 30 volumes. It cannot have lasted very long, because 14 years later Bishop Tozer brought up the

[1] Another member who carried on a running battle with the Committee on a legal issue and won in the end was Colonel Henry Newnham (e. 1831). For a whole decade (1854–64) he challenged the Club's right to deduct Income Tax on debenture interest, reducing the Committee to a state of almost hysterical pig-headedness until the 1864 A.G.M. finally voted in his favour by a large majority.

[2] The Rt. Rev. W. G. Tozer had been a Missionary Bishop in Central Africa, and was later translated to Jamaica. At the time of his death in 1899 his *Who's Who* address was The Oriental Club.

idea *de novo*. Again there was a subscription (headed by the Bishop) and though progress was rather languid, the practical step was taken of providing an extra gas burner in the Servants' Hall for the benefit of readers.

Bishop Tozer also kept an avuncular eye on the Club's Page-Boys, taking them to German Reed's Entertainment[1] at Christmas and on other treats. Those boys—an extinct race today, but until just before World War II a sprightly element in the Club's life. During the nineteenth century they varied in number between five and seven, looking no doubt very smart in the brown uniform with gold braid which was introduced in 1868. Apart from the usual hall duties, they were charged with collecting and posting mail, but were forbidden to go round the Clubhouse badgering the members for their letters; the correct procedure (according to a notice of 1885) was for the boy on duty to 'announce in a loud voice', 15 minutes before the postal hour, that he was about to clear the boxes. The last time he did this, poor little creature, was at 1 a.m., and when Mr. Allen queried (June 1878) whether it was really necessary to keep a boy up as late as that, he was told that the Committee had already considered the point, but as the duty was taken in turn, there was no serious hardship.

One's guess, however, is that the pages, whatever their hours, were the usual cheeky and resilient tribe, and that hall-boy Varney who slid down the banister of the main staircase (ideal for the purpose) on 22 July 1870, was following a revered tradition. The unlucky thing in his case was that he overbalanced and, as the Secretary recorded—his pen slithering like young Varney in the excitement—

> He fell on the ottoman at the bottoman

and had to be taken to Middlesex Hospital for repairs.

Apart from the Servants' Hall Library and outings for the boys, staff conditions generally showed a slow improvement. The servants numbered some 50, including 15 waiters, 10 in the kitchen, and (considering that there were no members' bedrooms) a rather formidable corps of six housemaids. In 1865 the first attempt had been made to rationalise staff pay with a commencing rate for each job,

[1] A popular Christmas show put on year by year at the St. James's Hall.

rising by £1 increments to a fixed maximum[1]. Some specimens: Carver (Woodcock) £30–35 a year; Head Waiter, Strangers' Room (Collins) £55–£60; Under-Butler (Carpenter) £28–£35; Night Porter (Howard) and House Porter (Green) £25–£30 and £22–£25 respectively; Coffee Room Waiters and most others £25–£30; Steward's Room Boy £6. Only six of the staff drew lodging-out allowances (£5 a year) at this period.

About one servant in 10 seems to have settled down to long service with the Club, but for the first 35 years after 1824 there was no talk of pensions when they could carry on no longer. One man did indeed draw a sort of pension, though in freakish circumstances. This was a lampman called J. Weaver. In December 1842, he was badly hurt in a gas explosion and was granted an allowance of 10s. a week until he could support himself.

Five years passed and the Committee, feeling that 'he ought e'er this to have found other service', decided that for only one year longer they would give him 5s. a week, plus an outfit allowance. Whereupon Weaver himself, backed by the Club surgeon, appeared before the Committee to show the 'utter uselessness of his hands'. And as his luckless situation was caused by his obeying 'a very imprudent order of the late Secretary' ('*take a candle and look for the leak*' perhaps?), the 10s. a week was reinstated until further notice. In fact, until Weaver's death in the London Hospital on 12 December 1876, when the long account was closed with a payment of £3 to his daughter for funeral expenses.

A year later another lampman, J. Davies, was given a genuine retirement pension of 12s. a week after the extraordinary period of 48 years and two months in that humble employment. By then, there was quite a list of pensioners, headed by Samuel Smith, Coffee Room Superintendent, who in 1859 was granted 50 guineas a year after 30 years service (a motion to make it his full salary of £60 was turned down). W. A. Collins, Strangers' Room Head Waiter, whom we have met before, got £50 in May 1880 (47 years service). He only lived two years to enjoy it, but an extra quarter's pension was voted

[1] Including, one presumes, the quaint institution of 'hat money'. When the Club first opened the servants were entitled to one new hat annually. This was commuted in 1843 for 16s. a year; it was abolished for newly joined staff from 1876 onwards.

to his widow, 'left almost destitute'—the old story. Finally, just before the 1884 A.G.M., there was a pleasing little revolt by the members; they insisted that Mary Hewright, Head Housemaid for 29 years, should get 10s. a week instead of the 5s. recommended by the Committee.

On the whole, the latter were far from hard-hearted. One feels (without knowing the circumstances) that they might have helped Anne Adams, Housemaid, when, forced into retirement by rheumatism after 20 years, she 'solicited a little assistance towards purchasing furniture for a room', but on the other hand they took a lot of trouble over getting the servants into hospital when they were ill[1], and usually paid their funeral expenses when they died; they were indulgent over petty crime, 'sackings' were frequently remitted if due penitence was shown[2], and no notice was taken when an anonymous letter informed the Chairman that one of the waiters had been in prison for bigamy.

Drunkenness—a little less prevalent perhaps than in the earliest days—was dealt with fairly sharply. On 6 January 1862, comes a Minute never, I am sure, to be duplicated in the lifetime of the present holder of the name and office:

> Harris, the House Porter, drunk twice last week. Ordered to be dismissed.

Serious notice had to be taken, too, when (as in all the world's catering establishments) things began 'going out through the back door'. In January 1859 there was a near-mutiny because one of the waiters was stopped by the police on the way home, and 'bread, meat, sugar, soap, etc.' were found in his bag. He got two months, and the staff were furious at what they believed to be a system of spying on them. The row was smoothed over, but no doubt the leakage continued, judging by a serio-comic incident in June 1880, when

[1] As an alternative, when Richard Cook, Coffee Room Waiter, was away sick, he was granted two bottles of port a week until he got better.

[2] A typical case was that of John Davis, another Coffee Room Waiter ('improper behaviour to the Under-Stillroom Maid', and other complaints). He pleaded 26 years service, a wife and five children, and was reinstated by one vote. This so incensed a Committee member, Lieut. Fowlis, that he threatened to resign (9 October 1854), but could not resist the temptation to return and move a resolution with regard to Irish stew.

A. Sinclair, Strangers' Room Waiter, was found 'drunk, and in the act of packing one of the Club's napkins with cutlets, curries, etc.'. Yet the thought of a hungry young family waiting somewhere obtrudes. . . .

One positive gain in security and well-being came rather late. For many years the Committee regularly voted the staff a sum of about £1 per head as a Christmas bonus, as well as providing a 'feast'. The latter indeed developed gradually into a Servants' Ball and a Christmas dinner, to which relatives and friends could be invited. But both these entertainments were stopped for a long period after an incident in 1861, when the Billiard Room money boxes were raided and 'many other gross irregularities' took place.

It was not until 1894 that the members were given the chance of supporting a Staff Christmas Fund. Subscription books were placed experimentally in the Coffee Room and Drawing Room and the response was immediate; between 6 November 1894 and 15 January 1895, £148 3s. 6d. was subscribed, compared with the Committee's own grant of £54 the previous year. In 1895–6 the figure went up to £160 16s. 0d. and in 1897 to over £193.

One day in May 1862, Captain Frank Crossman was standing on the steps of the Club smoking a cigar. The Hall Porter approached him, displaying (as he had been told to three weeks earlier) the notice forbidding the practice. Captain Crossman pointed out that it was raining in torrents and he was only waiting for a cab. He was shown the notice again. He went on smoking. At the next Committee meeting he was reported for 'a distinct and formal refusal to conform to the rule' and was severely censured.

Only a few months before an argument about smoking had led to a fracas in the Large Billiard Room (where tobacco was forbidden), between Mr. W. M. Anderden and our old friend the Rev. J. O. Oldham. The latter and a guest apparently insisted on lighting up, which so infuriated Mr. Anderden that he walked round and round the billiard table for 10 or 12 minutes uttering invectives against the Club—'the worst managed in London'!

Now it is a commonplace of clubland that some of the fiercest internal battles of the nineteenth century related to smoking. We have already met one club, the Alfred, which is reputed to have broken up on this question. And there is no doubt that the practice was widely disliked. We have all read stories of male guests in country houses puffing smoke surreptitiously up the kitchen chimney, but even in the masculine society of barracks and mess-rooms smoking was absolutely forbidden until the Duke of Cambridge became Commander-in-Chief in 1856.

Yet if there was any club in London where tobacco might have gained an uncontested foothold it was the Oriental. Smoking was habitual in the East; if only to discourage flies and as a vague defence against 'noxious effluvia'. It is inexplicable that our 'Indian' gentlemen should have been prepared to drop the whole thing when they came Home. The Club's attitude was in fact ambivalent. The right to smoke was fought room by room, decade after decade. Yet from at least 1850 onwards the Committee was making substantial purchases of cheroots, and certain waiters were allowed to retail them to members—an arrangement which invited 'irregularities' and got them.

The cheroots (and later cigars[1]) poured in, 10,000, 20,000 and 30,000 at a time, direct from China in some cases, or from William Dent or A. Gouger (£8 per 1,000), and if they were at all defective —or worse still worm-eaten, like some of Mr. Wood's in 1867— they went straight back. You could buy and buy, but hardly anywhere could you light up—not even, as we have seen, on the front steps, though once again the Club showed its split mind by providing a permanent gas jet (1885) for the very purpose!

The strongest testimony to the opposition's success in keeping tobacco out of the main rooms is that for over half a century the growing demand for smoking facilities had to be met in the most expensive way possible—by building additions to the Clubhouse! Decimus Burton's 'Smoking Divan and Smoking Billiard Room' of 1853 soon proved inadequate, and for an entire decade (1861–71) the Committee mulled over one extension scheme after another. The climax was perhaps reached in May 1869, when, as the result of a tangle of resolutions at the A.G.M., 'the eminent architect, Mr. Clifton' was commissioned to produce completely new plans. The

[1] An experimental order for *cigarettes* is recorded in January 1866.

result was a block-buster. Mr. Clifton not only suggested alterations embracing 'the Entrance Hall, a new Strangers' Room, Smoking Room and Billiard Room, alterations to the Card Room and Library, and consequent changes in the Servants' Bedrooms and Basement', but made it clear that in his view nothing worthwhile could be done to the building for less than £10,000. Miserably, the Committee paid him 100 guineas and turned him loose.

Another proposal was to buy the freehold of No. 18a Hanover Square, next door, but that was in multiple tenancy and too difficult to handle. At last, general support was given to a plan by Henry Burton (of the same firm as Decimus); this simply provided a new Smoking Room above the Kitchen, to cost, with its furniture and fittings, no more than £2,663. Thus was acquired the large, comfortable, rather gloomy apartment at mezzanine level which, with its famous 'quarter deck', almost at once proved more popular than the majestic but strictly 'non-smoker' Drawing Room facing Hanover Square.

Henry Burton's scheme was of course akin to the 'westwards' proposals turned down by Decimus many years before. But it did not encroach on Conduit Yard (as the Stables were still sometimes known), though considering the endless trouble and frequent financial loss[1] to which this area gave rise, it is a mystery why it was never, from 1828 until 1959, absorbed into the Club premises.

In the early years the tenants were cab-owners or livery-men. They perennially failed to pay their rent and put in lugubrious excuses—'I now have three as good broughams as any in London, and there they stand for days and not a job do they do' (Christopher Teesdale, 1855)—until at last, tired of seeing the brokers' men mooching about their backyard, the Committee decided 'no more cabs'. After an unsuccessful bid by Messrs. J. Schweppes, the buildings were finally let at £120 a year to Mr. William Phillips, auctioneer, whose successors, Messrs. Phillips, Son and Neale, have been near neighbours ever since. He was there from 1856 until 1880, and it was a long time before there was another settled tenancy.

Many applications for the premises came in (including such familiar names as Messrs. Savory and Moore) and there was a nibble

[1] 1854: Net loss on Stables £227 15s. 4d. (including £120 19s. 6d. for repairs).

from the Secretary of the Hanover Square Club, who also mentioned, apparently as an inducement, that the Oriental had tried unsuccessfully to poison his dog. . . . But the most significant enquiry was from Messrs. Loft & Warner in 1882: Could the stables be used as a 'centre' by Swan's Electric Light Company? The Committee was scared of the new element and long remained so, and eventually sought a rather Gilbertian escape from their troubles by having the stables demolished altogether in 1884.

For seven whole years the site lay vacant, while upholsterers, gunsmiths, more electric light companies, and the faint suggestion of a Club squash court were passed despondently in review. At last the spell was broken by Mr. Lucas, coachbuilder, who in January 1892 was authorised to erect a two-tier workshop in return for a rental of £150.

And here we might as well complete the electricity story. Many schemes to light the Clubhouse were put up, including one by the Club accountant, Mr. Ball, who was prepared to rent the Tenterden Street site for the purpose. This went no further; nor did an offer from the 'American Brush Light Co.' (1885); nor did a scheme to obtain light from a dynamo belonging to the Medical and Chirurgical Society at 20 Hanover Square. At last, in March 1892, the Committee were prepared to take the subject seriously. Tenders were invited for wiring practically the whole house, and the contract went to the Westminster Electricity Supply Co., whose 'low tension system' was preferred to the London Electricity Supply Co.'s 'high tension'.

The immediate result was that the cost of lighting the Clubhouse went up from £52 to £64 in a typical month, but in spite of this—and a 'partial extinction' during darkest November—the new system was highly approved; only in the Billiard Room (which suffered from draughts) were both gas and electricity maintained as alternatives, 'according to the temperature'.

Another symptom of modernity, the telephone, though several times discussed, had to await the new century, but a forbear of the 'tape' takes us back to 1867. This was a contract with Reuter for hourly Parliamentary and Racing Telegrams at a cost of about £25 for the half-year—an arrangement which seems to have debarred the Club from taking the Press Association's 'Telegrams from the Seat of War' during the Franco-Prussian conflict of 1870.

Such innovations apart, the day-to-day life of the Club did not differ greatly in the second half of the century from what it had been in the first. Europe's long and—as it now seems—dreamlike freedom from inflation ensured that Coffee Room prices remained stable, except that oysters, served at the Dickensian price of 1s. per doz. (dinner) or 1s. 3d. (luncheon) in 1864, had soared to 2s. 7d., including bread and butter, by 1869.

Members continued to keep a sharp eye on their bills, and this led Mr. William Arbuthnot to proffer the following excellent conundrum: 'Why, when I have claret for breakfast, do I have to pay more for fish?' 'Quite simple', replied the Committee:

> If a member takes tea or coffee for breakfast the charge is 1s. 2d. This includes bread, rice etc. and any relish, served at nearly cost price. But a member who takes claret for breakfast does not pay the 1s. 2d. but merely the cost of the wine. Therefore any fish etc. has to be charged at a higher rate. . . .

Other members looked after the pence by smuggling their own supplies into the Club and either having them cooked there, or consuming them *en nature*. Both Colonel de Winton and Mr. Hutt had to be reminded that only game[1] was allowed to be introduced in this way, but when the latter fumed that he had been bringing in his own sardines for 40 years, he was given a special dispensation. Later (after an argument with Dr. Winchester over strawberries) the concession was extended to fruit—but 2d. to be charged for the sugar!

Allowing for more elaborate menus and primitive equipment to prepare them, the pressure on the kitchens was much greater than in modern times, particularly of course in the evening; dinner was the great Club meal in the days when quite a large proportion of members were old bachelors or widowers living within walking distance from Hanover Square. It is recorded that on 16 March 1863 120 persons dined in the two rooms—no wonder there were no oysters in the pie and 'the whole of the sweets were written off the bill of fare'. No wonder, also, that there were kitchen rows from

[1] But not a *bear ham* please, Mr. de Berg, even if you shot the bear yourself—only small game which can be consumed at one meal (Ruling of June 1881).

time to time, and that cooks seldom lasted long, whether English or, more fashionably, Continental. Richard Terry comes to replace William Cherry ('though I will leave the good Countess with much regret'); M. Greliche is given notice after six months—a little matter of discounts to tradesmen?—and M. de Boeuf from the United University Club steps in. Exceptionally, he stays six years but, when he resigns in February 1882, MM. Cavernay, Lebelle and St. Martin whizz through the kitchens in less than 12 months.

It seems that there was a corresponding period of unease in the upper regions of Club management. It began in February 1871, when Mr. J. H. Hilton, who had succeeded Mr. Sturt as Secretary in 1851, sent another of those sad little letters of resignation to the Chairman. He declared that, 'shattered in health with long continuous work and adverse circumstances', he must give up the job, though it meant almost total ruin. He went on:

> Having a very large family I intend to emigrate to California if I can possibly raise the necessary funds, but even by selling up my home and some promised help from a friend, I can only raise £100 or £200.

Taking into consideration Hilton's 23 years as Secretary and four as Clerk before that, the Committee granted him a pension of £100 a year, but who knows whether he ever got to California? At any rate his pension was paid until his death on 25 April 1880.

Over the years Hilton's salary had risen from £160 to £350, and his successor Captain W. F. Dadson began at the same figure. But he only stayed two years and the Committee now saw (or thought they saw) a means to economise. Instead of having a Secretary and Steward they would appoint a General Manager at £250 a year, with a Clerk to the Committee (£150) and a Coffee Room Clerk (£70) —a saving of £100 a year. But such devices seldom work, and it is no surprise to find the General Manager, Mr. Lester, retiring after only seven months. Further juggles followed. On 16 March 1875 William Lane, the Committee Clerk, was promoted to Secretary Manager[1]. Then in June 1876 after allegations of 'waste and extravagance', it was realised that there were no short cuts to good

[1] Rather oddly, Mr. Lane and his father had also held the contract as Club launderers from 1874 to 1877 at £350 per annum.

management, and a separate Secretary and House Steward were appointed once more.

Lane's successors were Mr. Fry, from the Pall Mall Club (resigned after only two years), Mr. R. D. Fryers (four years), Major C. Cecil Clayton, appointed out of 281 applicants (five years) and Mr. Arthur Stirling (six years). It was at the time of Mr. Stirling's appointment that the Club realised that there might be something to be gained by raising its Secretary's status, and at the 1887 A.G.M. the Committee proposed that he should be eligible for Honorary Membership. In favour, Mr. Hugh Inwood urged that the Secretary ought to be able to dine in the Coffee Room and 'see what was going on'—an argument turned inside out by others who feared he might then act as a spy on the members!

The proposition was carried, and though modern Secretaries have not necessarily been made Honorary Members, they take their places in the Dining Room on a friendly (and non-spying) basis[1].

At the beginning of this chapter I mentioned various post-Mutiny influences which tended to make the Club a little less inward-looking than of old. These did not include any marked relaxation in either the rules for or the general character of the membership. Repeated attempts between 1826 and 1840 to broaden the latter by admitting 100 'noblemen and gentlemen not connected with the East' had not been renewed, and it was only reluctantly that the members agreed (Extraordinary General Meeting, 10 July 1843) that certain classes of V.I.P.s[2] who *were* connected with the East might be admitted by the Committee without ballot.

Nevertheless a non-Eastern element did slowly infiltrate the once homogeneous body, otherwise we could hardly have found Mr. H. Peregrine Birch, solicitor and Committee member, putting up his son, his partner Mr. Cartmell Harrison, and one of their articled clerks successively during 1873–4. He carried the process just too

[1] A delicate point of London club 'politics', this. In quite a number of cases, Secretaries still eat their meals in seclusion.

[2] Governors-General; Members of the Board of Control, H.E.I.C.; Governors of St. Helena, the Cape of Good Hope and Eastward thereof; Indian Bishops and Archdeacons. The list was much shorter than had been originally mooted. Lord Auckland (Governor-General 1836–41) and Lord Elphinstone (Governor of Madras 1837, and later of Bombay) were the first to be honoured under this rule.

far, however, and when he produced yet another articled clerk for the members' approbation, they blackballed him. Whereupon Mr. Birch and his entourage 'entered into a combination' and blackballed every single candidate at the next election.

As the latter was then by open ballot, with one black ball in 10 excluding, it can be understood that four or five determined saboteurs could easily hold the gate against any normal turnout of voters. There was a tremendous row and the Committee issued a printed resumé of the situation to all members, but at an Extraordinary General Meeting they failed to get the necessary two-thirds majority for the expulsion of their colleague.

As a precaution however, it was decided to transfer the right to ballot to the Committee—two black balls in under 12 votes, and three above that number, to exclude. It was not until 1879 that the general membership got their voting rights back, and retained them until 1947[1].

The Harrison affair could only be regarded as a setback to anyone who wished to widen the area of membership. But the fact remains that on 11 November 1884 it was agreed to change the description of the Club in *Whitaker's Almanack* from 'Eastern Empire and travellers' to 'Social' and that in May of the following year Mr. Whitehouse Q.C., referring to a proposed enlargement of the Club-house, prophesied quite fairly that this would lead to 'opening it to members who wanted to entertain, instead of keeping up the character of hospitality combined with homeliness'.

[1] At that year's A.G.M. it was urged that the system of open ballot had become a 'farce', and a resolution was moved on behalf of Sir James Donald that in future there should be an Election Committee consisting of the General Committee, reinforced with six representatives of the membership at large. After some reactionary murmurings, this was carried *nem. con.*

6 *Books and Pictures*

I have had to consume much more than my natural ration of dirt in making . . . an examination of many of our treasures.
Alexander Baillie

A new century and a new reign are in front of us, but before embarking on them we must spare some pages for two subjects which have been almost ignored up till now—the Club's Library and its collection of pictures. Both were essentially formed between 1824 and about 1870, and in this chapter we will follow their fortunes from the foundation of the Oriental until the end of the nineteenth century. Neither has been or is wholly a source of pride.

'I must touch upon our Library; but I confess that I approach the subject with a good deal of hesitation.' So wrote Baillie in 1901, and so write I (though without having to echo his other remark about his diet!). Quite apart from its recent vicissitudes (see page 213), the Library of the Oriental Club, in contrast with some of its coevals in Pall Mall, has seldom had the benefit of a consistent policy or of expert care.

At the start, no special funds were earmarked for buying books, and even when in 1828 the Library Committee was voted the comfortable-sounding sum of £203 17s., it turned out that £195 was to be spent on maps. In order to fill the shelves, members were urged to make voluntary gifts, especially of their own writings, and it is no surprise to find Sir John Malcolm setting a good example. Other gentlemen 'through whose politeness some very valuable books have been added gratuitously' were Colonel Ranken, who presented 19 volumes of Swift's works, and Mr. G. L. Prendergast, who weighed in with the 'very splendid and acceptable present of *The Journals of the Houses of Lords and Commons*, complete from the earliest to the latest period in 152 volumes folio'. An imposing sight they must have made, and they continued in undisturbed majesty until half a century later, when the run of *Journals* having increased to 332 volumes, the Committee directed that 283 of them should be sold off.

Most gifts, however, were on a less massive scale. A pamphlet on *The Spikenard of the Ancients* from Mr. Swinton ... a poem *Alfred The Great* from Mr. Thomas Newnham ... a *Topographical Survey of Ancient Thebes* from Mr. Wilkinson ... how often (or seldom) did a grey head nod over one of these in the stillness of a Hanover Square afternoon? There was a sprightlier welcome, one surmises, for Mr. Bayley's present of five volumes of the *Bengal Sporting Magazine*[1], and on at least one occasion (March 1837) the members took the initiative and persuaded the Committee to buy *Bentley's Miscellany* and *The Pickwick Papers*.

By way of reinforcement, the Club almost from the start subscribed to a circulating library. Its first contract was with Mr. Hookham of Bond Street, to supply 40 volumes at a time for £15 15s. a year—soon increased by 10 guineas 'in view of the time that members kept books'. In January 1835 Hookham tried to put up his charges still further, and the Club's custom was transferred to Churton of Holles Street, who made a surprisingly bold offer to supply 'every new book as soon as published', though with the same limit of 40 volumes at a time.

Another form of subscription involved the Club in a somewhat absurd tangle with the Royal Asiatic Society. This concerned the Oriental Translation Fund, which the Society sponsored. The Club had been supporting the Fund for several years when in January 1838 the Committee decided to withdraw on the ground that the publications were 'very seldom looked into by the members'. And in fact when the volumes were brought before the meeting, it was found that the pages had not even been cut.

So much, one would assume, for the O.T.F. Not at all. On 1 December 1842 the Committee, as though they had never heard of the subject before, again gave directions—'Subscription to the

[1] Sold in 1961, with some additional volumes, for £22.

Oriental Translation Fund to be given up'. Then suddenly someone remembered January 1838—surely the Club had not been paying all this time? In a sense it hadn't, but, alas, not the least of the crimes of the late secretary, Mr. Cornish, was that just before the crash he had suddenly polished off seven years' arrears. Feeling that the Royal Asiatic really might have put in an invoice earlier, the Committee sent them a copy of the original resolution, and 'asked to have 50 guineas back'. The Society retorted that they had applied every year in writing and made two personal calls, but Mr. Cornish alleged he could not bring the Library Committee together. In short they dug their toes in, and in spite of further pressure the Club never retrieved its 50 guineas.

Quite a few of these volumes are still in the Library, from HAOUKEWCHUEN, *or The Fortunate Union* (1829) to *The Popular Poetry of Persia* (1842), and all with a pretty individual book-plate, which the Royal Asiatic Society apparently printed for each subscriber.

Some time between 1838 and 1968 the pages have been cut.

The first real effort to achieve a collection worthy of the Club's position in the Anglo-Asiatic world came in the 1840s. It was decided to add a guinea to the entrance fee for the specific purpose of book-buying and, as already recorded, the old Card Room was merged with the Library, thereby more or less doubling its size. This Back, or Inner, Library, as it was variously called, achieved a certain social success, though at the expense of gravely annoying Mr. Thomas Haviside (Original Member). It was the warmest room in the house and 'much resorted to by members of a delicate constitution'. This, of course, led to chatter. The famous Snodgrass globe was located there, and when some members grouped around had begun arguing about 'the geographical location of part of the Oregon territory', Mr. Haviside rattled the poker deafeningly. Another evening, Mr. Viveash and Colonel Hodges were peacefully at chess, and Captain Chapman made some harmless observations on the game. Mr. Haviside kicked the fender in an intolerable manner.

Finally there was the day when, finding the door between the two libraries open, he sardonically flung the windows wide as well —an unseasonable proceeding in the first week of March. The

Committee intervened to avert a 'distressing collision' between Mr. Haviside and the other members. News of the little fracas then disappears from the Minutes, only to surface again *five years* later, when we find Mr. Haviside still keeping the doors closed against all comers.

There was at least one member who did not resort to the Library merely as a hothouse for his delicate constitution. This was Lieut.-Colonel James Hough, an Original Member and voluminous writer on Indian affairs. He used the Library as his work-room, and in one of his books which is still there, *Political and Military Events in British India, 1756 to 1840* (London, W. H. Allen, 2 vols., 1853), both the Preface and the Dedication are dated from the Oriental Club. Sooner or later there was bound to be trouble. In April 1855 Colonel Hough was told he could not continue to occupy so large a portion of the Library tables and shelves. The reply was indignant. The Colonel had been confident that his standing as an officer and the use he had been to the Service would preclude him from 'the injury of being deprived of finishing my book, now within a few days of being completed'.

Some kind of compromise must have been reached, because shortly afterwards Colonel Hough began a flow of benefactions to the Library which continued for years. It started in June 1855 with *Widow Burning* and *Precedents in Military Law*, and ended in January 1862 with *Essays and Reviews*, *The Chronology of Creation* and other theological works[1]. The only setback to his generosity was when he offered *Sketches of the Late Trial of Palmer*, which he thought 'could not fail to be interesting to members'. But the Committee would have no part or lot with the famous Rugeley poisoner.

The difficulty all along was that no one really knew what the function of the Library should be. Mr. Francis Nichols thought it was deplorably deficient in the works of standard authors—Fielding, Ben Jonson, not to speak of Ford, Massinger, Congreve, Sheridan . . . The Committee balked at first, but afterwards took action, starting with Mr. Nichols' first choice, Fielding. Even so, Mr. Nichols had to hint that in buying the works of poets and

[1] To these the Club hastily added, as a counterweight, *The Lays of Ancient Rome* and *Ruff's Guide to the Turf*.

novelists the choice should be made of 'such editions as can be held in the hand'. The Committee meekly promised that, when bound, Fielding would be divided into two volumes. Still keeping the tone high, Mr. Manning suggested (December 1869) that *The Odes and Epodes of Horace* by Lord Lytton would make an agreeable addition to the shelves. The Committee abruptly ruled that only books of reference and history should be obtained and then, in their inimitable way, forgot all about this, and only six weeks later authorised Mr. Burgess to spend £5 to form the nucleus of a small library on Law, Physic and Theology!

Even Eastern lore brought its own problems. In February 1856 there was a delicate correspondence with Colonel de Winton about *The Empire of the Nairs*. Nagged by him into buying this work in four volumes, the Committee were horrified to find after all that it was 'unfit to be placed in the Library', and asked the Colonel to relieve them of the purchase[1]. Soon afterwards the whole Club seems to have had an outbreak of *Arabian Nights* fever. It began in 1887 with Colonel Siddons[2] presenting *Supplemental Nights* by Sir Richard Burton, followed by another volume in December. A month later the Committee bought the *Thousand and One Nights* for £21. Colonel Siddons came back in May with Lane's version of the *Nights*, and in November with the final volume of *Supplementary Nights* and an unexpurgated translation of *Sadi Gulistan*, for which the thanks of the Committee were especially cordial. No wonder that by November 1891 Burton had to be rebound. After that the craze died down, and Colonel Siddons' many subsequent gifts were of a cooler cast: *Eton Songs*, *Addiscombe—its Heroes and Men of Note*, Bruce's *Travels to the Source of the Nile*, with only one belated relapse, *Hypnotism, Mesmerism and the New Witchcraft* (July 1897).

It was all rather hit-and-miss. Sometimes there was a Library

[1] *The Empire of the Nairs* no doubt described among other things the rather unconventional marriage customs of the Nayars in South India.

[2] So recorded, but can be identified with Colonel W. Siddons Young (e. 1869)—the name is given both ways. As he asked leave to display notices about a Mrs. Siddons Memorial, he evidently claimed descent from the great actress. The Club had an earlier link with her through the Sanskrit scholar H. H. Wilson (e. 1833), whose father-in-law George John Siddons (Bengal Civil Service) was her son.

Committee, at others (e.g. between 1870 and 1876) there was not. In fact a report of 1880 said that during the whole previous decade the Library had been 'grossly neglected' and few books had been added. There was still space for another 1,000 volumes, and the Library Committee wanted to spend £500 on filling the gaps. This was turned down, but they were voted £193 lawfully due to them from the £1 special subscription, and in a particularly choice Minute of 6 July 1880 the Committee agreed that: 'Menus, fish papers and artificial flowers, charged against the Library Account, should be transferred to Provisions.'

By the time Baillie wrote, the Library consisted of about 5,000 volumes, many of great interest and value, but matters of cataloguing and finance were in as much confusion as ever. For a Club many of whose members made lasting contributions to history and letters, the failure to grapple with the fairly simple problems of a nineteenth-century library was strange indeed.

When, in the year 1910, the Committee invited members to subscribe to a fund for buying pictures (including one of King Edward VII), they began by saying that no addition had been made to the collection for nearly 70 years. While this, as we shall see, was quite erroneous, it did underline the fact that the majority of the Oriental's pictures belong to the first half of the nineteenth century. This has its advantages. Painters such as R. R. Reinagle, Pickersgill, Brigstocke and Nathaniel Dance were not inspired artists, but, working still in the Reynolds/Lawrence tradition, they knew how to produce solid, impressive and straightforward likenesses. What might have followed in the way of tedium and sentimentality can be seen on the walls of any club which tended to honour its late-Victorian worthies.

Though there is something of interest, however brief, to be said about most of the Oriental's early nineteenth-century portraits, I will refrain from inflating this chapter with pages of catalogue entries. Instead I will try to illustrate, from a few examples, how the collection was originally built up, and the Club's later management of it. The details will be found in Appendix II. But even there I shall be more succinct than was Baillie, and for a good reason. He loved to describe the paintings themselves at some length, with much detail about the uniforms and orders worn by the sitters, and their various background attributes. I shall not, because in most cases these features have ceased to exist!

It is natural to have mixed feelings about the decision—taken when the move to Stratford Place had been settled—to cut the majority of the Club portraits down to head-and-shoulders' size. The critical can argue, (*a*) that to mutilate a whole series of works of art—even mediocre ones—is a barbarous act; (*b*) that you cannot produce a satisfactory close-up simply by lifting the face out of a full-length composition; (*c*) that a valuable record—if only of military costume—has been lost.

All three points have validity, but there was not really much choice, short of dispersing the collection. The Hanover Square building, like most of the old clubhouses, seems almost to have been designed to accommodate pictures seven feet high and four feet across! In the much smaller rooms of Stratford House, several of which are panelled or with delicate wall decoration, they would have looked utterly out of scale[1]. So farewell to clouds and pillars and palm trees and trousers and sashes of the Bath—all that acreage which it may be suspected was filled in by pupils rather than by the artist himself. One can at least be grateful to Messrs. Leggatt, who carried out the 'reductions' so efficiently, and to Lord Inchcape, who generously paid for the work.

Coming down to some sample acquisitions, I suppose that pride of place should be given to the Club's founder, Sir John Malcolm, and its first and only President, The Duke of Wellington.

I have already touched on Malcolm's career, and on the inadequacies of the Club's portrait (*Pl. 3*). It is, incidentally, a good example of what can happen when a full-length is reduced to a close-up—the crude and summary painting of the collar distracts one's eye. This is a posthumous likeness—it was in June 1833 that subscriptions were invited for a portrait of the late Sir John Malcolm 'to whom the institution [the Oriental Club] may be said mainly to owe its existence'. The cost was not expected to exceed £100; in

[1] Whether this applies to the Drawing Room and Writing Room, or whether they might actually have benefited if two or three of the more spectacular full-lengths had been preserved, is open to argument.

fact 'Mr. Lane of 60 Greek Street'[1], when commissioned, obligingly stated that he would paint it 'for any sum that might be in the hands of the Committee' and in any case for not more than the £110 which he was charging the 'Senior' for Lord Exmouth. The Club might have taken a little more trouble over its founder.

Wellington presented quite a different kind of problem. The acquisition of a portrait was first discussed in Committee in April 1834, but the members were aware that the Duke was being eternally pestered for sittings by all manner of artists and institutions, and that it would be useless for the Club to join the queue. However, in July he told Sir Pulteney Malcolm that he was about to sit to Pickersgill at the request of Lord Hill, and from that it was an easy step to bargain with the artist for a replica. Pickersgill, when approached, said he would 'forgo 100 guineas of his usual price' and provide a full-length for 200 guineas. At that stage only £177 had been subscribed, but no doubt the full amount was quickly made up.

The Wellington portrait (*Pl. 2*) was engraved by C. E. Wagstaff, as a speculation by Messrs. Cornish (the defaulting Secretary of the Club), W. B. Laver (his partner) and Pickersgill himself. It was the subject of a legal action between them and Wagstaff in 1846.

An example of the Club's dealings with an individual artist is presented by Thomas Brigstocke. Several of his works were acquired and one particular portrait, that of Mehemet Ali (see page 66) he seems to have regarded as his *chef d'œuvre*. For that reason, as well as for its documentary and picturesque qualities, I feel it is among those which might have been kept intact. In its full length state it depicted Mehemet Ali as a mild and grey-bearded old gentleman, seated Turkish fashion on an ottoman, a scimitar held negligently in his right hand. At his feet were a number of scrolls showing the route not (as has been vaguely supposed) of the future Suez Canal, but of the Cairo-Suez railway. This was a project dear to the Viceroy's heart, though it was not completed until after his death.

The story of the painting is that Brigstocke, wanting an excuse to

[1] If all the works of Samuel Lane were forgotten (as could happen without difficulty), it should still be recorded of him that he gave unswerving friendship to John Constable.

visit Egypt, told the Committee in January 1846 that he would provide them with a portrait of Mehemet Ali, free of charge, if they would provide him with credentials. The bargain was struck, but it was not until December 1849, after the picture had been 'shown in the Exhibition' (i.e. the Royal Academy[1]) that the artist announced that it was ready for hanging. The Committee thanked him warmly, offered to pay for the frame and invited him to 'do them the honour to select the most eligible light for the picture'. (Some readers will remember it hanging, soot-darkened and in a most ineligible light, over the Smoking Room fireplace in Hanover Square.)

However, the Committee's consciences still troubled them, and in January following a subscription list was opened to make an 'acknowledgement' to Mr. Brigstocke. The latter, for his part, treated this particular picture like a favourite child. He tried to get it into the Paris International Exhibition of 1855, and though it arrived too late, he seized the opportunity to touch it up and clean it. In January 1857 he asked that 'his pencil should be represented' by Mehemet Ali at another Exhibition (unspecified) and this was agreed.

Five years later the precious canvas was in peril! The then Viceroy (Said Pasha) had caused it to be borrowed to replace an inferior work in the Egyptian Court of the South Kensington Exhibition of 1862. But Brigstocke found it 'so placed that people can and do sit against it' and he asked that it should at once be removed to a place of safety. This was done, and so far as we trace it did not leave the security of Hanover Square again until the guillotine fell.

Also by Brigstocke are the portraits of Outram (the only Mutiny hero to figure in the Oriental gallery) and Sir William Nott, as commander of the Army of Kandahar in the Afghan War of 1844. The ever-zealous painter saw to it that these portraits were borrowed for the 1866 Exhibition of the Art, Industry and Products of Wales 'as the best specimens of a Welsh artist'—he had been born in Carmarthen in 1809.

Starting with Thomas Snodgrass's presentation of the (? Reynolds) portrait of Stringer Lawrence in 1824 which may be said to have

[1] Described in Catalogue as: 'Painted at Cairo previous to his [Mehemet Ali's] illness, etc. Mosque of Sultan Hassan in distance'.

founded the collection, the Club has acquired about half its pictures by gift. Motives have no doubt been mixed—family pride, admiration for the subject, affection for the Club, and lack of house-room! For an instance which manages to embrace them all we may cite the case of Lady Isabella Fitzgibbon and the portrait by John Smart of Sir Jamsetjee Jejeebhoy, Bt., the great Parsee philanthropist.

The transaction took place in 1852, after a correspondence worthy of so noble a donor, but also reminiscent of Lady Catherine de Burgh (as mediated by the Reverend Mr. Collins). First, Mr. Robert Williamson informs the Chairman (The Rt. Hon. Holt Mackenzie) that Lady Isabella has resolved to present to the Oriental Club 'the magnificent Portrait of Sir Jejeebhoy painted for her brother, the late Earl of Clare'[1], and that it would be delivered to any person who should be sent to her Ladyship's house, 35 Lowndes Square.

The reply is in just the right key:

> The Chairman of the Oriental Club begs to acquaint her Ladyship that the bearer, the Secretary of the Club, has been instructed to wait upon her for the purpose of receiving the portrait at such time as it may be convenient for her to appoint . . . The picture will be valued by everyone who has taken an interest in the welfare of British India, and we will gladly avail ourselves of the opportunity of giving it a place of honour.

An easy return, this, for Lady Isabella. She cannot but experience regret at parting with something which her lamented brother valued so highly, yet

> she feels grateful to the Club for allowing a place more worthy of it than that which it *now* occupies, and one which she feels will prove most flattering to the esteemed original.

We leave it to Baillie to hint that all this merely camouflaged her Ladyship's desire to find a home for 'a somewhat cumbersome piece of household goods'—her 'Battle of Assaye' in fact—since in its original form (*Pl. 8*) the Jejeebhoy portrait was enormous.

[1] A banquet given by Sir Jejeebhoy to Lord Clare on his retirement as Governor of Bombay (February 1835) is described in Jahangir R. P. Mody, *Jamsetjee Jejeebhoy* (Bombay, 1959) (O.C.L.). This book has the Club portrait (full-length) as colour frontispiece, but gives no further information about it. In 1935 a suggestion that the portrait might be transferred to the Jamsetjee Jejeebhoy Hospital, Bombay, was turned down by the Committee, but an engraving of Sir Jamsetjee was given to the present Baronet in 1959.

The question of 'copies' and 'replicas' is much to the fore whenever portraits of popular celebrities are involved. Baillie devotes several indignant pages to two of the Club pictures, Samuel Lane's of the 1st Marquess of Hastings and F. R. Say's of Lord Metcalfe. His grudge is against the *Descriptive List of Pictures at Government House, Calcutta*, issued in the 1890s. There, copies of these two portraits, made by J. Hayes, are described as originals, and the Oriental versions as copies. The fact that permission to the H.E.I.C. to have the Club's pictures copied for Calcutta is recorded in a Committee Minute of May 1857, clinches Baillie's case, and one wonders whether Calcutta has ever made amends! *The Illustrated Catalogue of the Victoria Memorial, Calcutta* (1925) (O.C.L.) includes a copy of the Club picture of Metcalfe, correctly attributed, but this was one formerly in the Calcutta City Hall.

It should be added that in Metcalfe's case some confusion is pardonable, since a wilderness of copies of this rather harsh and unattractive work exist in various parts of the world. As recently as 1937, Edward Thompson in his biography of Metcalfe[1] reproduced it from an engraving and stated that the original was 'believed to be in Ottawa'! The 'cutting-down' process has at least excised a lot of gaudy paraphernalia.

Such are a few of the relics of an age when portrait-painting was the staple occupation of the artist—his highest challenge as well as his bread-and-butter. Much of the copying and recopying that went on merely reminds us that photography had not been invented[2]; but the constant requests by exhibition organisers to borrow Oriental Club portraits shows the popularity of the *genre* and the good standing of this particular collection.

Finally, the Committee jibbed. When the Council on Education applied for seven pictures for the National Portrait Exhibition at South Kensington (1868), there was heated argument about the liability for damage as between the Committee and/or the Trustees, and the final decision, though favourable, came too late.

[1] *Charles, Lord Metcalfe* (London, Faber, 1937).

[2] It emerges in February 1857, when Colonel Philip Anstruther (e. 1827) suggests that the Club paintings should be photographed. He is authorised to go ahead and do it. In pre-photographic days many of the portraits were engraved, and there are a number of examples still at Stratford House.

No more loans are recorded for many years after that and a request for Warren Hastings from the Committee of the Indian Exhibition (1895) was turned down 'in accordance with a decision some time back'. Recently, however, there has been some relaxation—Lake was lent to the Grenadier Guards for their Tercentenary Exhibition in 1956 and Pottinger to the Ulster Museum's 'Great Irishmen' in 1965.

In a class by itself, for historic value as well as sheer size (though not perhaps as a work of art), is Mather Brown's[1] picture of 'Earl Cornwallis receiving the Sons of Tippoo Sahib as Hostages', which now occupies most of one wall of the Bar (*Pl. 12*). There are things to be said about this vast 'machine' (it measures 9 ft. 2 ins. × 7 ft.) from at least four aspects—its subject, its painter, its provenance and its ownership by the Oriental Club. On neither of the last two points is the evidence as full as one would wish.

However, we will start with the fourth. The first mention of the picture in Club records is a Minute of 13 February 1883, directing the Secretary to accept with thanks the handsome offer by Mr. Osborne Aldis of what they cursorily call 'the picture of Earl Cornwallis, etc.'. They also agree to spend £17 on doing it up. Later in the year they decide that the portrait of Sir Jamsetjee Jejeebhoy be removed from the staircase to make room for the Cornwallis picture, which was then presumably placed in the final position where (as a member of the staff has reminded me) 'it used to catch your shoulder as you went up the stairs'. There followed a silence of thirteen years—broken in September 1896, when Mr. Aldis asked for his name to be inscribed on the frame. Agreed.

Who was Mr. Aldis, how had he acquired this enormous work, and why did he deposit it in Hanover Square? In spite of every enquiry, all we can say is that he was a member of the Club (e. 1878), that we do not know how Earl Cornwallis came into his possession, and can only make guesses (including the usual uncharitable one) about his reasons for the benefaction.

The artist? Mather Brown was an American, a New Englander, born in 1761 in fairly humble circumstances, but claiming descent from

[1] For a recent Mather Brown acquisition by the Club see page 232.

the famous Massachusetts Puritan, Increase Mather. He is first heard of painting miniatures and peddling wine in what one would imagine to be unpromising territory around Worcester and Springfield, Massachusetts. But he soon came to Europe, studying under Copley in Paris and Benjamin West in London. Thus equipped, he started sending portraits and *genre* subjects to the Royal Academy, which accepted no fewer than 80 of his works between 1782 and 1831. He followed a fashionable line—lived in Cavendish Square, hunted with the King at Windsor, and so on—but towards the end of his life he lost his vogue and retired to the North of England. An article in *The Dictionary of American Biography* vigorously denies the 'imputation of imbecility' made against Brown (and repeated by Baillie), adding that his correspondence shows him as a 'disappointed but not embittered man of keen mentality'. He died in 1831.

To us, the interesting sentence in the D.A.B. article is as follows:

> His 'Marquis Cornwallis receiving as Hostages the Sons of Tippoo Sahib'[1] was exhibited, admired and engraved.

In other words the picture ranked as Brown's masterpiece and the irritating thing is that though we have been told a lot about the engraving, we do not know where the original was exhibited or who in particular 'admired' it. However, it is well worth going back to the start of the whole project.

Next to the death of Nelson and the meeting of Wellington and Blücher on the field of Waterloo, no battle theme has proved more attractive to artists in Britain than the series of campaigns against Tippoo Sahib between 1790 and 1799. The formidable character of the Sultan of Mysore, the two sieges of Seringapatam, and the final death of the tyrant, all helped to generate an insatiable demand for paintings and engravings. This iconography has never been properly explored—one can only refer in passing to such works as 'Sir David Baird Discovering the body of Tepu', by Sir David Wilkie, 'The Death of Tepu', by H. Singleton and 'The Storming of Seringapatam' by Sir Robert Ker Porter, 'an artist of no ordinary

[1] Cornwallis did not actually receive his Marquessate until some months after the incident of the hostages. The old form 'Tippoo Sahib' (for Tipu Sultan) has been retained in this book.

kind', as one can well believe—his picture was 120 ft. long and would have made Mather Brown's look like a postage stamp[1].

Brown, however, had the advantage of a subject certain to 'send' a sentimental public—the surrender of Tippoo's second and third sons as hostages at the end of the first siege of Seringapatam in 1792. The youth and grace of the two boys—Abdul Khaliq was aged 10 and his brother Mu'izz al-Din eight[2]—and their 'paternal' reception by the great Governor-General made an irresistible appeal. It was not necessary, of course, to be on the spot to reconstruct such scenes; Robert Home, for example, happened to be in India and Arthur Devis, whose charming version hangs in the United Service Club, made sketches there; Mather Brown, John Zoffany and David Wilkie had no such advantage.

Just how Brown set to work with the help of the Rt. Hon. Henry Dundas, Secretary of State, is told in a wonderful and vain-glorious 'blurb' which was issued in order to publicise the engraving made of his picture by Daniel Orme. As regards the exhibition of the original, it may seem strange that Brown did not send it to the Academy, but it is likely that the publicity value was so great that, like Benjamin Haydon and many others, he took a special gallery or room for it and charged admission. The show may also have included two smaller paintings with which Brown completed the narrative and which were engraved by Bartalozzi and Orme respectively—'The Departure of the Sons of Tippoo from the Zenana' (and a very tender scene it is) and 'The Delivery of the Definitive Treaty by the Hostage Princes into the Hands of Lord Cornwallis'. A final point about the engraving of the main work is noted by Baillie; the Governor-General is shown without the cummerbund which he wears in the original—Baillie thinks this may have been added later as the result of criticisms of the cut of Cornwallis's waistcoat and breeches!

Brown's picture has characteristically consumed a lot of my space, but earns it not only by its intrinsic interest but, as the key now

[1] See Miles and John Hadfield, *Gardens of Delight* (London, Cassell, 1964). There is a fine group of reproductions in Mildred Archer's Victoria & Albert Museum pamphlet *Tippoo's Tiger* (1959).

[2] Enchanting miniatures of them by one of the John Smarts are in the British Museum.

hanging near it shows, because the group of officers on the right includes the founder of the Oriental Club, Colonel (later Sir John) Malcolm, at least one other Original Member, Colonel (Sir Patrick) Ross, and the ancestor of a notable Club dynasty, Colonel (Lieut.-General) Alexander Dirom (see page 216). How pleasant if the 'hostage princes' had also graduated to Hanover Square! But as we have already seen, it was Tippoo's ninth son, Jameh-ud-Din[1], who eventually made his way thither.

The Oriental's more recent (I will not say modern) pictures, together with a few older ones acquired since 1900, are among those listed in Appendix II. They included several vast and flaccid full-lengths from Edwardian and later times, which have certainly benefited by surgical treatment. Numerous drawings and water-colours of Indian scenes, including the sports of the East, have been presented to the Club at various periods, and are mostly to be found in the upper corridors, though an interesting group has recently been placed on long-term loan at the National Army Museum. With a few exceptions noted in Appendix II, a large collection of *busts*, which as recently as 1950 was rendering the old Billiard Room unusable, has happily disappeared.

The last paragraphs of this chapter would be the natural place to mention other gifts to the Club by nineteenth-century members. But there were virtually none, which is most curious for a society of 'nabobs'—many clubs less opulent in origin seem to have done far better. Silver candelabra from Mr. John Rutherford in 1880 'to mark his 50 years membership', a snuff-box from Mr. Cardwell in 1896 'as a token of gratitude for many happy years' of Club life—that is all I have been able to mark down.

A certain number of trophies of the chase did find their way to Hanover Square, but mostly after 1900. Earlier, the Committee tended to look these gift carcases rather carefully in the mouth. Mr. H. Brereton's stag heads from Kashmir, offered in 1857, were refused because setting them up would have cost £10; in contrast,

[1] More strictly, Jami 'al-Din Sultan, though in sending an ancient manuscript to Lady Seymour in November 1837, the Prince preferred Jamh O Deen! The MS, with his autograph inscription, is in the India Office Library.

the members were prepared to risk 10s. on dressing Dr. Culham's tiger skin (1869)—'method of mounting to be settled later'.

Acquisitions of Eastern bric-a-brac have been mercifully few. Those envisaging the Oriental Club (as some may even today) as a place where yellow-faced *sahibs* are waited upon by dusky retainers amid a welter of Benares brass, have always been well on the wrong road. Even when its membership was almost 100 per cent East Indian, it was in fact an English gentlemen's club in the purest, most antique mould—the perfect setting, I have always thought, for Chapter I of *Round the World in Eighty Days*.

7 *Club Life in Full Bloom*

CLUB—a weapon used by savages to keep white women at a distance.

George Augustus Sala

The only place in London where my wife cannot get at me—and am I to lose this boon?

Member at Annual General Meeting, 1905

Witnesses by the hundred thousand—some still alive, others who have left written testimony—tell of the trauma caused by the death of Queen Victoria on 22 January 1901. They describe a wave of universal sorrow, but also the feeling that a new and perhaps more buoyant epoch had begun. It seems that the members of the Oriental Club—contrary to what one might expect—took the less sentimental view. A week before the Queen's funeral, when men and women and even their entire houses were swathed in deepest crape, the Committee passed a resolution that the staff were not to be 'placed in mourning'.

Moreover, a subscription opened on 12 February to buy a portrait of her late Majesty obtained but tepid support. By 16 April only 27 guineas had been promised, by 4 June £78 15s. (of which £42 had been paid in) and by 16 July £100 15s. od. Clearly this would not go very far, and in November application was made to the new King to allow a copy to be made of a portrait of his mother by Benjamin Constant, which he had bought from Sir William Ingram. Permission was not granted, and the fund (still only £113 7s. od.) was quickly and quietly wound up.

The members showed a more lively interest in what might be called a memorial to themselves. On 19 February 1901, when the portrait subscription had just opened, the Committee received a letter from Mr. Alexander F. Baillie asking permission to place in the Drawing Room a subscription list for 'the history which he is now completing'. The Committee agreed, subject to the heading being vetted.

The story of this project may be of interest—especially to those who may have erroneous ideas on how long it can take to produce a Club history! It was on 19 December 1893 (only two years after his election) that the Committee heard from Mr. Baillie for the first time. They took note that he was 'compiling a History of the Oriental Club' and agreed unanimously that he should be given every assistance and access to documents; a month later he was allowed to put up a notice on the subject.

In other words this was, most unusually, a personal enterprise by the author and his publisher, instead of being a commission from the Club. *The Oriental Club and Hanover Square* was not Baillie's first venture. He had begun with a book about Paraguay, and in 1890 had published *Kurrachee, Past, Present and Future* (Calcutta, Thacker, Spink & Co.). This was in fact a massive piece of 'promotional literature' for the rising port which we today call Karachi. The author was connected with the family of Baillie of Dochfour, and a whole covey of his relations had served with distinction in India and had been members of the Oriental Club—Colonel John (1722–1833), M.P. for Inverness, after whom the Baillie Gate at Lucknow was named; Henry James (1803–1885), also M.P. for Inverness and Under-Secretary of State for India; Colonel John's son, Neil Benjamin Edmonstone, Indian jurist and Club Committee man; and others less notable.

As the title of his book shows, Baillie was out to catch the public with a piece of topographical and social history (a good precedent), as well as to chronicle the Oriental Club. The result was an imposing volume in the style of the day, but not quite so exhaustive as it looks at first glance. Excluding appendices etc. there are 279 pages of large type with wide margins, out of which 35 are devoted to Hanover Square, and no fewer than 67 to the Club's picture collection. The book is dedicated (why, one wonders?) 'To a generous patron of literature and the Arts, BARON ALFRED CHARLES DE

ROTHSCHILD' and though it has obviously been compiled *con amore* by a faithful Oriental Club man, there is not a word, introductory or otherwise, to acknowledge the help, or even to recognise the existence, of the Committee and members!

The Oriental Club and Hanover Square did not actually come out until 4 December 1901. The archives of Messrs. Longmans, Green & Co. must be in fine trim—when I applied to them for information they answered by return that they published the book at their own risk, paying the author a royalty; that 1,000 copies were printed; that the price was 25s. net; and that Mr. Baillie died on 28 January 1909.

The Baillie history seems to have made a good impression, and on 18 March 1902, just nine years and three months after it had been mooted, the Committee passed a formal resolution thanking Mr. Baillie for his labours 'in narrating all that is interesting in the past history of the Club'.

I doubt whether clubland has seen a similar transaction.

One of Baillie's chapters is headed 'Our Conservatism'. A powerful ingredient indeed in the character of the Oriental Club, as even non-members, glancing through his book or mine, will recognise. But social, like political, Conservatism can only conserve by adaptation, and we now have to watch the Club coming to terms with the twentieth century.

Of the forces *against* change, the most potent was the fact that the overwhelming majority of the members habitually using the Clubhouse were retired men—'home from the East', with their life's work behind them. They had seen enough, done enough, and made money enough to last them the remainder of their days, and now they only wished to enjoy (or at any rate to frequent) their Club in peace. I have already quoted from Sir John Kaye's reference, in his biography of Mountstuart Elphinstone, to the eminent Civil Servant, William Butterfield Bayley (Original Member) coming home in the prime of life, with 'a boyish freshness and cheerfulness about him which afforded the most remarkable contrast ever seen with the traditional moroseness of the retired Nabob'. The Edwardian members may not all have been nabobs in the financial sense, but they shared many of their characteristics. And of course, a large number of them were extremely old[1].

An album belonging to the Club preserves some jottings made in about 1930 by Francis Mathewson (e. 1900), and one of his stories is to the point:

> Thirty years ago a young, or even middle-aged member was a rarity. A recently joined member was being shown over. Apparently the scene recalled one of those enclosures in Bengal in which the kindly Jain (who may not kill) interns those domestic animals which are past work. The new member, to the horror of his sponsor, ejaculated, 'Good gad, it's a *Pinjrapole*!'.

Appropriately, it was at this very period that the Club said good-bye to its first but not (as we shall see) its only centenarian. One day in 1900, Mathewson records:

> A new arrival sits down next to an elderly gentleman in the Coffee Room.
>
> 'I gather, sir, from what your friends said in welcome, that you have come from Calcutta? I wonder whether it has much changed since I left?'
>
> 'If you will tell me, sir, when you left India, I could reply to your question'.
>
> 'Let me see, it was in May 1834 . . .'

The first speaker was Mr. James Macauley, who was born on 11 November 1800, and died in his rooms at No. 3 Tenterden Street on 11 March 1901. Strangely enough, he was far from being a senior member. Mathewson says he was already 87 when he joined the Club and tried to get a reduced entrance fee, but the Committee refused. Mathewson congratulated him on reading *The Times* without spectacles on his hundredth birthday, to which he replied that he had worn them most of his life but as his eyesight had recently improved, he had given them up.

Baillie, too, devotes several fascinated paragraphs to Mr. Macauley.

[1] As a result, the Club annals were always rich in 'links with the past'. One of the most striking had been severed as recently as 1872 with the death of Lieut.-Colonel William Nicol Burns, Madras Infantry (e. 1849). He and his brother James were given Indian cadetships in 1809, and I remember Mr. Ivor Brown commenting many years ago on the extraordinariness of the two sons of Robert Burns by his wife Jean Armour ending up as Indian Army colonels, 'with subsequent retirement to Cheltenham'.

He describes him as a short, slight figure with long hair (only tinged with grey) and long beard:

> His breathing was laborious, and the exertion of mounting the staircase to the Smoking Room was painful to himself and to those who witnessed it; for he still smoked after he was a hundred years old, was fond of his champagne, and was a chivalrous squire of ladies . . . We always supposed him to be unmarried, but it is stated that after his death a wife appeared, from whom he had been separated for fifty years.

A tantalising Committee minute of 12 March 1901 (the day following his death) refers to a draft letter of 9 March and states that 'A reply from the late Mr. Macauley was read'. Had he been complaining about the quality of the champagne?

It must be taken for granted that a minority of members remained antiquated in social attitudes as well as years—sometimes with an unwelcome overlay of Edwardian ill-breeding. Witness the case of Mr. E.N., which came up in 1906. A lady had called for him and 'as none of the Club servants went out to her carriage', she entered the hall. A page boy told her 'in a most rude manner' to go round to the ladies' entrance, where she was kept waiting *nearly five minutes.* Mr. E.N.'s complaint continued:

> The Secretary told me in effect that he could not be responsible for the manners of the Club servants, but as he is a paid employee of the Club it is surely his duty to ensure that the Club is not inflicted with ill-mannered servants. I submit that the page-boy who insulted my visitor should be instantly dismissed, otherwise I shall resign.

The Committee took this very calmly—said the page boy had been adequately reprimanded for his mistake and they had no intention of going any further. Mr. E.N.'s reply carries us into a rather disagreeable corner of the world of Hilaire Belloc and Cecil Chesterton:

> I regret that the Committee should condone such an offence—particularly when a lady was the victim—but their decision is merely another instance of the spirit which has caused the Oriental to sink from its position of a great club to one where lower-middle class merchants, business managers and Jews are put up by members with whom they have business transactions and because they are 'good' for the entrance fee and subscription.

Inevitably, the venerable phrase about 'disturbing the harmony and good order of the Club' had to be invoked, and Mr. E.N. was expelled.

The members' feelings over this sort of thing were unmistakable. Fortunately they also realised that fresh life must be injected into the 'Pinjrapole'. Mr. Buckle, who resigned in February 1905, did so on the following crisply stated grounds—'No bedrooms, no cards played, no country membership'. He could hardly have chosen a more irrelevant moment, so far as his first criticism was concerned. Only 10 weeks before, Mr. T. H. Watson had been appointed 'Club architect' in connection with a vast scheme for the extension of the Clubhouse and on 10 March a circular put the proposals in front of members. It involved building two further floors of bedrooms and 'residential chambers', and since it will be remembered that Decimus Burton had already added one floor to the original two-storeyed building, the ghost of Benjamin Wyatt might reasonably complain that whatever the shortcomings of his own design, the Clubhouse in its final phase (*Pl. 6*) looked like an advanced case of elephantiasis.

Practically speaking, however, the advantages of the scheme made a strong appeal to members. The three top floors would now provide eight sets of residential chambers (two to be let at £250 each, two at £225 and four at £200); four permanent bedrooms (£100); and 10 temporary bedrooms, for which the charge—present readers will note with a sigh—was 6s. a night, including bath, lights and attendance. The total cost was estimated at £18,000 plus £3,300 for furniture and fittings, and the revenue hoped for was £2,650 against extra annual expenses of £1,970—profit £680.

To many members, the questionable element was the space given up to residential chambers. It did not appear—and later generations have seen the point—that the aim of revivifying the Club would be achieved by providing permanent lodgings for a select number of its old gentlemen. Moreover, as the Chairman (Mr. G. P. Field) remarked at the Extraordinary General Meeting where the subject came up,

> It might lead to scandal—a man might take upstairs his sister or his aunt, *so-called* . . .

But there was an element of compassion in the proposal. It had been explained that 'the houses opposite (Nos. 2 and 3 Tenterden Street), which provided some 16 bedrooms, are about to be closed and will no longer be available for the use of members'. It was of course at No. 3 that old Mr. Macauley had recently breathed his last, and though it is not clear whether the Club itself rented these houses (or the rooms in them), or whether they were someone's private speculation, several devoted adherents of the Club were obviously about to be unnested.

The temporary bedrooms, on the other hand, marked a real and beneficial revolution. They meant above all that for members coming on leave the Club could provide a cosy though transitory shelter and not just a port of call. How Jos Sedley would have appreciated that! A 'temporary' bedroom could in those days be engaged for up to a fortnight, with further extensions unless it was wanted for someone else, while the 'permanent' rooms could be occupied for periods of three months and thus could cover an entire home leave.

So Mr. Buckle's first grounds for resignation were removed—what of the others?

(*a*) *No card-playing*. Rule I in every reshuffle of the Club's accommodation is that the card-players lose out. We saw an earlier example on page 79. After the 1871 extension (Smoking Room, etc.) they had obtained the use of a quite spacious apartment over the Strangers' Room, but when the demands of private hospitality increased, the obvious solution was, Evict the card-players!—and in February 1900 this was duly done. Their room thereupon became the Private Dining Room which remained in constant use until the end. The resolution rather curtly added 'Cards can be played in the Smoking Room'. Grumbling continued and finally, on 24 January 1905, the Committee decided that Room No. 22 on the Third Floor (they meant the Second Floor) should be appropriated to card-playing.

(*b*) *No country membership*. This was another old grievance[1], and

[1] It goes back at least to 1832, when one of the reasons which Major Robert Thew (e. 1827) gave for resigning was that though he lived *20 miles* from London, he had to pay the same subscription as members resident in town.

various resolutions on the subject had been rejected in the past on the deeply-held but somewhat irrational ground that membership of the Club was one and indivisible, and that none should enjoy concessions not open to all. Mr. Buckle got no satisfaction here and even in April 1907, when Mr. S. R. Turnbull asked whether there was 'any probability of a new rule being passed' on the subject, he was flatly told, 'no probability'. And so things remained until 1941.

It seems at first sight an anomaly that as we get nearer to our own time, our sources of information tend to wither away. As I hope my earlier chapters have suggested, the Committee Minutes were at first reasonably uninhibited, and quite a lot of 'human interest' can be squeezed out of them. But by the end of the nineteenth century they tended to be shorter and drier, and finally became very summary indeed. This was mainly because of increasing delegation to the House Committee, whose own Minutes have always been markedly laconic. Perhaps 2 October 1900 marked the end of the old ways, when the full Committee was specially summoned to consider the Superintendent's report about 'card-playing on a Sunday, jam-puffs in the Smoking Room and the Coffee Room being used after 1 a.m.'

Even so, one's curiosity is occasionally set working. For instance, on 29 March 1904, a letter from Mr. Tarbett Fleming (e. 1886) asks the Club's acceptance of a Bronze Elephant and suggests that it should be placed in the inner or outer hall. This is cordially accepted, and Mr. Fleming's elephant has greeted visitors to No. 18 or to Stratford House ever since[1].

An appropriate gift, one might say, in view of the Club's badge. But what *is* the Club's badge and when and why was it acquired? The records are silent! As far back as the 1830s the Secretary had been instructed to buy snuff-boxes with 'the club badge' (unspecified), but the very first reference that I have noted to the elephant as such is a Minute of 1 July 1864, when the cost of 'introducing the elephant onto the D'Oyleys' was 3s. 6d. a dozen. Already

[1] It is traditionally said to have been 'found on a scrap-heap'. It was much admired by the late J. C. ('Elephant Bill') Williams (e. 1946), who estimated that the animal represented was 45 years old.

there was much uncertainty about the design, and three years later Mr. D. I. Money is complaining of 'the incorrect figure of the elephant' on table-cloths, dishes, paper, etc. I reproduce here three 'figures of the elephant' and it is anybody's guess which is the 'correct' one.

The Fleming gift also reminds us that for years the Club had been in elephant trouble of another kind with the General Post Office—the story has a pleasant touch of the absurd. It began in October 1885 with the decision of the Committee to register the Club's telegraphic address as 'Elephant London' at a cost of one guinea. This was refused by the G.P.O. (no explanation given) and on 20 October it was agreed to try 'Oriental' or 'Tiger'. No go once more, but a fortnight later there is a note that 'Cobra' had been accepted. End

Fig 1 The Elephant steps out. (*Left*) Nineteenth century; (*Centre*) First half of twentieth century; (*Right*) Today

of argument? Not by half. On 6 April 1895 the G.P.O. suddenly ordained that the address must be 'Care of Cobra'. But even this went wrong—it was discovered that the Eastern Telegraphic Company was sending all the Club's foreign cables to a City firm which also had a claim on 'Cobra'. The Committee decided to try again, while retaining 'Cobra' for inland telegrams. At this point the story—like so many in this history—goes underground for seven years, to emerge in January 1903 with a bright thought from the G.P.O.: Would the Committee like 'Clubcone'? The Committee decidedly would not and, still hankering after elephants, countered rather wearily with 'Hathi'. Silence once more, but somehow finality was reached, because by 1905 the Club was using 'Ganpati'[1] and has continued to do so ever since.

[1] The elephant god.

What neither party to this dialogue can have wholly realised was that all the time 'Ganpati's' rival was creeping up on him and soon would sharply reduce his status. In Chapter 5 it was mentioned that several attempts to get a telephone installed were voted down during the 1890s. By May 1900 the Committee had actually decided to take action, and were prepared to sign a five years' agreement at £17 per annum. But this was only carried by a majority and four months later the whole thing was still 'under consideration'. It was not until March 1902 that application was made for a number on the Mayfair Exchange; the estimate was that this would take at least 12 months to achieve—the pace has slowed down since then! The apparatus arrived at last and was placed 'close to the entrance door', but that was as far as the spirit of innovation went for the moment; a proposal in December 1912 that there should be 'a second telephone instrument' was voted down.

The Club's reaction to two other novelties can be quickly dismissed. During May 1896 a notice was posted in the Hall: 'Bicycles are not admitted inside the Clubhouse'; and in December 1905 the Committee agreed to take part in and to support any action arising from a public meeting to protest against 'motor-omnibuses standing in the Square'.

This 1905 move, incidentally, was only one of a whole series in which the Committee had essayed to protect the dignity of the Square and its garden or, contrariwise, to modify it to the members' advantage. In 1879–80 we find them trying to eject a row of cabs which had settled down in front of the Tenterden Street windows and to have a proper cab-stand established on the north or west side of the Square. Opposition was fierce, but the shelter still to be seen on the North side is a monument to their success. There was always a lot of tetchiness over the garden, as this sequence shows:

1872 Club asks permission for members to play croquet. *Vetoed by Hanover Square Committee.*
1882 Lady Harewood tries to get the garden opened to local children. *Successfully opposed by Club.*
1885 Group of residents want to introduce lawn tennis. *Club says no.*

So the garden remained, shabbily inviolate—until, in fact, the exigencies of World War II gave rise to 'odious growths' (mostly concrete) which took a lot of removing. Those who have picked their way through the bodies that strew the railless lawns in any sunny lunch-hour today will find it hard to credit that, as recently as 1949, the old enclosure was reconditioned, and though the public was allowed in at stated times, the Club held a key so that (as the Committee poetically minuted) the members could 'take their ease in the cool of the day'.

Pardon this digression back and forth! One thing which never seems to have troubled the Edwardian members in planning the future of their Clubhouse was the rapid evolution of Hanover Square as a social unit. By 1900 it was far down the slope towards becoming a business rather than a residential quarter; in fact for 20 years past there had been virtually no private residents on the west and north sides. Later in this book we shall be savouring the aristocratic hush of Stratford Place. Yet it can hardly have exceeded that of north-west Hanover Square in its pre-commercial phase, when both Tenterden Street and Harewood Place were closed by chains or bars[1], and, if the clop of hoofs was heard at all, it was as likely as not an Oriental member approaching the Clubhouse on horseback. Baillie has a telling passage about this. Sometime in the very early days, he says, the Secretary drew the attention of the police magistrate to the number of idlers who hung around the Club door 'waiting to lead about the members' horses' and he adds,

> Imagine for a moment ten or a dozen well-groomed cobs and thoroughbreds being led in procession round and round Hanover Square. At the present day it would be an attraction to us that would outrival those that we now possess—the visits of fair women in elegant carriages to the fashionable modiste who rules the establishment in front of us, and the coming and going of the no less fair students of the Royal Academy of Music.

The cobs and thoroughbreds had gone in Baillie's time and the carriage folk and music students in ours, and though the smart dressmakers have disappeared as well, their successors (less gracefully known as the rag trade) are in greater force than ever. But it is

[1] The Tenterden Street bar seems to have been removed in 1895, though its posts were still in place within the memory of the older Club servants. Harewood Place was opened up about the same time.

interesting that Baillie should mention, though not by name, the pioneer of all this infiltration—'the fashionable modiste who rules the establishment in front of us'. This is a reference to Lady Duff Gordon, who rented No. 17 (see page 45) from Sir John Dashwood in the 1890s and set up as Lucile, perhaps the most famous dress-house outside Paris[1]. Later Sir John wanted to come back to his house—the ancient family connection lingering on—and Lucile had to move to No. 23[2].

It was not only Lady Duff Gordon, parading her 'mannequins' under the Angelica Kauffmann ceilings that had once looked down to Mrs. Jordan, who made the Oriental Club a natural magnet for shopping ladies, and helped towards its fairly rapid 'opening up' in Edwardian days. It was far and away the nearest Club to the great shops of Regent Street and Oxford Street, then in their aristocratic zenith, and it was still 'an easy drop down from Harley Street', the stronghold no longer of nabobs, but of doctors as fashionable as the *modistes*. In fact, the pastime of visiting one's doctor was somehow on a par with visiting one's dressmaker and in either case a cup of tea at the Oriental would nicely round off a strenuous afternoon.

Nor did the old 5 to 7 rule long keep the ladies within bounds. Though, as already mentioned, the Committee's Minutes became steadily less revealing, there is the compensation that those of the Annual and Extraordinary General Meetings began to be recorded verbatim in 1903. We now get an idea of just what earlier Secretaries meant by the not infrequent phrase, 'the meeting then broke up in some confusion'. The Yost Typewriter Company's shorthand writer has left us a spirited transcript of the 1903 Annual General Meeting, when the question of admitting ladies to lunch between 1 p.m. and 2 p.m. was broached. Mr. G. H. M. Batten (always a reformer), moved that they should be. Clubs, he said,

> are not recruited from old gentlemen. They are recruited from young men, and those young men require to find themselves surrounded by the institutions [*he presumably means young women*] which they are accus-

[1] The story is told, with many a feminine flourish, by Lady Duff Gordon herself in *Discretions and Indiscretions* (London, Jarrolds, 1932)—an ingenuous work which will be enjoyed by the most disingenuous reader.

[2] Sir Francis Dashwood, Bt. kindly informs me that his family still owns No. 17, and granted a new lease of it only 10 years ago.

tomed to . . . Last year one gentleman seemed to think that if we admitted ladies, we would see nurseries of children sprawling over the floor in the Smoking Room. But ladies would be confined—(*Heavy guffaws*)

We need not continue. The meeting got into a fine old tangle, but the significant thing is that the members, with repeated remarks about 'the spirit of the age' ringing in their ears, voted overwhelmingly for the change; even the fearful threat that ladies admitted to lunch might 'stay on to tea' did not deter them.

Mr. Batten, a master of tactics, next brought forward a cautious little suggestion (A.G.M., 1904) that ladies should be allowed to *dine* in the Strangers' Room on Wednesdays and Fridays. What, and hang about the Club all the evening? a member interjected. Not to worry, replied another Batten supporter, Mr. Crozier; he was quite confident that these females would 'clear out about 8.30 p.m. and go to the theatre'. Once again, the spirit of the age prevailed, and a mere six hands were raised against the proposal. To complete this revolution, in 1905 Sir George Mackenzie got Sundays added to 'ladies' nights', and soon they were only excluded on Thursdays, which were kept for big 'men only' dinners until 1937.

Thus the lady shoppers of Oxford Street steadily enlarged their bridgehead, and, at a time when the catering side was losing money steadily (the Coffee Room alone was £21 per week in the red during 1902), an immediate rise in Strangers' Room luncheons from 1,574 in 1902 to 3,696 in 1903 was most welcome.

Even from the male point of view, the unique location of the Club continued to have its advantages. There may have been few private houses left in Hanover Square, but not far away was the humming hive of residential Mayfair, again with the Oriental as one of its few easily accessible clubs. In *Club Makers and Club Members* (London, T. Fisher Unwin, 1914), T. H. S. Escott puts the case with period unction:

During the twentieth century's second decade, to its manifold attractions as a comprehensive place of social reunion, the Club adds the special recommendation of being a Mayfair paradise for inhabitants of the Grosvenor Square district in the dead season. The family is out of town, the servants are on board wages, but the head of the house is obliged to postpone his departure, though the only room he finds habitable is his library. Happily for him he belongs to the Oriental. There within ten minutes walk of his book and his domestic cigar box, he finds all he needs in the way of material consolation for his desolate dining room and closed kitchen.

By the time Escott wrote, the Edwardian age was already over. For our purposes, the passing of its King was chiefly notable because it touched off a new wave of picture-buying by the Club—I have already recorded the Committee's belief that nothing had been added to the collection for 70 years. The problem of King Edward was tackled by the same method as had been attempted with Queen Victoria, only more successfully. A circular to members disclosed that, subject to the permission of the new King, Sir Luke Fildes would be prepared to supply a replica of a portrait he had recently completed. It would be 'practically an original portrait' and his charge would be 1,000 guineas.

One thousand guineas for a replica—truly an opulent age!

From then onwards there was a fairly steady flow of accessions—none of them, alas, outstanding as works of art. But at least the Committee achieved their rather naively expressed ambition of 'filling the large vacant wall spaces in the Inner Hall'.

We are now very near the age of living testimony. The election on 7 October 1913, of Alfred Donald Pickford reminds us of a great guardian of the Club's traditions whom hundreds of members can easily recall, even though 'Pickie' himself is gone. But it was a full year earlier that Walter Kenneth Warren, of Calcutta, joined the Club, after a longish spell on the waiting list, and he is still in regular attendance as senior Honorary Life Member[1]. Two other H.L.M.s of almost the same vintage are Messrs. J. E. J. Taylor and E. A. Mitchell, both Calcutta men and both elected in 1914.

Well-known characters from the 'pre-1914' era who, though no

[1] It was in 1934 (though there had been an individual case once before) that it was decided that the Senior Member, provided he was of at least 50 years standing, should be entitled to Honorary Life Membership. The first beneficiary was Major R. N. Sutton-Nelthorpe (e. 1877). The privilege was later extended to all those with half a century's membership. In addition to those named above, there are at the moment three H.L.M.s *honoris causa*—Sir Arthur Bruce, Mr. W. Gibson (on his retirement as a Trustee in 1962), and Lord Butler.

longer with us, lived to serve on the Committee or otherwise to make their presence felt in comparatively recent times were: among Calcutta men, Sir James Leigh-Wood (e. 1901), James McGowan (e. 1909), Thomas McMorran (e. 1910), Stephen Anderson (e. 1908) and whole tribes of other Andersons, Magors, Marshalls and Robertsons; a great public servant who became a great Oriental Club man, Sir John Prescott Hewett (e. 1904); from Burma, Charles Findlay of Rangoon (e. 1904 and Chairman in the mid-thirties); on the Ceylon side, Sir Edward Rosling (e. 1907), Percy Bois (e. 1909), Sir Stanley Bois (e. 1913) and Walter Shakspeare (e. 1912); and a renowned representative of Australia, Major-General Sir Charles Ryan (e. 1911).

They had, on the whole, a more relaxed world than our own to look back upon. If the opening years of the twentieth century had introduced a certain *douceur de vie* into the Oriental Club, it was because it had begun to serve a somewhat wider social purpose. Cheerful mixed luncheon parties in the Strangers' Room, the comings and goings of temporary residents, many of them young men on leave from the East, had modified the *pinjrapole* image, though the old and dozy no doubt continued to hold tyrannic sway in the Smoking Room and other favoured corners.

Recruitment and finance had responded well to the various innovations and it was not until the period 1910–12 that some loss of impetus was again being felt. The annual surplus, one notices, fell from £882 in 1910 to £528 and only £80 in the succeeding years, this being traced mainly to a temporary decline in elections and hence in entrance fees. As so often before, the Committee took this as a challenge to expand rather than to retrench, and thus in February 1914, less than a decade after the last great building scheme had been completed, another was put before the members. This time the proposed scene of action was that old 'debatable land' to the west, once known as Conduit Yard. The buildings happened to be untenanted and as the chairman (Mr. D. B. Horn) put it, this seemed to be the moment to take over the whole thing and 'secure for ever our ancient lights'. A scheme costing about £5,000 was put forward and it was with obvious reluctance that everyone finally agreed that the financial return would not justify the expense.

What was the proposal? I have already hinted much earlier in this book that it is of doubtful profit to mull over abortive plans for altering a now-vanished building. I will only say that not just in 1914 but in 1920, as a Centenary project in 1924, and less formally at intervals since then, an assortment of glittering visions was held out, including a fine Ladies' Drawing Room, a 'proper Card Room' (of course), more bedrooms, better staff accommodation. Indispensable to all schemes was a reshuffling of the three old jokers in the pack—the Coffee Room, the Smoking Room, the Drawing Room. There is a certain irony in the forecast with which Baillie concludes his chapter on 'Our Conservatism':

> The Smoking Room is situated immediately above the kitchens, and probably in course of time will be converted into a Coffee Room; while this room on the Ground Floor . . . will probably be ceded to the lovers of tobacco, and will be the prize of the victors in the long war that has been waged for half a century . . .

But all the course of time brought was *another* half century of argument and good intentions. Until the last moments of 18 Hanover Square, invisible to the members and perhaps unknown to most of them, relays of boy carriers continued to pass and repass along the 30 yards of passages which separated the kitchens from the Coffee Room, with a lift intervening. As for the alternative and even more frequently canvassed switch of Drawing Room into Smoking Room and vice-versa—this never came to fruition either. The anti-smoke lobbyists were too cunning. To Mr. C. A. MacDonald, Chairman in 1918, they were the exact equivalents of the 'backwoods' peers of 1911. Referring at the A.G.M. to the temporary use of the Drawing Room for smoking during redecorations, he said:

> I have been told that there are a certain number of members living in remote parts of the country who have been deprived of the greatest enjoyment of their lives, which is coming to the Club for one purpose only: namely, to oppose any proposal for the smokers having the use of this room.

However, the end was at hand. As the result of a motion passed at the 1924 A.G.M. smoking was eventually allowed in the Drawing

Room as well as the Smoking Room, the non-smokers being given the Library as their final retreat.

Physically, therefore, the Clubhouse remained unaltered from 1905 until the bulldozers moved in. It simply grew older, in an ever-deepening patina of dark mahogany, dark carpets, huge dark pictures and a great deal of buff-coloured paint. In a queer sense, it was one of the most functional buildings in London.

Reverting to 1914, when the Committee saw their proposals come to nothing, they let the yard to a fencing organisation called the Sword Club. The surprising result was that 'Conduit Yard' now entered on the most useful period of its rather hangdog career, and even achieved a mild degree of glamour. The Sword Club (a breakaway from the London Fencing Club) reconstructed the old coachbuilders' premises, and though World War I naturally upset their programme, competitions were held there in 1915. To complete the story, after the War the Sword Club moved out to reunite with the London Fencing Club and 1a Tenterden Street (the correct designation) was taken over by the Bertrand Fencing Academy. Here the great Felix Bertrand and his son Leon ('Punch') carried on with *éclat*. The majority of the British Amateur Foil Championships from 1921 onwards were held in their rooms, and from them Mr. Charles de Beaumont gave the first-ever B.B.C. commentary on fencing.

World War II brought a period of dereliction and a further change. In 1948 the London Fencing Club obtained a tenancy and 1a became virtually the headquarters of British fencing. Yet to the Oriental members and their staff it was always 'The Sword Club', with cheerful memories of boxing evenings and Christmas parties, and it was sad that the move to Stratford Place meant that the L.F.C. lease had to be cancelled. As though to emphasise the end of an era, the whole place was virtually demolished by fire on the night of 16 June 1962.

Yet, without the benefit of foresight, many Oriental Club members thought that the seven-year lease granted to the Sword Club in 1914 was much too long—they still hoped to see the Club's expansion scheme revived.

The events of August 1914 brought all such dreams to an end for the time being. It would be a mistake to assume, however, that

World War I—or even World War II—affected the Oriental Club in any fundamental way. The most they did was to accelerate the three historical processes which really have modified the character of the Club, and to which we shall return. They are: the decline in the number of British expatriates in the East; the effect of taxation on the habits and hospitality of the professional classes; and the withdrawal of residents from Central London. The wars themselves merely gave rise to a certain number of day-to-day problems either common to the whole country or peculiar to old-fashioned institutions in the West End. In coping with them the Oriental showed a considerable quiet talent for self-preservation.

8 *Two Wars and a Darkening Scene*

I believe that no objection will be raised by any member to being served by a nice tidy girl wearing a clean white apron.
Robert Williamson at the Annual General Meeting, 1916

The first Committee meeting held during World War I was on 25 August 1914, when in view of what the Chairman mildly called 'the unsettled state of the country', it was decided not to have an annual closure. Mr. J. M. G. Swanson suggested that the able-bodied staff should be encouraged to enlist, and terms were quickly worked out which included half-pay to men in the Forces and allowances to the relatives of some of them. The younger members themselves went off to the War, while most of the older ones found jobs of some sort—Mr. D. B. Horn remarked in a rather charming postwar exchange of letters with the Committee that the reason why he had been chairman so often (1910–11, 1913–15, 1917) was that he was 'one of the few idle men in the Club'.

Some loss of income was inevitable and this, as well as a generous impulse, was no doubt behind the decision to invite any members' sons serving with the Forces to become Honorary Members and to make use of the clubhouse 'for the duration'. A list of the 130 who responded is extant. However, by the end of 1917 a whip-round was necessary, mainly to cover the special staff allowances, and 450 (out of 680) members contributed a useful £3,218.

War charities were of course supported. They started near home, so to speak, with a 100 gns. donation to the Indian Soldiers' Fund, but spread ever wider till they finally embraced a gift of used playing cards to the Chinese Labour Camp at Folkestone (November 1917). The drama of Kitchener's death in 1916 touched off a 'general wish' among the members to possess a picture of him, and the ever-obliging John Collier supplied, for £315, a replica of his 1911 Academy portrait. Heavily cut down, it is now in the Smoking Room.

Sometimes 1917 seems to merge into 1940, as when the Club was fined £4 because a member failed to do what was not yet called 'the black-out' in his bedroom. The Committee rather superbly reminded him that 'as a citizen of London and a member of the Club' it was his duty to pull down the blind and his moral responsibility to refund the £4. He was at first defiant, but in the end paid up.

Rationing was the next bother. As most of us remember from World War II, Club catering, with all its shortcomings, did in fact shield the members to some extent from the rigours of the domestic coupon. But a surviving note on fuel-rationing is more evocative—it takes us straight back to the era of the universal open coal fire. By calculations of a delightful complexity—212 scuttles per month for bedrooms, 1½ barrows per day for the kitchen—it reveals that on a three year average, the Club fireplaces, ranges and boilers swallowed up exactly one ton of coal every day, 365 tons per annum. However the Controller's allocation of 292 tons for the year 1917–18 was not too crippling.

At the deepest level of all, the cost of a long, stern war came home to every member, not only through the casualties in his private circle, but through the ever-lengthening roll of those young Club servants who had been 'encouraged to enlist' and who would not now return to Hanover Square. Let it be put on record that they represented more than a quarter of the total with the Forces—nine killed or missing out of 34. This aspect of World War I needs to be allowed for when we come to the only serious question of policy with which the members had to deal and which they settled promptly and unanimously—or so they thought!

On 26 May 1915 the Committee issued a circular stating that 'in pursuance of the recommendation of the members present at the Annual General Meeting of the Club on the 11th instant', they felt it imperative that 'no person, though naturalised, who is of German, Austrian, Hungarian or Turkish origin should use the Club during the continuance of the war, whether as a member or a guest'. The

Committee added that they recognised that many of these naturalised British subjects were completely loyal, but this was no time for discrimination.

At the A.G.M. in question the lead had been taken by Sir John Hewett who, declaring himself a strong anti-German, urged that in view of 'the outrages, the scandalous outrages' committed by the German Government, they should not consent to lead their lives with Germans, naturalised or otherwise. He believed that 10 were still members of the Club and in his opinion 'we should turn them out and stand the shot'. Mr. William Beaumont followed in a similar vein. He supported the view which had been expressed in Committee that these men should be expelled; this was seconded by Sir Edward Rosling, there was no opposition, and the meeting turned to other matters.

On now to an Extraordinary General Meeting convened on 26 November 1918 to discuss the following Committee resolution:

> Whereas in pursuance of instructions from the General Meeting of May 11th 1915 the Committee have called for and received explanations from those members of the Club who are of enemy alien origin, it is hereby resolved that no further action be taken.

Hell then broke loose. Headed by Mr. Beaumont, member after member pointed out that the intention in 1915 was not to 'call for explanations' from the naturalised members but to eject them. Why had the Committee not only failed in this, but had actually done nothing at all until February of this very year 1918, when rather mild letters of enquiry had been sent to four of the villainous Huns—and what about the remaining six?

The Committee defended themselves as best they could. They said their enquiries had in fact started earlier; they read out replies from two or three of the naturalised members ('became a British subject in 1884 . . . 30 years in Rangoon . . . never visited Germany in my life . . . two sons in the trenches and a third in Charterhouse O.T.C.', and so on); produced their solicitors' warning that the Club's rules about expulsion were strictly drawn and could not without grave risk be 'bent' to get rid of a member just because his father was a German; and finally played their trump card—there had been no resolution at the 1915 meeting at all. *No resolution?* No, just a proposition that something suitable ought to be drafted, and acted upon in due course. The members gasped, but Sir Edward Rosling weighed in with what sounds like a deliberately naive elucidation:

> I seconded the motion, not that there was any motion before the meeting; but there was a strong feeling that something should be done, and I seconded what I believed Mr. Beaumont was going to frame afterwards and did not frame...

This did not placate anyone, and then and there, 15 days after the Armistice, the members rejected the Committee's resolution and passed one of their own that the naturalised enemy aliens must be got rid of, by whatever means. The Committee took up this task, no doubt with the same distaste which had clearly caused them to back-pedal from May 1915 to February 1918, and so far as can be traced the few remaining crypto-Germans resigned.

The sequel was strange. During the 'between Wars' period the rule (IVa) remained in force that 'No person who, or either of his parents is or was a German or Austrian[1] (whether such person or his parents have been naturalised in Great Britain or not) can be proposed for membership of the Club'. Then, in the rather inapposite year 1937[2], the Committee brought to the A.G.M. a resolution 'that Rule IVa should be expunged'. In support, the Chairman (Sir Henry Wheeler) urged that the bitter passions which produced it had died down, that nations should try to live in amity, and perhaps a small contribution would be to eliminate words which were in a way a reproach to two European nations. The 'blood business' had sometimes given rise to extraordinary instances of oppression, and in any case most of the English members of the Club probably had some Germanic blood in their veins! These arguments impressed the members in the year before Munich, and the resolution was passed with only two dissentients. The rule was not revived during World War II.

One more event of the 1914–18 period has to be noted—of

[1] The Turks and Hungarians seem to have got off the hook at quite an early stage.
[2] A similar resolution had been put down in 1932, but was withdrawn for technical reasons.

passing significance at the time, but members still have cause to be grateful for it. It was on 2 November 1915 that the possibility of employing waitresses was raised in Committee, but action was not taken until the following summer. The first few candidates who presented themselves shied off—a little intimidated, no doubt. However, on 14 August 1916 Mrs. Hunt's agency in Marylebone Lane sent along a girl called Ellen Elizabeth Moore, who had just refused a job at the Piccadilly Hotel at 18s. a week. She liked the look of the Club and the Club liked the look of her, and offered her 19s. 3d. She started work at once as the Oriental's first waitress, and remains in its service to this day.

Though 'Alice', as she mysteriously became, was the daughter of a master builder, her mother ran a hand laundry in Queen's Park, Kilburn, then the laundry quarter of London, and Alice helped her. The war put paid to that and brought Alice to 18 Hanover Square, but it accounts for the unforgettable feature of her appearance—the beautiful frilled and starched apron and other accoutrements, unchanged in style since 1917 (*Pl. 1*), which Alice still launders herself with professional skill.

At the end of the War, it was resolved gradually to dispense with the girls. Alice stayed on, however, and as Senior Drawing Room Waitress developed a unique relationship with the members, particularly the older ones, whose vagaries amused her but whom she delighted to 'mother'.

It is high time, in fact, to say something about the relationship generally between staff and members, as it evolved in the present century. In Chapter 6 we left the Club servants wallowing along rather grimly in a Dickensian ambience of drink and black beetles. But the public school spirit was already active and it worked its way through to the staff of the Oriental, as of other Clubs, mainly via the encouragement of sport. By the 1890s a regular cricket fund had been established, love of the game being especially fostered (according to Baillie) by the Hon. Robert Grimston, an 'Alfred' recruit and 'one of the kindest and best-hearted men who ever entered the Club doors'[1]. Then came the era of rifle-shooting which followed the

[1] He was also an impassioned diner, and it was dangerous for even a fellow member to speak to him while engaged upon this rite.

South African War and the vigorous propaganda of Earl Roberts, and in 1912 we hear of Captain Lockwood 'taking the Staff Rifle Club Contest: Winners, C. Smith, R. Gale and E. Stevens'.

For the remarkable development of sport after World War I we have the first-hand testimony of Jack Parsons, the Club's Head Valet (*Pl. 28*), with a record of service only second to Alice's—he joined on 17 November 1917. Parsons looks back with relish to the days when the Club's young men and boys, with himself as one of the keenest, played cricket and football on Paddington Recreation Ground, shot at the Polytechnic, boxed at the Sword Club and swam in the Serpentine. Cricket, the initial favourite, became more organised but no less fun—Lord Lilford (e. 1885) gave a Cup for the best bowler, the team competed in the Inter-Clubs League and later there were summer outings to Sir Bertram Hornsby's place at Iford in Sussex or to Dr. Crouch's at Ascot, where members and staff joined in the matches.

'How did you find time for all this, Parsons?'

'Well, I don't know, sir, but of course we nearly all lived in, and somehow though we worked longer hours, things weren't so *tight* as they are now...'

By this time, the old Cricket Fund had been expanded into a Staff Recreation Fund, well supported by the members, but more was needed to make the Club something of a little 'welfare state' for its faithful employees. The gap was partly filled by the Provident Fund founded in December 1919, on the basis of five per cent subscriptions from the wages of staff and a 50 per cent bonus added by the Club. Personal contributions and legacies by individual members helped to swell the total. The period 1923–7 seems to have been particularly fruitful in legacies. In more than one case, as Alice can testify, it was some old gentleman noted for eccentric frugality in his lifetime ('wouldn't pay for as much as a biscuit with his cup of tea') who surprised the staff by a post-mortem gesture.

If the Club is blessed today with a small group of very long service employees, it had even more of these veterans between the Wars. Such a one was Cunnington, the Wine Butler, who retired in 1938 after more than 40 years in the Coffee Room. He kept a very strict control over his stocks and, says Parsons, 'we boys loved to play tricks on him. When he was out serving, someone would make a noise like a cork being drawn [*demonstration*] and he would come rushing back—"*Who opened that bottle?*"' Another seasoned character was Stanley, the Hall Porter, who once earned commendation by detecting a thief who had got into the Club disguised as a member. Then there was Dumastière, the tall and stately Chef, first appointed in 1908, recalled to the colours in the efficient French way at the first stroke of war, welcomed back in June 1919 and still in full control of the kitchens up to 1933; and Emily Davies, his right-hand woman, who used to get in at 6 o'clock in the morning and wheel great barrow-loads of coal about—'a job no man would touch'. The retirement of these old stagers was marked not only by a pension but usually by a members' subscription—in Cunnington's case as much as £450.

There seems to be a good deal about money in this book. Too much, considering that we are dealing with such a gentlemanly topic, a very old West End club? But the truth is that never in the whole of its existence has the Oriental paid its way for more than a few years together. Even during the non-inflationary epoch before 1914 the Committee was at almost predictable intervals forced into 'economy drives' which encroached equally on the security of the staff and the comfort and good temper of the members. I have not mentioned the half!

One of the few intervals of seeming affluence came in fact immediately after World War I, with plenty of money about and men back from France or the East all set to enjoy the pleasures of club life. The Oriental felt the benefit—94 candidates came forward in 1919, 85 in 1920, and optimism expressed itself in various ways. The entrance fee, which had stood at 31 guineas for so long, was hoisted to a rash 50 guineas. Recruitment at once fell off, but it was not until the depression of 1931 confirmed their growing doubts that the Committee, rejecting any half-way house, recommended a return to the old figure. The annual subscription, too, after maintaining its 1882 level of nine guineas even through the stresses of 1917, now started to climb. In 1919 it was fixed at nine guineas for old members and 11 for new; in 1921, 11 and 12; and in 1922, 14 and 15 guineas.

The brevity of this boom period—it hardly lasted three years—also put paid to the grandest of the expansion schemes already mentioned. This time the architect *in potentia* was Mr. Guy Dawber, a name worthy to stand beside Wyatt and Decimus Burton. He proposed to turn 18 Hanover Square upside down and back to front at a cost of up to £70,000, so that though the still extant photostats of his plans are a pleasure to peruse, it is not in the least surprising that they never went beyond paper. Mr. Dawber remained 'Club architect' for several years, but his talents seem to have been dissipated on sordid little jobs like alterations to pantries.

Even a much less ambitious scheme intended to mark the Centenary of the Club in 1924 had to be scaled down when the flow of contributions stopped well short of the £5,000–£6,000 required, and in the end only some modest improvements to the 'ladies' side' were carried out.

In general, the Oriental, reticent as ever, made no great *tamasha* over this Centenary affair. As often happens, there was a choice of suitable anniversary dates—e.g. 4 February 1824, when the decision had been taken to nominate a Committee and to issue a prospectus; or the next stage (some time in March) when the necessary 400 members had been enrolled to bring the Club formally into being; but the Committee's choice fell on 8 July 1824, the day on which the first Clubhouse in Lower Grosvenor Street opened its doors. The central event, needless to say, was a dinner, and on 8 July 1924 some 120 members did themselves rather well at two guineas a head:

	CAVIAR d'ASTRAKHAN
Pale Dry Sherry	TORTUE CLAIRE au MADERE
Graves Superieur	TRUITE SAUMONEE a la NEVA
Veuve Cliquot (1915)	ESCALOPE de RIS de VEAU CLAMART
Gruaud la Rose (1915)	SELLE d'AGNEAU RICHELIEU
Taylor Vintage (1904)	TERRINE de FOIE GRAS LUCULLUS
Fine Champagne	SOUFFLE GLACE au RHUM
Courvoisier	FRIANDISES
Liqueurs Various	CASSOLETTES ORIENTALES
	DESSERT

The memory no doubt lingered on, but for a more permanent memorial—apart from the abortive building scheme—the Committee invited Mr. Stephen Wheeler[1] to compile the Club's *Annals*. Wheeler evidently had no wish to compete with Baillie or even to go on where he left off—he aimed at something quite different. *Annals of the Oriental Club: 1824–1858*[2] consists in fact of a nine-page historical introduction, followed by brief biographies of about 300 out of over 2,000 members elected from the foundation of the Club until the dissolution of the East India Company. The principle of selection is not very clear, since some conspicuous personalities are absent, while other entries consist of no more than a name and a date. But even as it stands the list represents an immense labour, and its value to the Club's latest historian has been incalculable.

Unless (as is likely) Wheeler had been accumulating notes for several years, his tempo was a distinct improvement on Baillie's, though he did not quite catch up with the Centenary itself. The *Annals* seem to have been commissioned some time in 1922, a prospectus (undated) was sent out in either 1923 or 1924, and on 15 June 1926 Messrs. W. H. Smith delivered 1,000 copies at a total cost of £248 7s. 6d. Of these, 400 were bound and 600 unbound, the prospectus having rather curiously offered the work in either form at a price of half a guinea or 7s. 6d. respectively. How many of each were taken up is not known, but we must record (with some apprehension) that by 1928 'surplus copies' could be had for 2s. . . .

Apart from a bonus of one week's pay to the staff, that was about the whole of the Centenary story. A cynic might reflect that the members would have been more impressed with the wonders of being 100 years old if so many of them were not already—but let us move on to other themes.

The administration of the Club showed some interesting trends after World War I. This has always veered between the sprawling and the succinct—sometimes a proliferation of Sub-Committees with wide powers, sometimes the virtual dictatorship of an 'inner cabinet'. The 1920s were certainly a period of concentration. The

[1] Elected as far back as 1887, Wheeler had acted as Honorary Librarian for a number of years. It was on his advice that 8 July was chosen as the Centenary date.

[2] Privately printed by the Arden Press for the Oriental Club in 1925.

first big step came in 1925 when the General Committee was reduced from 24 to 12 members. This meant less distinction in size between it and the House Committee and less tendency to delegate minor decisions to the latter, until in 1928 the two became a single body, and so continued for six years.[1]

The result was a temporary return to the 'good old days' of General Committee minutes. Once more, a draft answer is gravely prepared to Sir J. P. Hewett's complaint about muffins; the right judicial tone is chosen to appease Mr. Justice Harrison—'it was decided to say that the servant who had failed to carry out his desires about soup had been admonished'; a pretty sharp letter is sent to the member who had infringed by-law XVII by taking more than two guests upstairs, one of whom had also infringed the laws of God and man by being sick on the Smoking Room carpet; while to calm the age-old suspicions of Sir Ludovic Porter the Secretary is directed to reply that:

> The Committee regretted that Sir L.P. has cause to complain, but assures him that the remnants of the week are not used for service on Sundays.

In one case, the self-restraint of these long-suffering Committee men must be admired. A Strangers' Room guest had been justly annoyed when his daughter's dress was splashed with gravy, but it was hardly his place to complain that the meal provided by his host was inedible; however, the letter was simply passed to the host in question.

After the run of short-term secretaries recorded on pp. 100-1, there was a series of more stable incumbencies. Perhaps the most conspicuous figure was Lieut.-Colonel Godfrey Bird who held office for 13 years (1909–1922), including war service. It is extraordinary, but true, that he accepted the post at £250 a year, £50 *less* than Mr. Thomas Cornish reached just 80 years before. However, by 1920 his

[1] The full vicissitudes of the House Committee would be tedious in the telling. It was reconstituted (two members plus Sir Alfred Pickford, Honorary Secretary) in 1934, but must have lapsed again, since the Chairman's statement circulated before the 1949 A.G.M. announced: 'We have, *I think for the first time*, constituted a permanent House Committee of two members and the Chairman'. The words I have italicised were later withdrawn!

salary had doubled, and since then the graph has shown a steady, gentle rise. . . .

There have been two interregnums. The first was when Major R. C. B. Williams resigned the Secretaryship in 1934 and the Committee, hard-pressed as usual, realised that they could save money by appointing an Honorary Secretary from among their number. Luckily the bed of nails was accepted by Sir Alfred Pickford, and he held office from November in that year until 1937. There has already been mention of 'Pickie' in this book, and there is no doubt that among Club 'characters' he ranks high. My own first memory of him was in 1945 when, as a newly joined employee of the International Tea Market Expansion Board, I was confronted by this gigantic monocled figure, attired, unnervingly, in the shirt and shorts of a Boy Scout (I did not know then that Pickford was one of Scouting's great international figures). He seemed rather formidable, though another thing I learnt about him later was that there was a sensitive and even diffident being inside that massive carapace. Living in the Club year after year, exerting his honesty and common sense in its service whether as Committee man, Honorary Secretary or Chairman, 'Pickie' left it only to die, and when he did so (7 October 1947) he bequeathed his entire holding of £2,200 debentures to the members.

The second period of honorary secretaryship was during World War II. In 1941 Colonel Dallas Smith, 'Pickie's' professional successor, went off to the Army and Mr. H. A. Gardner carried on with a most thankless task until 1945. The world heard something of his success, since during the war years and just after, the Oriental, most uncharacteristically, used to be the subject of fairly regular paragraphs in the 'Peterborough' column of *The Daily Telegraph*, and elsewhere, no doubt the work of a member then on the staff of that paper. One of these chatty pieces (10 April 1945) rather amusingly attributes the Club's good standard of war-time catering to the fact that it lay 'far off the Whitehall lunch route'; it was one of the few places where one could get a meal 'without being trampled under foot by that howling mob of starving Civil Servants'.

Food apart, World War II more or less duplicated World War I as far as the Oriental was concerned. There was the same problem of allowances to staff in the Forces (though thank God not the casualties); the same abrupt decline in income calling for a whip-round[1]. Physically, the old Clubhouse got through successive blitzes with a minimum of damage—the only direct hit was from one of our own anti-aircraft shells which came to rest near the Hall Porter's box, but did not explode. More damage was in fact done when fire broke out accidentally in the boys' dormitory—as one of the servants expressed it, the Brigade quite enjoyed having 'a genuine fire' to deal with.

One long-sought reform precipitated by World War II was the institution of country membership. This the Committee had always side-stepped because of the immediate financial loss involved, but with resignations flowing in during 1940 and 1941, it was felt that if the Oriental followed the example of almost every other club in London, it might do something to stop the rot. The first Extraordinary General Meeting called to consider the proposal (2 December 1941) failed to get a quorum of 50, so there was a free-for-all debate in which 'Pickie', as Chairman, enjoyed himself vastly, but at a repeat performance the new rule went through.

The formula (still in force) was that members who 'do not live within 100 miles of Oxford Circus or have their regular place of business in London' could elect to pay a lower subscription—at that time 10 gns. Though only 50 members actually took advantage of the rule in the first year, it definitely helped to stabilise the membership.[2]

It was a happy chance that the date chosen for the 1945 Annual General Meeting—8 May—turned out to be V.E. Day, so that the 33 members who turned up did so in an atmosphere of national rejoicing. But the victorious mood did not last very long within the management of the Oriental Club. After World War II there was little of that buoyancy (however ephemeral) which followed the first

[1] Three Club servants were killed or died on active service. The whip-round raised over £6,000, just twice the 1917 figure, though of course at lower money values.

[2] A great effort by the Committee and other senior members actually produced 60 new entrants in 1941, after two years of virtual stagnation.

Armistice—only continued food restrictions and rising operational costs, above all in wages.

For a time, membership and finance stood the strain, but from about 1949 onwards crisis came in full force; 1951 will always be remembered as the year when five General Meetings were held and a specific proposal for the dissolution of the Club and the sale of 18 Hanover Square was decisively rejected by the members.

Even the most committed readers of this book would not thank me for dragging them step by step through that interlude in the Oriental's history. The difficulties of clubs and the devices by which they have to be propped up nowadays are a too familiar tale. During the 1951 debates everything from turning the upper floors of the Clubhouse into flats (or the ground floor into shops) to the use of paper napkins was mulled over again and again. Ideas from the remote past, too, were unconsciously dredged up—for example, raising a cash sum by allowing the older members to compound their subscriptions for life, as was done after the Cornish debacle of 1842.

It is more useful to ponder what was behind a member's remark at the first of those five General Meetings (1 February 1951):

> It seems to me that 10 years ahead those who follow us will have no use for such a club as this.

The founders of the Oriental, as we saw, planned it as a refuge for East India Company servants from the loneliness and unfamiliarity of 'home'. This concept was weakened by the withdrawal of the H.E.I.C. element to St. James's Square and made finally obsolete by the dissolution of the Company itself in 1858. From then onwards the pace-makers were drawn from commerce—typically, the 'No. 1's' of the great merchant houses of Calcutta, Bombay, Madras, Colombo, Rangoon, Singapore. But these were not necessarily retired men, as in earlier days; still vigorous on their return from the East, many of them took up directorships in banks or shipping companies, or in City firms with which they had been linked, from a distance, all their lives. They formed in fact the 'inner ring' of the Club and there was a belief (not wholly apocryphal, or wholly approved by outsiders) that the affairs of certain plantation industries—above all tea and rubber—were largely decided in comfortable corners of the Oriental's Smoking Room.

Between the Wars, however, there was a slight reversion to the past in the shape of an influx of Indian Civilians, some of them with a big part to play in the Club's affairs. Sir John Hewett (Lieutenant-Governor of the United Provinces 1907–12) I have already mentioned; others were Sir Henry Wheeler (Governor of Bihar and Orissa 1922–7), four times Chairman of the Club (1932–3, 1936, 1938), Lord Carmichael (Governor of Bengal, 1912–17), Sir Harcourt Butler (Governor of Burma, 1923–7), Sir John Stratheden Campbell, Sir Godfrey Fell, Sir Hugh Stephenson and Sir Benjamin Robertson. All these belonged to the Oriental's great 1919–22 intake; a somewhat earlier comer was Sir Reginald Mant (e. 1915), Chairman 1932–33, and a later was Sir Charles Innes (Governor of Burma, 1927–32), elected in 1929 and Chairman during the latter part of the 1951 typhoon.

With the entry of such men the Club probably achieved as happy a balance of interests as it had known throughout its long existence.

But by 1950 the wheel had turned again. It was a decade since the last British entrants had been accepted for the I.C.S., and all over the East the expatriate official was (in the new jargon) being 'phased out'. It could not be very long before there would be no more 'K.C.S.I.s' and 'K.C.I.E.s' to grace the Club's Committee list.

Even among the merchants there was a sense of withdrawal. One of the points made at those 1950 meetings was that though there would still be abundant work for Europeans to do in Asia, it would be on the technical rather than the executive level, and technicians might be less likely to find the Oriental to their taste—'they would have no use for such a club as this'.

But the phrase can be slanted another way. Such a club as *this*. If the Oriental's function was obsolescent, so (it could be argued) was its form. To the town members of the nineteenth century it was their way of life—the place where they enjoyed, day by day and in familiar company, the simple pleasures of food and drink, cards, billiards, gossip. Living, most of them, within walking distance or a short drive away in a hansom, the evening was their choicest time; in fact they loved the old place so much that, as we know, it was the devil's own problem to get them to quit it at two o'clock in the morning.

Now, there were no more nabobs in Wimpole Street or Devonshire Place, and the last of the flats or 'chambers' which sheltered a few members round about were ripe for the bulldozer. The typical Oriental man, on the days he came to town, took the 5.30 home to Guildford or Haywards Heath. A great lumbering apparatus was still being provided for people who, in crude truth, needed nothing more than a lunch club or occasional bed-and-breakfast. And because the tax man was eroding private fortunes year after year, even the busy scene at midday had changed its character; plenty of members still lunched quietly by themselves or with their friends and families, but the takings were bulked out by that 'business entertaining' which, though a natural and enjoyable part of modern life, has no particular connection with Dr. Johnson's 'assembly of good fellows meeting under certain conditions'.

Dying on its feet, then?

> There are two ways of dealing with impending doom. One is the Eastern way of lying down helplessly and hopelessly and letting it roll over you; the other way is to get up and try and do something about it.

So up and spoke Sir Percival Griffiths at the last, decisive meeting on 11 October 1950, using an argument well adapted to his audience! But in any case they had already made up their minds. They were not going to let the Club, which most of them used so little, founder under them. Once the sale proposition had been turned down, the Committee, with extraordinary resilience and resource, got to work on a wide selection of the various remedies which had been put forward: associate membership for wives and unmarried sisters and daughters; suspension of the entrance fee and a rousingly successful recruiting drive in the East as well as at home; a reduced subscription for young entrants; a bar at last; and solid cash support which in the next year or two brought in a remarkable sum of nearly £50,000, one fifth of it as outright gifts, the rest in the form of interest-free loan stock[1].

[1] Mr. J. K. Michie (Chairman 1953) was elected an Honorary Life Member in 1954, in recognition of his efforts at this time. Mr. J. McFarlane (Chairman 1952) received the same honour in 1962, but lived less than a year to enjoy it. Mr. Michie died in 1967.

For the time being the Oriental was kept afloat, and there is no doubt that it gave great pleasure and a wonderful sense of 'belonging' to the scores of young men who had signed on at meetings in Calcutta or Bombay, and sooner or later came home to find themselves fully fledged members of one of the oldest and stateliest clubs in London. It was a cheerful time.

Unfortunately, the basic causes of weakness, as I have described them in this chapter, remained, and those of us who joined as town members at that period soon became aware of them. By about 1954, deficits and overdrafts were reappearing: there was a feeling of ossification setting in again; all the old questions began to be asked once more. The answers which were eventually found—so different from those of 1950—have already been revealed in the Prologue to this book.

II

STRATFORD PLACE

PROLOGUE

Concerning the Tyburn

In the inner hall of Stratford House stands a cylindrical wooden object about five feet high, hollow, bluntly pointed at one end, its blackened surface of the hardest texture[1]. It is in fact a water pipe, fashioned from the trunk of an oak-tree, and it is probably two centuries old at least. To remark to a visitor that it is strangely appropriate as the totem of the Club is to invite ribaldry, as the object is decidedly phallic in appearance, so one has to follow with a hasty exegesis, more or less as follows: the Oriental Club, in all its three locations—Grosvenor Street, Hanover Square and Stratford Place—has stood on or near the east bank of one of the most historic rivers in England, and its story is threaded by the water-courses to which this river and its tributaries gave rise.

To speak of the Tyburn as 'historic'—at any rate in the same breath with Thames or Severn, Humber or Trent—may seem too flattering. But consider it for a moment—first in space, then in time.

According to the best topographers, the Tyburn rises at Shepherd's Well, on the south side of Hampstead Heath. It meanders down past Swiss Cottage, and, entering Regent's Park by an aqueduct across the Canal, forms the beautiful lake there, emerging close to Baker Street Station. Thence its course is plotted by the windings of Marylebone Lane, which follows it faithfully as far as Wigmore Street. Here lane and river part company, the latter swerving away right-handed, to pass beneath the cellars of the houses on the west side of Stratford Place; to cross Oxford Street—the dip is still visible—near Bond Street Station; to traverse Mayfair, defining the boundary between the City Mead (of which more later) and Grosvenor Estates; to form a second dip a few yards from No. 16 Grosvenor Street and a third, much more famous, in Piccadilly; to enter

[1] But see page 242, note.

the gardens of Buckingham Palace and bestow upon the Monarch her own private lake; and to reach the Thames (amid a cloud of controversy) somewhere between Westminster Bridge and the Tate. Total course about five miles from source to mouth (or mouths).

Measured in time, a river incalculably old, but even during the last millennium setting a stamp upon London out of all proportion to its size. The northern reaches of the Tyburn named a great parish and later a Borough, for Marylebone is of course St. Mary-le-Bourn, 'the church near the stream'; at its outfall it is said to have formed Thorney Island, the sacred eyot on which Westminster Abbey was built. In between it gave its title to the Manor of Tyburn, sprawling along the north side of Oxford Street, and, by propinquity, to the fatal Tree at what is now Marble Arch and to the dolorous road thither[1].

But it also served the natural and homely function of any river or stream; it supplied water. All writers on mediaeval London give space to the City's 'conduits', applying the term both to the fountains or stand-pipes at which housewives and stall-holders filled their buckets and to the water-mains which nourished them.

Of these systems perhaps the most celebrated was the Great Conduit in Cheapside, fed from the site where Stratford Place now stands. In spite of all explanations[2], it remains extraordinary that even in the thirteenth century the City should have found it impossible to obtain 'sweet water' from its own rivers—the Fleet and the Walbrook, for example—and had to go miles into the country for supplies. But that is what happened. There is some argument whether the pipeline concerned actually tapped the Tyburn, or relied only on various freshets and springs alongside. However, the fact that the headquarters of all this activity was within a few yards of the little river's east bank strongly suggests that both were used.

It was in A.D. 1236 that one Gilbert de Sanford granted the City rights over 'certain springs' on his Manor of Tyburn. A year later a

[1] The old name, 'Tyburn Road', persisted into the second half of the eighteenth century, when it gradually gave way to Oxford Road or Oxford Street—see the Hon. Edward Stratford's petition (page 161).

[2] Cf. Stella Margetson, 'Bringing Water to the Capital' (*Country Life*, 22 June 1967).

group of merchants from Northern France astutely gained trading rights in exchange for contributing £100 'au Conduyt de ewe de la funtayne de Tybourne amener en la Cite de Londres', and later in the same century the records link this initiative with the Great Conduit in Cheapside.

It was quite a problem in hydraulics. Stratford Place stands just 30 ft. higher than Cheapside, but between them, barring the direct route via Holborn, is a slight hump at Oxford Circus. So a more southerly course was plotted—under what is now the Hog-in-Pound public house[1] and down South Molton Lane to eponymous Conduit Street and the St. James's Church end of Piccadilly, eastwards along the north side of the Strand and Fleet Street, across the Fleet River near Ludgate Circus, and so forward to Cheapside. That crossing of the Fleet . . . it seems to be quite happily accepted that sheer gravity would have kept a brisk flow moving along leaky wooden pipes all the way from Stratford Place to the top of Ludgate Hill. To me it appears more probable that there was a well-'skied' aqueduct over the Fleet or that pumping of some primitive kind was always resorted to—there was certainly a 'Pump House' at the Bond Street end of Conduit Street two centuries ago.

The mediaeval lay-out of what we may call the 'Stratford Place waterworks' cannot now be reconstructed, but Fig. 2 shows the kind of thing into which they developed. At first, an adequate head of water seems to have been obtained on the spot, from the springs and perhaps the Tyburn, but later there were one or more aqueducts bringing reinforcements from other Marylebone and Paddington sources, and these discharged into great cisterns and a subsequent 'receipt house'.

However, the City's interests did not halt at the Oxford Street line. The better to protect their springs and pipelines, the Lord Mayor and Corporation also took over an area of pasture land known variously as 'Conduit Meadow' or 'Conduit Mead' and still partly owned by them today under the name of the City Mead Estate. As Fig. 3 (p. 160) reveals, this very valuable slice of London

[1] Pieces of sculptured stone from the ancient conduit were found here, deep underground, in 1859 and 1875. It may be conjectured whether a vault uncovered on the site of No. 1 Stratford Place, in 1967, is not also part of the conduit system.

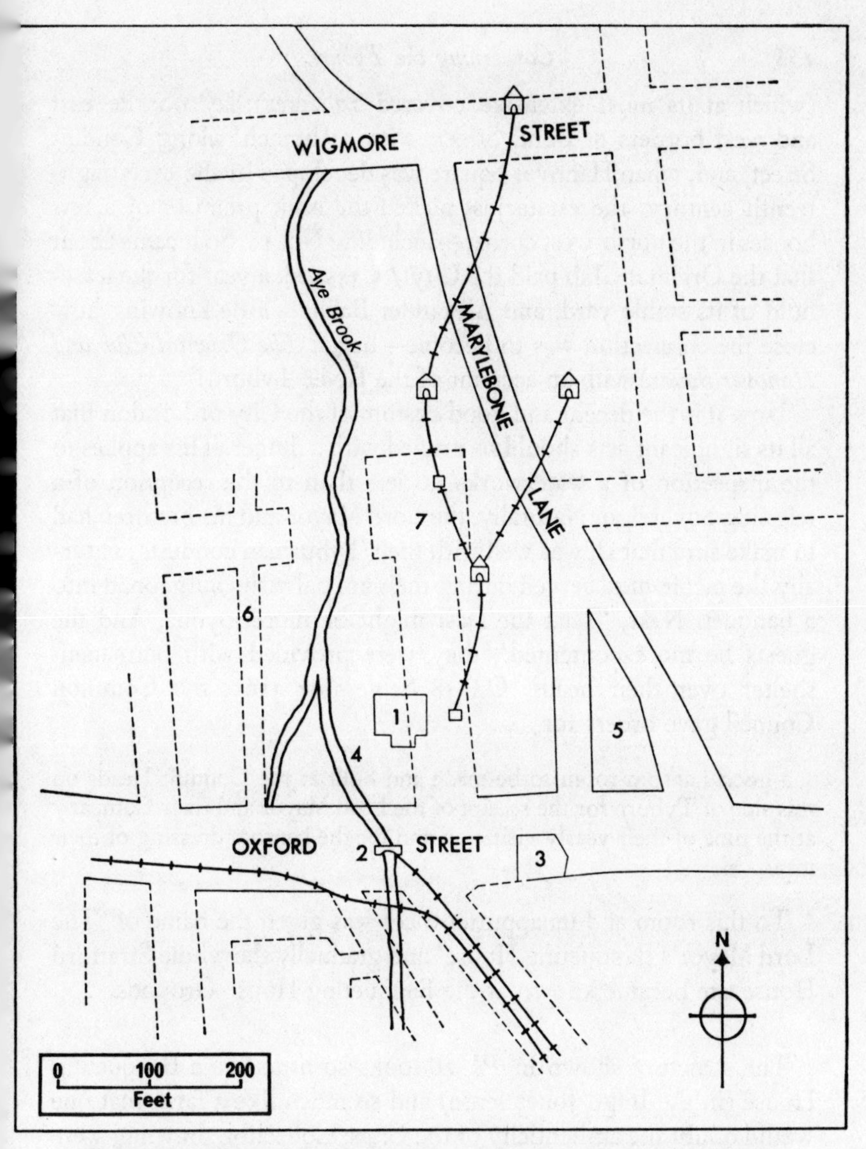

Fig 2 The Banqueting House Grounds and 'waterworks' in the late eighteenth century. 1. Site of Lord Mayor's Banqueting House. 2. Lord Mayor's Bridge. 3. Receipt House. 4. 1738 diversion of the Aye Brook (R. Tyburn). 5. Marylebone Watch House. 6, 7. Sites of future Gee's Court and Stratford Place. The various conduits and the 'heads' from which water could be drawn are also shown. (Adapted from the plan accompanying the paper, 'London's First Conduit System' by A. Morley Davies, *London and Middlesex Archaeological Society Transactions*, New Series, Vol. II, 1913)

(which at its most extensive covered 27 acres), lay on the east and west borders of Bond Street, with a 'branch' along Conduit Street, and, when Hanover Square was developed in the early eighteenth century, the estate just nicked the back premises of a few houses in the north-west corner—including No. 18. So it came about that the Oriental Club paid the City £3 15s. od. a year for the leasehold of its stable yard, and Alexander Baillie—little knowing how close the connection was to become—began *The Oriental Club and Hanover Square* with an account of the River Tyburn!

Now it is the decent and good custom of the City of London that all its significant acts should be ratified with a dinner. This applies to the inspection of a waterworks no less than to the reception of a reigning Sovereign. Naturally, the Lord Mayor and his brethren had to make sure that all was well with their Tyburnian conduits; naturally the picnic meal served during their annual visits burgeoned into a banquet. Next, 'That the feast might be more joyous, And the guests be more contented', they were provided with permanent shelter over their heads. On 18 September 1565, the Common Council gave orders for

> a good hansom room to be made and built at the Conduit Heads on this side of Tyburn for the receipt of the Lord Mayor and their Company at the time of their yearly visitation and for the hansom dressing of their meat.

To this room and its appurtenances was given the name of 'The Lord Mayor's Banqueting House' and gradually the whole Stratford House site became known as the Banqueting House Grounds.

The structure shown in *Pl. 16* looks so little like a Banqueting House (in the Inigo Jones sense) and so much like a farm that one would doubt the authenticity of the Crace Collection drawing, were it not confirmed by others. Contrary to a fondly held belief, it did not stand on the exact site of Stratford House, but nearer Oxford Street and slightly to the west—at the very brink of Tyburn in fact. And here came the jolly Aldermen to take a quick look at the cisterns, to hunt in the Marylebone meadows, to dine, and, with more raucous holloas, to hunt again. May I be of the company on 29

August 1974, when the Club Committee will assuredly mark the tercentenary of one 'memorable meal' by providing (perhaps out of the accumulated profits of this book) the following repast:

Poultry (to the value of £17 10s.)
Fish (£12 4s. 6d.)
2 Bucks (£10)
6 Shoulders of Venison (£1 5s.)
3 Dishes of Pigeon Pies (£1 5s.)
5 Dishes of Florentines [meat pies] (£1 10s.)
8 Dishes of Custards (£2 4s.)
4 Westfield [Westphalia?] Hams (£2 8s.)
8 Dried Tongues (£1 4s.)
8 Dishes of Fruit
4 Grand Salads
4 Rocks of Snow Cream
Syllabubs, wine, beer, ale, sugar, tobacco and oranges to the value of £45.

Total cost in 1674, including the hire of linen, forks, plate, etc.—£123 11s., a bill which by the time it was paid nearly four months later, had been 'abated' to a mere £115.

Such was City feasting in Charles II's reign, but within half a century the whole waterworks complex was fast falling into obsolescence. By 1725 the Banqueting House was reported as in poor condition, in 1736 it was 'ruinous', vandals having carried away large pieces, and in November of that year[1] the remains were ordered to be pulled down. They fetched £18. The cisterns were then arched over and though one 'aqueduct' remained, the three conduit heads on the site had lost their importance and on 31 January 1749 the once civic site was let to Henry Warrington, paviour, as grazing ground at a rental of £14 a year. He in turn sublet for a similar purpose to a fellow craftsman, George Shakespear, carpenter, whose cows remained in peaceful possession until the year 1771.

Meanwhile the City Mead Estate as a whole had had many vicissitudes. Gilbert de Sanford held from the Crown, but the City seems to have obtained the freehold, since this was reacquired by Henry VIII, and let to the Mercers' Company in 1514 for six shillings a year. Several times the City tried to get the freehold back, but had to wait until 1628 when Charles I, heavily in debt to the Corporation

[1] This was just three years before the foundation stone of the Lord Mayor's present 'banqueting house'—the Mansion House—was laid.

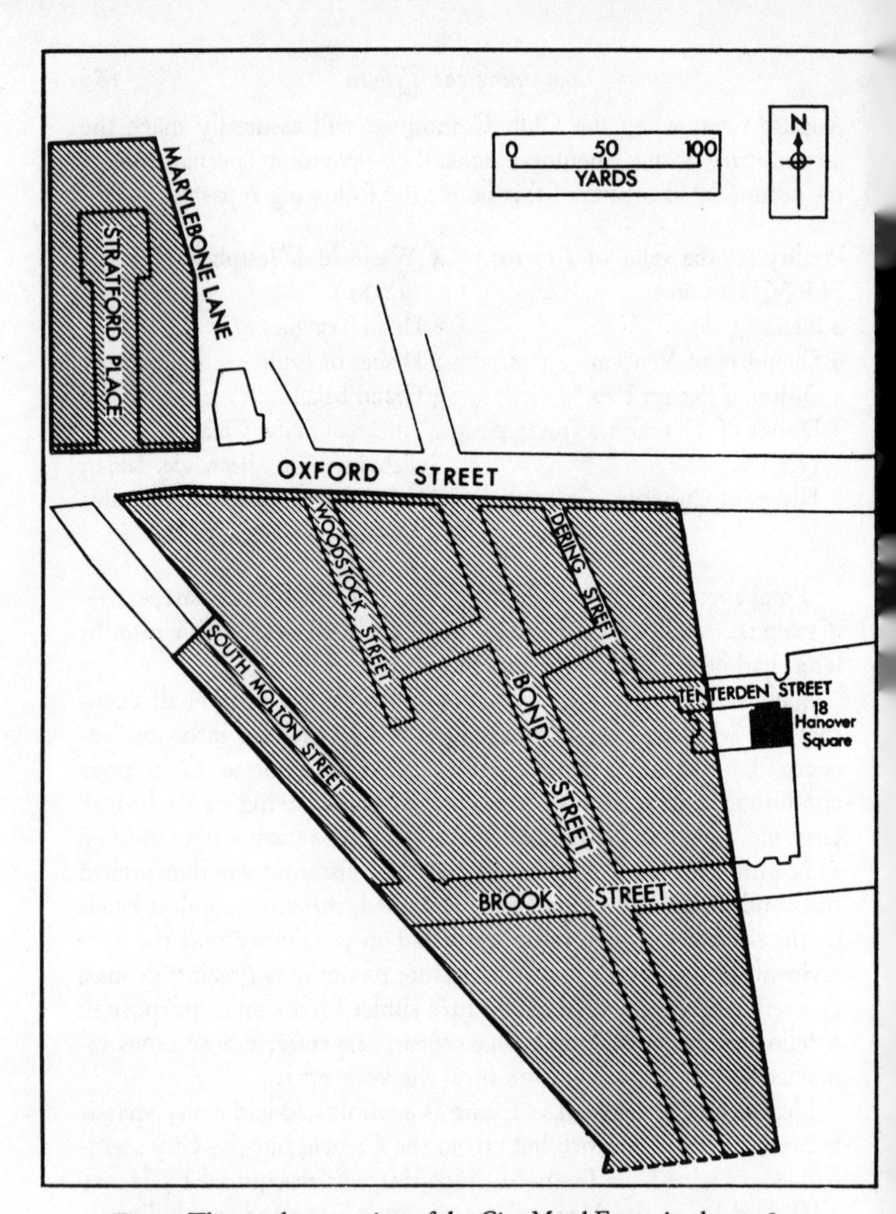

Fig 3 The northern section of the City Mead Estate in about 1800, showing how it took in part of the garden of 18 Hanover Square, the subsequent site of the Oriental Club. Shepherd Street is shown under its modern name of Dering Street. The Estate continued south as far as Hay Hill, with a narrow eastern extension along Conduit Street to Regent Street

as usual, sold it them for the equivalent of 36 years' rent (the latter having by then risen to £8 a year).

Yet, even when the development of Mayfair began, the long-sought purchase brought little financial gain. This was because of the Corporation's lax habit of granting perpetually renewable leases on very easy terms. By the mid-eighteenth century the whole thing had developed into a scandal—meat and drink, in fact, to such pamphleteers as the anonymous author of *The City Secret, or Corruption at All Ends of the Town* (London, 1744). We shall be meeting the same criticism of bad bargaining (though not of corruption), nearly 100 years later!

And finally, what of Tyburn itself? In spite of its history and achievements, it was never much of a river really—hardly more than a fair-sized brook—and as its waters dwindled through tappings near the source, it lost even its name and became known in fact as the Aybrook. By 1736 it had reached the final stage of degradation (suffered by virtually every London river in the end) and appears on a map of that date as 'the Aybrook or Great Sewer'.

Today, Tyburn is almost wholly enclosed in pipes and generally about 15 ft. underground. Building operations have sometimes exposed it, and its damp bed was once revealed to Mr. Nicholas Barton's father 'at the bottom of a very deep bomb-crater' near Stratford Place[1].

What we have seen is a whole system running down, and it was time for a change. The climactic moment came on Wednesday 5 June 1771, when the Common Council of the City of London received the following communication:

The Humble Petition of the Honble. Edward Stratford,
of Dean Street, Soho, sheweth

That your Petitioner is informed that the City are possessed of a piece of ground on the north side of Oxford Road commonly called or known by the name of the Lord Mayor's Banquetting House Ground, part of the City Mead Estate now occupied by Mr. George Shakespear for a term

[1] Nicholas Barton, *The Lost Rivers of London* (Leicester University Press, 1962). Sir Shane Leslie says his grandfather remembered the Tyburn above ground, and the carriages splashing through it, near the Guards' Club in Brook Street.

Which is near expiring and your petitioner conceives will admit of great improvement by erecting new buildings thereon.

That your Petitioner apprehends if the said piece of land was properly laid out and good Buildings erected upon it, it would not only be a great advantage to the City, but an Ornament to the rest of the City Mead Estate and as your Petitioner is desirous of embarking on the said undertaking and will give the full value of the premes,

Your Petitioner therefore humbly prays this Honourable Court will be pleased to grant him a Building Renewable Lease thereof on such terms and conditions as shall be thought fit.

And your Petitioner will ever pray, etc.

EDWARD STRATFORD

The Common Council briefly considered the petition, and referred it to the Committee for Letting the City's Lands. The modern history of the Banqueting House Grounds, now Stratford Place, had begun.

9 *The Squires of Stratford Place*

Considered as a whole, Stratford Place was of outstanding architectural merit and interest . . . As a composition dependent on a great house it was unique.

Mr. B. A. Barker, evidence to Stratford Place Preservation Enquiry, 1961

At the moment when the City Corporation received the scheme for developing their Banqueting House Grounds, the originator of it was a sanguine and energetic young man of about 28. In spite of a hyperbolic pedigree, in which the eighteenth-century heralds deduced the family coat-of-arms from that of Alexander the Great, the Irish branch[1] seems to have been fairly inconspicuous until Edward's father became Lord Baltinglass in 1763, taking his title from the Wicklow constituency which he had represented for some 40 years. Then in 1776–7, when he was over eighty years of age and had but a few months to live, Lord Baltinglass was caught up in a flurry of promotions in the Irish peerage, hardly less crude and venal than those which a few years later were to ease the passage of the Act of Union between Great Britain and Ireland. The tactics, in fact, were identical—to strengthen the Government's majority in the Lords with additional peers, and in the Commons by the election of compliant substitutes.

This 'mob of nobility', as Horace Walpole called it, included 18 commoners ennobled in 17 days between 18 July and 4 August 1776; seven Barons promoted to Viscounts between 1 and 24 July;

[1] It was founded by Edward's grandfather, who came over from Warwickshire during the reign of Charles II and died in 1699. His eldest son, Edward, was a strong supporter of the House of Orange; John, Lord Baltinglass, was the second son. Like the next Edward, they all seem to have extended their lands and influence by marrying heiresses.

and three of these Viscounts elevated to Earls during February of the following year.

In the process, Lord Baltinglass became in turn Viscount Aldborough and then Earl of Aldborough and Viscount Amiens. The last-named title was a salute to the district in France from which his ancestors in the female line, the Lupellas, were supposed to have 'come over with the Conqueror', and it was borne by his eldest son Edward until the old man's death on 29 June 1777. The creator of Stratford Place thus inherited as the 2nd Earl of Aldborough. He marked the event by changing the name of the mansion into which he had already moved to Aldborough House—the first of a series of rechristenings which one hopes has ended at last; in 1968 Stratford House is Stratford House once more, and may it long remain so!

The showering of titles on his aged father might suggest that the 2nd Lord Aldborough was himself a placeman, but at least he was sturdy in opposing the Union later on and had a certain intellectual character of his own. He was a Fellow of the Royal Society who consorted with scientists and connoisseurs, and spent the day before his father's funeral receiving the Degree of D.C.L. at Oxford. Above all, he was a passionate builder, leaving behind him not only Aldborough House, London, but Aldborough House, Dublin (a fine mansion still in existence, but now used as a Post Office store) and the model town of Stratford-on-Slaney, Co. Wicklow.

However, the money and perhaps some of the artistic impulse behind his London venture came from his wife, born Anne Herbert, daughter and heiress of the Hon. Nicholas Herbert of Great Glemham Hall, Suffolk. Anne's was a great virtuoso stock. Her father was the son of Thomas, 8th Earl of Pembroke and Montgomery, collector of many treasures at Wilton House, and brother to Henry the 9th Earl, one of Mr. Lees-Milne's 'Earls of Creation'[1], who left the Palladian Bridge as his undying monument. If it could be shown that the Stratfords possessed between them anything approaching the architectural flair of Mr. Lees-Milne's chosen Earls—Bathurst, Burlington, Leicester and Pembroke—nobody would worry much about the question which now confronts us: Who designed Stratford House and Stratford Place?

[1] James Lees-Milne, *Earls of Creation* (London, Hamish Hamilton, 1962).

I do not pretend to have solved—or even to have contributed anything new towards solving—this problem, which has defied the art historians up till now. The point at issue can be fined down to a sentence. Tradition attaches the name of the Adam brothers to the project; expert opinion does not.

Such facts as are available come from the records of the Lands Committee of the Court of Common Council, which received the Hon. Edward Stratford's petition of June 1771. A sub-committee to which the matter was referred reported back on 31 July. It seems to have been bear-led by George Dance the Younger, architectural adviser to the Council and designer of that lost masterpiece, Old Newgate Gaol. Most of the report deals with intricate negotiations with Stratford over rent and conditions, the final recommendation being that he should pay a clear yearly rental of £160, renewable every 14 years on payment of a 'fine' of five years' ground rent.

The contract was eventually signed on 20 November 1771 (the lease itself is dated 12 May 1772). It specified that Mr. Stratford should erect 'good substantial dwelling houses in brick and stone to conform with drawings or designs, deposited with the Comptroller, signed by him'. The crux of our problem is that though we have the very interesting plan and elevation (*Pl. 17*) which was attached to the lease, the original drawings submitted in 1771 have disappeared, and nobody knows whose name (apart from that of Stratford himself as developer) appeared on them.

One obvious candidate is Richard Edwin. Described in the Sub-Committee's report as 'Surveyor, of 29 Portland Street', Edwin twice attended meetings as agent for Stratford 'then absent in the country', and when the buildings went up he took No. 5 on the east side. We know just enough about him to make his status in the matter equivocal. He was certainly a pupil under Matthew Brettingham, the fashionable architect whose father (also Matthew) worked on Holkham Hall for another of Mr. Lees-Milne's 'Earls of Creation', William Coke, Earl of Leicester. While still a student (1764) Edwin competed successfully among the 'under-18s' for a Royal Society of Arts Premium in the Polite Arts, the subject being a detail drawing from Inigo Jones's Water Gate in York Place. Five years later he was in a strong field of competitors for the Royal Exchange,

Dublin, and in 1770 he sent a 'Design for a Temple' to the Society of Artists of Great Britain.

More importantly, Edwin submitted at least three architectural drawings to the Royal Academy. The first, in 1774, was in fact 'A Longitudinal Elevation of the West Side of Stratford Place, Oxford Street'; the second (1776), a section of the Concert Room in Hanover Square; the third (1777), a design for a villa in Surrey. The fact that he sent in these drawings is strong presumptive evidence, but not absolute proof, that he had a hand in the buildings concerned. Edwin died in 1778, when he must have been still under 32.

There has been some confusion over Edwin's Stratford Place drawing. The usual statement is that though submitted to the Academy it was not hung, and it does not appear in any of the 1774 catalogues that I have seen. Yet in Algernon Graves's great encyclopædia[1] of Academy artists and their works it is listed as No. 357 for that year, and Edwin's address given as 12 Great Castle Street, Cavendish Square. The extant catalogues end with No. 355, but Graves in his preface explains that in the early days they used to be produced in various editions and these no doubt took care of late entries, accidental omissions, and so on.

The question of attribution was well explored by Mr. B. A. Barker in his scholarly report[2] on Stratford Place prepared in 1961. Believing that the Edwin drawing was not hung, he suggested that this might have been because it was 'too akin to the work of the brothers Adam' to please Sir William Chambers, who then dominated the Academy Council.

If 'too akin to' why not 'by'? The first answer is stylistic. As everyone can see at a glance, Stratford House and the remains of Stratford Place as a whole are in 'the Adam manner'—but so are hundreds if not thousands of buildings all over Britain designed by other architects between 1765 and 1790. Sometimes they are charming near-masterpieces, like Boodle's Club in St. James's (by Crunden); often they are the routine work of unknowns who were

[1] *The Royal Academy of Arts. A Complete Directory of Contributors* (London, Henry Graves and George Bell and Sons, 1905).

[2] *Proof of Evidence, County of London* (*Stratford Place St. Marylebone*) *Building Preservation Order, 1961*. Submitted on behalf of the Historic Buildings Section of the then London County Council.

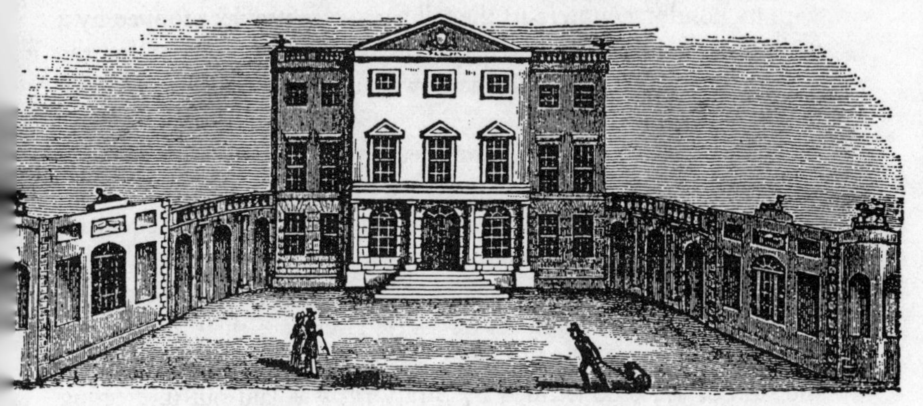

Fig 4 Aldborough House, Dublin

placidly swimming with the tide. Those competent to judge do not feel either that the 'Adamesque' decoration applied externally and internally to Stratford Place has the masters' touch, or that the lay-out of Stratford House, as originally planned, showed that resource-ful management of space which made Adam town houses, of what-ever size, liveable as well as stately. Another 'anti-Adam' argument also has considerable force. It is the simple fact that in all the surviv-ing mass of their drawings, notes and correspondence (8,000 draw-ings at the Soane Museum alone), there is not a single reference to the Stratford Place project, or to the Hon. Edward Stratford as an Adam patron.

Of course it remains possible that Robert or James Adam did pro-vide a generalised 'back-of-an-envelope' design, and that the client worked the details out for himself with the help of Richard Edwin, who was certainly lucky to get such a spectacular job while still in his early twenties. With this in mind it is interesting to read that Aldborough House, Dublin, was built 'on a very fanciful plan, agreeable to his Lordship's own views'[1], which does suggest an architect Earl employing a young technical assistant. Fig. 4 shows that though the Dublin façade had no order of columns, it shared

[1] Quoted in the Georgian Society Records, vol. 4 (Dublin University Press, 1912) from a *Tour of Ireland in 1813 and 1814* by 'An Englishman'. Aldborough House was begun in 1796. It was still unfinished in 1798, and it is doubtful whether Lord Aldborough ever lived there.

with its London counterpart the tall narrow centrepiece topped by a pediment. This seems to reflect Lord Aldborough's taste for the conspicuous—it is not in character with the Dublin mansions of his day.

The City Lands Sub-Committee expressed self-contradictory views on the architectural importance of the scheme. In one place they opined that the Stratford Place buildings would be 'equal to, if not exceed the most magnificent structures of Europe' (which sounds more like the Adam brothers 'selling' their Adelphi project than a description of our cul-de-sac!); elsewhere they merely said that the elevation of the buildings was not very material 'providing the sum of £40,000 [named by Stratford] was laid out in erecting good, substantial dwelling-houses ...'

This requirement was fully met, though not, as time went on, in strict conformity with the plans put before the City Lands Committee. The latter took some umbrage after an inspection in 1774, and Stratford retorted by producing drawings to show that his new designs were superior to the originals. His primary aim, beyond doubt, was to provide a graceful setting for his own majestic house; the commercial success of the speculation came second. Property rights did not deter him. The Marylebone historian, Thomas Smith[1], in addition to a eulogy of Stratford Place ('uniformity and neatness' are *his* epithets), has an illuminating reference to 'the Estate of John Thomas Hope Esq.'. This bore the significant name of Conduit Fields and lay immediately to the west of Stratford Place.

Smith explains that it had been intended to form a single long avenue through this estate, but the encroachments of the City of London, encouraged by the owner's 'unaccountable apathy', had curtailed the site. The situation was made worse by the action of the Hon. Edward Stratford,

> who in his anxiety to render Stratford Place the most magnificent pile of buildings of that period, made a still further encroachment on this estate by erecting the buildings on the West side of Stratford Place, over the brook which formed the boundary line between the two estates, but for which compensation has recently been made.

The result was that a warren of lanes was permitted to remain

[1] Thomas Smith, *The Parish of St. Mary-le-Bone* (London, John Smith, 1833).

alongside Stratford Place. Some impression of them can be gained to this day by anyone who dives down the crevice called Gee's Court[1].

Mr. Barker suggests that the fact that the westerly buildings were erected last and in a somewhat different style may have been caused by this very problem of building 'over the brook', whose vagaries were to worry the dwellers on that side for more than a century to come. The last houses did not go up until 1793.

The whole development was in fact carried out piecemeal. Some houses were erected by speculative builders. They included Nos. 2, 3 and 16, built by the brothers Lyster (one of whom, William Lyster M.P., occupied No. 3 for a time). Another was No. 22; here the developer was John Devall who, Mr. Barker tells us, was one of the mason contractors for Somerset House and whose father worked on the Palladian Bridge at Wilton, already referred to.

Other sites were leased by financiers who commissioned builders and then sold the resultant houses, while in two cases at least the future occupants themselves built to their own designs. These were Sir George Yonge, Bt., M.P., at No. 4 and Earl Poulett at No. 19. Earl Poulett—a familiar name, because many years later the family moved from the immediate neighbourhood of Stratford House to that of the Oriental Club in Hanover Square; more than once in the 1860s the Committee Minutes echo with the plaintive cries of the Countess Poulett, whose garden at No. 20 is being 'ruined' by smuts from the Club's kitchen chimney.

Lord Aldborough's own financial commitment is far from clear, but it was heavy enough to get him into difficulties as early as 1775. An endorsement on the original lease shows that on 9 May of that year, he raised £2,000 by transferring to a certain Mrs. Ann Wood of the Parish of St. George's, Hanover Square,

> part of the ground with six messuages built thereon in possession of Stephen Sayre, Sir G. Yonge, Thomas Selby, and Daniel Barnes or their under-tenants.

Preserved among the Aldborough Papers[2] is a copy of a rather

[1] Mr. Gee (or Jee) himself comes into the story! In 1772 he had recently died insolvent, leaving no representative, so the City Lands Committee agreed that his 'slip of land' at the south-west corner of the Banqueting House Grounds should be added to Mr. Stratford's estate.

[2] The Aldborough Papers consist of several hundred letters written by or to the

firm note dated 4 December 1776, from Messrs. Mayne & Co. (presumably his bankers) reminding him that he owes them £3,192 12s. 11d. of cash actually disbursed besides acceptances, and 'in the present scarcity of cash' they request Mr. Stratford to put his account in order.

Attached to this is an interesting memorandum (in précis form) from one of Stratford's men of affairs, Mr. D. Robinson of Warwick Court, who was evidently engaged in raising loans:

Sir,

I am favored with your Letter, have since been in S. Place and perceive the Buildings on the West Side of ye Square go on but slow, the Ground Floors not being laid, nor is there a Slate put on the East Side, [I] am inclined to think the Houses on the West Side of the Square will not be covered in so soon as January, the Time you say a further Sum of £2,000 will be wanted.

I know Mrs. Wood will not have any money to spare so soon as Jan. but think aft. the Month of March I can get the Sum from one other of my Clients. If Mrs. Wood advances the Money, well, I hope she will be able to do, [but I] think it but right you should deposite with her the original Lease from the City. You may have recourse to it when you please. As to the £4,500 I have it in View and will be glad to wait on you as soon as I hear you are in Town. Can say no more at present but that I shall be happy in having it in my Power to accomodate you.

Five years later (7 February 1782) a further endorsement was made to the lease showing that Lord Aldborough (as he had now become) was again raising money by transferring Stratford House itself to his wife, from whom he had already borrowed £10,000.

Rather pathetic begging letters—particularly from nieces—are a feature of the Aldborough correspondence; it is now easier to understand why they were usually brushed off.

Although, as we have seen in the case of Hanover Square, eigh-

2nd Lord Aldborough, or exchanged between other members of his circle. They provided the raw material for Ethel M. Richardson's *Long Forgotten Days* (London, Heath Cranton, 1928). Through the kindness of Sir Edward Verner, Bt. and Miss R. W. Verner, descendants of one branch of the Wingfield-Stratford family, I was able to reexamine the whole archive, but, apart from the one memorandum quoted here, it deals exclusively with Irish or family affairs. What must have been an enormous correspondence over the London Estate was evidently kept separate, and has vanished.

teenth-century London made much use of gates and chains to secure privacy, there was nothing quite to compare with Stratford Place for its sense of calm and ordered seclusion. Its buildings may not have been as 'magnificent' as claimed, but Edward Stratford did create a small masterpiece of planning, at once decorative and functional (*Pl. 18*). From the front pavilions facing Oxford Street, with their lion-topped sentry-boxes and elegant wrought-iron gates, to the little square at the far end, all was exquisitely proportioned to what Mr. Barker calls the 'great if attenuated elegance' of the lordly house which closed the vista. No unwanted strangers could penetrate this haven—even tradesmen's vans were unknown, since every house had its back entrance in one of the adjacent lanes. Only the occasional rumble of a 'chariot', perhaps bringing ladies to call or carrying one of the M.P.s away to Westminster, ruffled the sunny stillness.

Yet beyond the gates, and in full view of Stratford House, Tyburn Road roared and rattled by, as Oxford Street does today. One form of traffic at least passes the mouth of Stratford Place no more—the processions of victims on their way to Tyburn Tree. Did the well-dressed ladies and gentlemen stand watching at the drawing-room windows on such mornings as these? . . .

27 October 1773. Stratford House is just finishing. Here come five malefactors escorted by the sheriffs on horseback, with two persons in black walking all the way before them. They will take an hour and a half over their devotions before the hangman gives the signal.

30 November 1774. Edward and Barbara Stratford are happily settled in. Sixteen-String Jack (John Rann[1]) and five others pass by, engulfed in a riotous crowd, who when their friends have been swung off will try to burn down the house of one of the prosecutors.

17 January 1776. Start of a year in which titles will descend upon the Stratfords in a tinsel shower. Thirty thousand people pour along Tyburn Road to see the well-bred forgers, Robert and Daniel Perreau, fall from the cart together, their four hands clasped.

27 June 1777. The first Earl of Aldborough has two days to live.

[1] A local boy who did *not* make good. John Rann is said to have been born 'of very honest parents' in the parish of St. George's, Hanover Square.

Tyburn stages its greatest spectacle of all—the execution of the celebrated Dr. William Dodd. He perishes in spite of the strong petitions of Dr. Johnson and others.

And so to the terrible Tree's last victims—to the Rev. James Hickman, jealous assassin of Lord Sandwich's mistress, Martha Ray (25 August 1779) . . . Isabella Condon, coiner, strangled and then burnt (27 October 1779) . . . William Wynne Ryland, friend of Angelica Kauffmann and skilled engraver of her works, hanged for forgery (29 August 1783) . . . and ending the sad line, John Austin, convicted of robbery with violence (7 November 1783). He travels with great composure from Newgate to Tyburn, remaining calm even while the cap is drawn over his head. 'Christ have mercy upon my poor soul', he says as the cart is driven away, but the halter having slipped to the back of his neck, it is longer than usual before he dies.

Because the inhabitants of Stratford House whom we are going to meet are mostly gentle, civilised and fortunate (though not on the whole long-lived), we always need to picture them with Shepherd Street just across the way and the yells of the Tyburn mob within earshot.

The second Earl of Aldborough and his Countess divided their bustling days between Stratford Place and Ireland, where they had innumerable relations and the Earl could cut a figure in local affairs, such as the raising of the Irish Volunteers. But they were childless, and, when the Countess died suddenly in 1785, Lord Aldborough did not feel he could live on in the great house alone. So Stratford House (or Aldborough House as we had better call it for the moment) was let to Lord Talbot, a lawyer who held the office of Lord Steward and was himself to be advanced to an Earldom the following year. Lord Aldborough retired to No. 12 next door, which he had built as a Dower House but which had never been used for this purpose; it has remained linked with the fortunes of No. 11 until very recent times.

Earl Talbot, a not very distinguished legal figure and a tepid patron of literature, at least gave stylish entertainments at Aldborough House, and his death there in 1793, when he was only 43 years of age, must have been a shock to the Stratford Place folk. His widow stayed on in the house another four years but in due course the family, like the Pouletts later, homed to the Oriental Club corner of Hanover Square, where they occupied No. 19.

But already the Earl of Aldborough had acquired a new Countess —and heiress. Like some character in Jane Austen, he had met at Bath the pretty daughter of an Essex baronet[1], Miss Elizabeth Henniker, with £50,000. Within a year of poor Barbara's death they were married, and after a short interval of foreign travel entered upon a vigorous and expensive London life in the circle of the Prince of Wales and Mrs. Fitzherbert. But even after Countess Talbot gave up Aldborough House they did not return there, letting it instead to a member of the Carlton House set, the diplomat Robert Adair, for a term of one year (1797–8).

This series of fashionable but short-lived tenancies was continued when the house was next taken by the Earl of Jersey, whereby another of the Prince of Wales's mistresses enters our story, since it was of course Lady Jersey who detached him from his well-loved companion (and, save in the sight of the Royal Marriages Act, his wife) Mrs. Fitzherbert. Though Lady Jersey's reign was now near its close, 'Prinny's' equipage must often have been seen in Stratford Place, especially as he liked to frequent the studio of the artist Richard Cosway, who led an eccentric existence at No. 19 (see page 199).

While the Jerseys still occupied the family home, Lord Aldborough died on 2 January 1801, leaving no children. Within a year his widow married George Powell, barrister-at-law and agent to the Aldborough estates, but herself died almost at once. There is something *evanescent* about Edward Stratford—his own personality, his successive titles, his successive wives and their fortunes, all seem to shimmer and disappear, leaving only the stones of Stratford House to speak for him. There were still five more Earls of Aldborough to come—two of Edward Stratford's brothers and the descendants of the youngest, Benjamin—but they seem to have become steadily poorer and more Irish and the family might indeed have dwindled

[1] This was Sir John Henniker, later propelled by his son-in-law into the peerage as Lord Henniker of Stratford-upon-Slaney, during the Union promotions of 1800. His was one of 16 baronies dated 31 July in that year.

into squireens by now if the line had not ended with the seventh Earl in 1875.

None of these later Aldboroughs owned Stratford House. On the death of the 2nd Earl his London properties passed to Lieut.-Colonel John Wingfield, twin son of his elder sister, who had married Lord Powerscourt in 1776. The new owner took the name of Wingfield-Stratford, and though he did not move to Stratford Place immediately, he became in some sort its squire. No. 12, left vacant by the deaths of the Earl and Countess, was now occupied by the latter's widower, Mr. Powell.

In 1805, came another change of name for No. 11. Lord Jersey died, and Lady Jersey not wishing to stay on there, the next Earl sold the remainder of his lease to his cousin, the 6th Duke of St. Albans. So one royal mistress was succeeded by the descendant of another (Nell Gwyn). Apart from holding the not very onerous office of Hereditary Grand Falconer of England, the Duke was an inconspicuous figure, but in the end his occupancy gave a new and somewhat exciting twist to the story of what was now renamed St. Albans House.

These were the years when the great Napoleonic drama was thundering along. Austerlitz, Salamanca, Moscow, may have raised but mild ripples in the cul-de-sac off Oxford Street, but Leipzig, the Battle of Nations (1813) opened the way for a complete victory by the Allies and a period of 'summit' diplomacy to come. In March of the following year the Congress of Vienna opened, and the same month brought to London a Hungarian magnifico, Prince Paul Esterhazy. His immediate purpose was to arrange a sort of goodwill tour for two young Austrian Archdukes, John and Louis. The Foreign Office had its eye on Stratford House as a suitable lodgement for them, and Esterhazy's remit was to work out the details in conjunction with the Duke. The Hundred Days came and went, and by August 1815 everything was set for the visit, when once again there was a premature and sudden death in Stratford Place. On 16 August *The Times* announced that a fit of apoplexy had carried off Aubrey Beauclerk, Duke of St. Albans. The very next day the paper forecast that Prince Esterhazy would succeed the late Count Merveldt as Ambassador at the Court of St. James's.

The death of the Duke did not interfere with the plans for lodging the Austrian princes in St. Albans House. On Monday 23 October, they arrived at Dover—Archduke Louis about 30, serious and rather silent, Archduke John five years younger, much more animated, fair-haired and gaily dressed in a blue coat and green cloth cap. A lively cavalcade escorted them to Stratford Place, but, after courtesy calls on Queen Charlotte and the Regent, they relapsed into a fairly rigorous anonymity for their subsequent tour of industrial Britain.

It was a programme which seems to belong to the Prince Consort's epoch rather than to the Prince Regent's. Birmingham, Sheffield, Glasgow ... collieries, ironworks, glass-works ... the new Sunderland Bridge, the impressive effects of gaslight... The young men turned solemn eyes upon them all, and refused every attempt by Aldermen to entertain them to turtle soup and champagne.

They were away from London from mid-November until nearly Christmas, but Prince Esterhazy stayed on at St. Albans House while the decorators were at work on his chosen Embassy. This was none other than Chandos House[1], so even if the Oriental Club had selected Lord Kemsley's mansion instead of Stratford House in 1960, it would still have had a link with His Serene Highness, Prince Paul Esterhazy!

I feel that the connection does the Club credit. Esterhazy was very grand and very able, as well as very rich. He had been accredited at the particular request of the Prince Regent, who was obviously unaware that Metternich had instructed the new Ambassador to flatter him! This Esterhazy was well placed to do. He was in fact one of the few diplomats of that era who could hold his own in London against the wealth and self-assurance of the native leaders of fashion. Dinners and balls kept Stratford Place in an aristocratic uproar, with, as often as not, the Regent and his suite at the heart of it.

We need not, however, glamorise the epoch by imagining that all was gaiety and sparkle. The necessary corrective is supplied in half a dozen lines from one of Lady Harriet Granville's letters[2] to

[1] He lived there in great style. Messrs. Phillips, Son and Neale record that, when he gave up the Embassy in 1842, the sale of his *batterie de cuisine* alone occupied a whole day.

[2] *Letters of Lady Harriet Granville*, ed. the Hon. F. Leveson-Gower (London, Longmans Green, 1894).

her sister Lady Morpeth. They are undated, but clearly belong to the early months of 1816:

> Madame de Lieven, whom you enquired about, is become famous for civility and *empressements* to everyone . . . We dined there on Sunday. It was a dinner quite unrivalled in the records of dullness. The Archdukes scarcely utter, though the eldest looks intelligent, but the youngest is without vivacity, and it is said they are as bored as they look . . . Esterhazy crowned this flow of soul. He is silly and tiresome to the supremest degree.

Taken at its face value, this acidulous note would contradict much of what we have already recorded about the princely brothers (young John may well have been tongue-tied in such company), and about Esterhazy himself. But we shall see why the vivacious Harriet Granville is not totally to be relied on, where Lievens and Esterhazys are in question.

The two Archdukes finished their English visit during March 1816, sailing away from Dover to a jolly accompaniment of cheers and popping guns. A few weeks later Prince Esterhazy moved into Chandos House. Stratford House—'St. Albans' had gradually been dropped—was tenantless once more. What next?

Next was Princess Lieven. This celebrated lady was the wife of Prince Esterhazy's only serious rival in the Diplomatic Corps, the Russian Ambassador, Prince Lieven, whom in fact she dominated. Her name, her *bons mots*, her love affairs and her bony silhouette pervade, to the point of tedium, all the memoirs of the period. In spite of her brilliant position in society, her attitude to the Esterhazys had a curious touch of inferiority complex, and heavily influenced that of her bosom friend, Lady Harriet Granville. 'He is clever', she said of Prince Paul, 'but he is childish, and I do not like little boys of thirty-four.' To his wife, the 'small, round, black' Princess, she showed a 'hostile and perfidious politeness'.

Apart from that dull Sunday dinner-party, Princess Lieven impinges at least twice upon our story. Just before the two Archdukes left Stratford Place there arrived in England a royal visitor obscure up till then, but of extraordinary destiny. This was Prince Leopold of Saxe-Coburg. His errand was no less than to marry the heiress of England, the Prince Regent's only daughter, Charlotte. Though he

14 Edward Stratford, 2nd Earl of Aldborough. From the portrait by Mather Brown in the possession of the Oriental Club

15 Stratford House as originally designed. A nineteenth-century impression by P. Hosmer Shepherd

16 (*top left*) The Lord Mayor's Banqueting House. This adaptation by P. Hosmer Shepherd of one of the old views of the Banqueting House shows what a rustic-looking structure originally stood on the Stratford Place site

17 (*left*) The drawings attached to the Hon. Edward Stratford's May 1772 lease from the City Corporation. They are described as 'drawings or designs of Several Dwelling Houses to be erected on the Banquetting House Ground, Oxford Road' and are signed by Geo. Dance and J. Peacock on behalf of the City Lands Committee and by Edward Stratford. They show the entrance (*top*) and a side elevation—both modified later

18 (*above*) This print (from the Crace Collection in the British Museum) purports to show Stratford Place as completed. The gates (see p. 197) are suspect

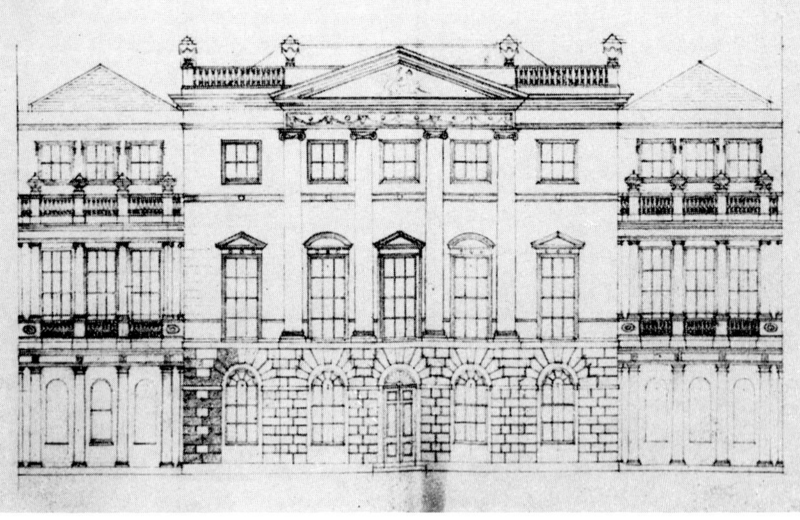

19 (*top left*) The first stage of enlarging Stratford House —Murray Guthrie raised the wings by one storey in the 1890s

20 (*bottom left*) A ponderous Edwardian scheme, prepared by J. MacVicar Anderson in 1908 but never used

21 (*above*) 'Derby House' (now Stratford House once more)—the front elevation by Romaine-Walker and Besant, 1908

22 Staircase detail

23, 24 The famous first-floor Drawing Room in two phases: (*top*) the photograph of King Edward strikes an appropriate note for the occupancy of Lord and Lady Colebrooke (1902–8) (the doorcases have since been raised); (*bottom*) as adapted for the National Gallery of British Sports and Pastimes (1949–50)

25 Lord Derby's ballroom, into the shell of which the Club has built two tiers of bedrooms

26 The banqueting room, another of Lord Derby's creations, is now the Members' Dining Room. Richard Jones (Head Waiter—retd. August, 1968) and Kathleen King (Cashier) mark up the reservations

27 The Entrance Hall, Stratford House, with its Wedgwood plaques and fine eighteenth-century chimney-piece. W. H. Harris (Head Hall Porter) has been in the service of the Club since 1935

28 Jack Parsons (Head Valet) on the Rear Staircase. In the background, landscape capriccios believed to have been brought from Italy by Lord Derby

came at the invitation of the Regent himself, no appropriate arrangements seem to have been made for accommodating him. All that happened was that Count Münster, the Hanoverian Minister, engaged a bedroom for him in Bond Street without so much as a sitting-room attached to it. It does not seem that his landlady provided him even with 'bed and breakfast', since the next morning he had to share that meal with the Archdukes 'at their residence in Stratford Place'.

Strange enough, but more surprising still is the fact that this was the *second* time that Stratford Place had provided Leopold with a refuge from inferior London 'digs'. Two years before he had come to London in the train of the Emperor Alexander of Russia. He himself wrote the story for Queen Victoria many years afterwards, referring to himself in the third person:

> I forgot to mention a subject which has been since told as a proof of the great poverty of Prince Leopold when he was in England in 1814. He came with the Emperor Alexander, and as long as the Emperor remained himself in England, the lodgings of the persons who had come with him were paid by him. The Russian Ambassador, Count Lieven, had the charge of locating the suite, and as they lived in Harley Street, they lodged the people near it, and had taken a rather indifferent lodging for Prince Leopold in High Street, Marylebone. The Prince had nothing to do with the choice of that lodging, and as soon as the Emperor had left, he lodged himself in Stratford Place, in a house where General Count Beroldingen, the Würtemberg Minister, lodged[1], and where he remained till he left London.

In justice to the Lievens (it was always the Princess who made the domestic arrangements) they were under heavy pressure during the grandiose visit of the Emperor Alexander. Leopold was very small fry, and no doubt a room two floors up over the grocer's shop of Mr. Hole (three guineas without candles) seemed good enough for a hard-up young attaché[2].

By contrast, when in 1817 Princess Lieven was faced with more or less the same problem as Prince Esterhazy, she found the same

[1] The Minister is not recorded as a Stratford Place resident—the phrasing in fact suggests that he had merely taken apartments for the season.

[2] There are a number of versions extant of Prince Leopold's 1814 visit, but his own is to be found in Appendix A of Lieut.-General the Hon. C. Grey, *The Early Years of H.R.H. The Prince Consort* (London, Smith Elder, 1867). The 1816 break-

solution. In other words she had a really important royal visitor to park, and decided there could be nowhere better than Stratford House for the purpose. Apart from its convenient nearness to her rickety old embassy among the Oriental Club nabobs of Harley Street, the charm of Stratford House itself no doubt cast a spell, and there was the further attraction of complete quiet and security.

The visitor in question was the Grand Duke Nicholas, brother of the Czar, and destined shortly to mount the Russian throne himself as Nicholas I. He was of course much heavier metal than the young Archdukes. He had fought with the Allied armies against Napoleon and (like most Czars of Russia, unfortunately) was more interested in military display than in glass factories—'mania for uniforms', sniffed Princess Lieven. We need not pursue him on his rounds, but it is clear that Stratford House at this period was to an even greater extent a centre of gaiety, gossip and diplomacy than in its Esterhazy phase.

It was at about this time, while Congress danced in Vienna, that one of Austria's most celebrated exports, the waltz, was supposed to have made its English debut under the painted ceilings of Stratford House. As far as I know, no contemporary evidence of any kind survives. On the contrary, there are indications that various forms of the dance were popular in England, though not in upper-class circles, during the last quarter of the eighteenth century. Miss Mitford daringly practised it at her finishing school round about 1800 and by 1805 it had gone so far up in the world that it was performed, rather shakily, by 'Prinny' himself at the Pavilion at Brighton. So one slight basis for the Stratford House tradition could be that Lady Jersey introduced H.R.H. to the waltz during her tenancy (1799–1805). But a more likely clue, to my mind, is the fact that Lady Jersey, Princess Esterhazy and Princess Lieven were all Lady Patronesses of Almack's[1], and the third-named is known to have set

fast with the Archdukes is mentioned in Chapter I, Joanna Richardson, *My Dearest Uncle* (London, Jonathan Cape, 1961). I am grateful to Mr. Denis Campbell for putting me on the track of Leopold in Stratford Place. The later history of the young Prince—his 18 months' happy marriage to Princess Charlotte, ended by her death in childbed, and his later reincarnation as the first King of the Belgians and Queen Victoria's wise 'Uncle Leopold'—is a familiar but still moving story.

[1] The ultra-exclusive dancing and gambling club in King Street, St. James's.

society waltzing there round about 1814. Indeed, according to the dandy and diarist Thomas Raikes, our latest Stratford House inmate sometimes led the revels:

> You may remember the present Emperor Nicholas fourteen years ago in London, when he lived in the large house at the end of Stratford Place, now occupied by Sir John Beckett. He was then one of the Grand Dukes of Russia, travelling for his amusement; a fine-looking youth, making a conspicuous figure in the waltz, and whirling our English beauties round the circle to a quicker movement than they had previously learned to practise[1].

It is natural enough, surely, that Stratford House, its three dazzling hostesses, its Grand Ducal lodger and the introduction of the waltz, should all have become blended into an inextricable legend!

Nicholas stayed on only until March 1817, but it was announced that his brothers the Grand Dukes John and Michael would be the next to follow the London trail. John arrived during the summer and had a short tour under Countess Lieven's pilotage. Michael did not turn up until the following June.

Meanwhile Stratford House had once more reverted to the dynasty which gave it its name. Lieut.-Colonel Wingfield-Stratford had quickly obtained possession of No. 12 from Mr. Powell, and with the expiry of the lease which had been granted to the Earl of Jersey and which had devolved upon subsequent tenants, he was now poised to reoccupy the big house itself, along with his wife Fanny and their three small children.

Once the Grand Duke Michael was out of the way there seemed nothing to delay the move but—*will the line stretch to the crack of doom?*—yet one more princeling appeared on the horizon. This time it was the Archduke Maximilian of Austria, arriving under Esterhazy auspices and insisting on being put up at what was now the recognised reception centre of Grand Dukes and Archdukes alike.

By Christmas he was gone, and at last, in the early months of 1820, Stratford House was occupied, for the very first time in its short but varied history, by a *family*. There will not always be children

[1] *A Visit to St. Petersburg, 1824–30* (London, Richard Bentley, 1838). Raikes himself may have been a witness of these gyrations—in 1815 he lived at No. 5.

about during the next century or so, but the scene does become more domestic and our curiosity shifts from the historic rooms of state to the less known ones where people actually lived.

I could wish that we knew more about these rooms. There were not many of them. It is easy to smile at Lord Derby, when he came on the scene, marvelling how any family could have fitted itself into such a bandbox, yet it is true that though we have been using the words 'great house' and 'mansion', there was astonishingly little living space in Stratford House until Murray Guthrie and his Lordship got to work. Apart from service quarters, the original building Fig. 5 (p. 204) consisted of the following (current use in italics):

GROUND FLOOR. Dining Room (*Bar*) in front; Library (*as now*)[1], Morning Room (*Ante-Room*) and perhaps one more sitting room (*Billiard Room*) behind.

FIRST FLOOR. Ballroom (*Drawing Room*) and Drawing Room (*Writing Room*) in front; probably two main Bedrooms[2] (*Smoking Room*) and a Dressing Room or two (*Card Room, etc.*) behind.

SECOND FLOOR. A few attic-like bedrooms, some of them used as nurseries.

And that was absolutely all. Crewe House, easily the smallest of Beresford Chancellor's 'Private Palaces of London', had 18 bedrooms!

How those vast Archducal suites were bedded down, what happened when 40 people came to dine and 450 to the subsequent reception is beyond imagining (the sanitary problem we encounter later!).

Moreover the house had the great drawback, especially in London, that whereas the State rooms (which did not particularly need it) got maximum sunshine, the family quarters giving on the garden faced due north—a circumstance that has some subconscious influences on Clubhouse life today.

However, the Wingfield-Stratfords tucked themselves in somehow, and there was plenty of youthful fun for Fanny, Isabel and John, as well as more elaborate gaieties for their parents. Unfortun-

[1] At one stage, however, this room was known as the 'Green Drawing Room'.

[2] Or perhaps one only, the western section of the present Smoking Room, the eastern section being an additional Drawing Room.

ately, Mrs. Wingfield-Stratford's death in 1829 caused a break in this ordered existence, and when the Colonel married again three years later, he followed an Aldborough precedent in leaving the family house and retreating down the cul-de-sac—first to No. 9 and then to the old Dower House, No. 12.

There followed one of the longest tenancies in Stratford House history. The in-comer was the Rt. Hon. Sir John Beckett, a hard-shell Tory politician from Yorkshire, who had received a baronetcy in 1813. A fact significant for the future was that his wife was Lady Anne Lowther, daughter of the Earl of Lonsdale, and that her sister was married to Lord William Bentinck.

Sir John was a supporter of the Duke of Wellington and though they did not always see eye to eye (e.g. over Catholic Emancipation) he had held legal office during the Duke's 1823–30 Ministry. Naturally, therefore, the Duke was a frequent caller at Stratford Place, and we can please ourselves with the fancy that before or after such visits he would drop in at what was easily the nearest of his innumerable clubs, the Oriental.

Sir John Beckett died in 1847. From now until 1871, Stratford House becomes the home of a dowager, and at last of a blind old lady. For towards the end of her long life Lady Anne Beckett lost her sight completely, and her only excursions from the twilit rooms and corridors were into the garden, round which she would feel her way with the help of a hand-rail.

If we know little about the interior mechanism of the house, how much less about the garden! Sometimes we hear of it as shabby and dull, a real London cat-run, sometimes it is suffused with the scent of roses, brought there by a later owner. The only constant feature is the fig-tree on the south-facing wall, which is supposed to be coeval with the house. In Victorian times this was a struggling thing which 'never fruited'. At the moment of writing these lines (13 August 1967) it had a fine show of figs on it, though they did not look as though they were going to ripen. Shortly afterwards some drastic pruning took place. The main thing is that the old tree is in magnificent heart; in fact I am assured that it has burgeoned considerably since Stratford House was Hutchinson House only eight years ago.

At last Lady Anne followed her husband, and one of the last hatchments seen in London was hoisted over the front door. The property was left to her nephew, the Rt. Hon. George Bentinck, M.P. He was wondering what to do with it when he got a telegram with an offer to purchase from his wife's brother, Mr. John Leslie, of Castle Leslie, Glaslough, Co. Monaghan.

10 *A Great House and its Fate*

How ever a big family got into this house I do not know.

Edward, 17th Earl of Derby

The exact terms of Mr. Leslie's offer are not on record—tradition says that he bought the remainder of the Becketts' lease for 'under £9,000'—but it was quickly accepted by their nephew. And so Stratford House, built by one spirited Irish family, passed into the occupation of another.

The Leslie phase is by far the better documented. Not only is it much nearer to us in time, but the story has been told, with plenty of picturesque detail, by two grand-children of John Leslie, Sir Shane and his brother Seymour (who was born in the house) and by the former's daughter Anita[1]. They have recalled the easy-going Hibernian atmosphere which was imported from Monaghan along with the servants, the carriages, the horses and the hens, and we count as old friends the footman drowsing in his ancient hooded chair beneath the soot-blackened Venus of Milo in the front hall; the Leslie girls clattering out of the stables and trotting their ponies along Oxford Street to Rotten Row, while their mother drove out in the 'sociable' and pair to leave cards; the generations of housemaids carrying shining cans of hot water up to the queer old bedrooms ('stone kennels').

Above all, we have been made free of the sanitary arrangements. They seem to have had a horrid fascination for the family chronic-

[1] Their books include: Shane Leslie, *The Film of Memory* (London, Michael Joseph, 1938), Seymour Leslie, *The Jerome Connexion* (London, John Murray, 1964) and Anita Leslie, *The Fabulous Leonard Jerome* (London, Hutchinson, 1954). 'The majestic mansion at the bottom of Stratford Place', and even its entrance hall 'props', also appear, virtually undisguised, in Sir Shane's novels, *The Cantab* and *The Anglo-Catholic*.

lers, and no wonder. Throughout the whole Leslie occupancy (and before their time as well, one presumes) there were only two w.c.s in the house—one for ladies (opening into the servants' bedrooms) upstairs and one for men (not opening into anything) under the great staircase—you may detect it in Fig. 5. Sir Shane records that Stratford House was pervaded by a powerful *smell* and his daughter tells how healthy young Irish footmen, brought over for the season, began to droop and die after only a few months of living and working in the basement. This led to the discovery that everything drained, not into the main sewers of London, but into a gigantic cess-pit beneath the staircase hall. The Leslies, all for 'Nature', remained unmoved . . .

This blackish comedy was rendered the more macabre because Stratford House, from the moment they took over, was not only permissively Irish but socially grand. Sir John Leslie (as he became in 1876) had behind him a substantial fortune derived from 130,000 acres of agricultural land. Humanely administered, these great estates in Ireland were still a financial asset—in fact they were supposed to be worth £20,000 a year in golden, almost tax-free sovereigns.

But the foundations of a brilliant London success had been laid long before. Born as far back as 1822, John Leslie went on the Grand Tour, collected Old Masters destined to hang gloriously in Stratford Place and Glaslough, and moved among musicians from Rossini onwards, while with the other half of his personality, so to speak, he rode steeplechases, shared a 'tiger' with Count d'Orsay and inherited his valet. In 1856 he married Constance Damer, an orphan of 18[1]. After Glaslough had come to him through the death of a bachelor brother, the couple lived for a time in Berkeley Square before moving one step down (as they considered it) by crossing Oxford Street into Stratford Place. However, they made up for this social *dégringolade* by entertaining the whole 'great world'—aristocratic, political (Tory only), literary, musical, artistic. Several accounts exist of the evening when Mr. Disraeli himself slowly mounted the grand stair-

[1] The Leslies' titles need an explanation. John Leslie was made a baronet by Disraeli; his wife, a Colonel's daughter, became known as Lady Constance Leslie when her brother inherited the Earldom of Portarlington from an uncle.

case, looked tortoise-like about him and with his famous economy of speech, murmured to his hostess, 'Vistas!'[1]

Sanitation or no, this was a happy heyday at Stratford House, incomparable setting for the handsome pair who had brought it back to life. It was a home as well as a headquarters, and to illustrate its aura Sir Shane draws 'a perfect pre-Raphaelite picture' from the reminiscences of Augustus Hare:

> Called on Mrs. Leslie in her glorious old house in Stratford Place, which is beautiful because all the colour is subdued, no new gilding or smartness. She herself sat in the window embroidering, with the bright sunlight just glinting on her rippled hair and sweet face, at once a picture and a poem[2].

Best of all, as in the 1820s it was a family house, and what a family! The four daughters, Mary (Mrs. Crawshay), Constance (Lady Hope), Dosia (Lady Bagot) and Olive (Mrs. Murray Guthrie) were a lively crew enough, but their only brother 'Jack', though vague and easy-going himself, brought a further infusion of dazzling energy into the circle by his marriage to Leonie Jerome.

It would go far beyond my brief to chronicle the works and days of Leonie, of her father Leonard, king of the American turf, and of her two sisters—Clara, who married Moreton Frewen, and Jennie who became Lady Randolph Churchill and the mother of Sir Winston. The tumultuous tale can be read in the books already cited. Sufficient to say that they all dwelt at one time or another in or near Stratford Place, if not in Stratford House, and that the latter was their society spring-board and, incidentally, the scene of the pugnacious little Winston's first meeting with his childhood's idol, Rider Haggard.

These events have taken us past an important epoch, when the final link between the Stratford family and their ancestor's creation was broken. The death of the last Earl of Aldborough in 1875 did not, as I have shown, affect the situation one way or another. But when Mr. John Wingfield-Stratford died in 1881 he was succeeded by

[1] In another version, 'Perspectives!' But whatever beauties Stratford House had or has, a classical enfilade of State rooms is not among them. Dizzie's graceful insincerities are well known.

[2] Augustus Hare, *The Story of My Life*, Vol. IV (George Allen, 1900).

his son Edward who seems to have spent money at a torrential rate, since within a year or two not only the Stratford Place property, but the family estates in Kent and Ireland had to be sold to meet his debts. Today only a few family portraits and exquisitely illuminated pedigrees remain of what should have been a stunning inheritance.

Henceforward, Sir John Leslie held Stratford House in his own right, subject only to the City's ground rent. But as he grew older it became a burden to him and Lady Constance and they moved to something smaller though still highly dignified in Manchester Square. 'Jack' and his wife settled in Great Cumberland Place, Marble Arch, next to Lady Randolph, and when, years afterwards, their beautiful Adamish house had been demolished and the foundations of the Cumberland Hotel were being dug, Leonie Leslie threw a rose into the grave[1] . . .

Stratford House, meanwhile, passed not to Sir John Leslie's son Jack but to the wealthiest of his sons-in-law, Walter Murray Guthrie M.P., merchant banker and Chairman of the venerable firm of Chalmers, Guthrie & Co. He paid £16,000 for it, but the cheque was never presented—in fact Sir Shane Leslie tells me it was found stuffed in a drawer and forgotten after Sir John's death.

Like so many earlier owners of the old house, Guthrie was good-looking, bonhomous—and short-lived. He continued the tradition of grand parties, and even did something about the sanitation. He was also the first owner to change the outward face of Stratford House, when he added an extra floor to the wings (*Pl. 19*). Finally, he provided it with its ghost story! The extraordinary incident in which the apparition of one of his former loves appeared at his bed-side at the moment of her attempted suicide is not at all unlike some accounts of the 'Stratford House ghost', as seen about the upper floors to this day.

To help with their parties, Guthrie and his wife summoned one of the most picturesque characters in our whole story—Mrs. Rosa Lewis. In the Club's own pamphlet about Stratford House she is described as having been a 'kitchen maid' there, but that is a little

[1] André Maurois based a story on this. Sir John Leslie's death took place in 1916, so that, as his grandson Seymour puts it, 'he who had talked to Sir Walter Scott on a mail coach lived to see and hear the first air raids'. Lady Constance survived until 1924, dying at the age of 89.

off-beam[1]. By the time the Guthries took over the house and its hospitalities in 1894, the young woman who had been born Rosa Ovenden was already well in orbit as London's most sought-after 'job cook' or, in our more pompous modern phrase 'contract caterer'. Whisked out of obscurity by her service with various members of the Orleans family and the subsequent attentions of the Prince of Wales, she was cook to Captain Charles Duff in Lennox Gardens, Pont Street, when in the year 1893 she married the feckless Excelsior Lewis and bought 55 Eaton Terrace as a base of operations.

From then onwards Rosa was never 'in service', but cooked by appointment for the great hostesses of the day, including Lady Randolph Churchill and Olive Guthrie. How long the family employed her we do not know—according to Sir Shane Leslie she became too expensive even for their long purses. However, Murray Guthrie retained a friendly interest in the spirited Rosa until at least 1899, since in that year he recommended her as caterer to White's Club—'I shall do all in my power', he wrote to her, 'to make it a success. I am sure that your own personality will do that without any outside help'.

The impact of that personality on White's, the story of how Rosa finally left after calling a member of the Committee 'a damned old woodcock in tights' and how two years later she bought her immortal Cavendish Hotel, has nothing directly to do with Stratford House, and thither we must return.

The Guthrie period was certainly a brilliant one, but it did not last. Murray Guthrie was diabetic, there was no insulin in those days, and he found the pace too much for him. In the year 1902 Stratford House was sold once again, and by 1911 Murray Guthrie was dead at the age of only 42.

The new owner was, from the special angle of this book, one of the most interesting of them all. Sir Edward Colebrooke, 5th Baronet, was neither an East India Merchant nor a member of the Oriental Club, but his progenitors were both and several had been prominent in Club affairs. The first of the line was Sir James Cole-

[1] In *Rosa* (London, Peter Davies, 1962) Michael Harrison sorts out the chronology. See also Daphne Fielding, *The Duchess of Jermyn Street* (London, Eyre and Spottiswoode, 1964).

brooke, who is said to have made money out of the South Sea Bubble, and sat for the 'rotten borough' of Gatton. With his son, Sir George, 2nd Baronet, the connection with the East began—he was Chairman of the East India Company. Then came three generations of Oriental members—James Edward (1761–1838), 3rd Baronet, Member of Council, Bengal, his brother Henry Thomas (1765–1837), and the latter's second son, Thomas Edward (1813–90), 4th Baronet. Of these by far the most distinguished was H. T. Besides being a judge (President of the Court of Appeal, Calcutta, 1805) he was simultaneously Professor of Hindu Law and Sanskrit at the recently founded College of Fort William. *The Dictionary of National Biography* goes so far as to describe him as 'the first great Sanskrit Scholar of Europe'. On his return to London in 1814 he took the lead in founding the Royal Asiatic Society, and as early as May 1825 he became a member of the Oriental Club Committee of Management.

H.T.'s second son, Thomas Edward, had been a member for two years when he succeeded as 4th Baronet in 1838. We have already met him in 1842 (page 73) needling the Committee into taking a more liberal attitude towards 'strangers'.

Sir Thomas lived until 1890 and, with the succession of his son Edward, the Colebrooke family history took quite a different turn. By marrying Alexandra, the seventh daughter of Lord Paget and a god-daughter of the Princess of Wales (later Queen Alexandra) in 1889, he had entered into a brilliant social sphere. He received a peerage in 1906 and became a Lord-in-Waiting. Wealth, and good taste in making use of it, were also his, and there could have been no couple more suitable than the Colebrookes to carry on the social traditions of Stratford House.

Inevitably there was more 'tinkering' with the ancient structure. A primitive lift was installed, there was better accommodation for the children on the top floor, but the most spectacular change was the complete redecoration of the room that is now the Club Library. Colebrooke took endless trouble to reproduce Adam motifs, and the craftsmanship of the mahogany panelling and ormolu work is exceedingly fine. But the whole thing is a little too rich and glossy to be mistaken for the 'real thing'.

It was the Colebrookes, too, who filled the garden with roses.

Some memories of those days were brought to life when in December 1967 I had the pleasure of walking round Stratford House with Lord Colebrooke's daughter the Hon. Lady Packe, who spent several years of her girlhood there. She told me that, like so many of the children of grand houses in those days, her life was lived almost entirely apart from that of the grown-ups; there were only occasional descents from the schoolroom to the drawing room (*Pl. 23*), the library or her mother's first-floor bedroom. Thus, like the Leslie children before them, the young Colebrookes' main view of the adult world was over the balustrade (now swept away) above the main staircase, where they watched the tiaras and uniforms come sailing up from the hall.

Like the Leslies too, the Colebrookes rode in the Row; Lady Packe remembers how she would mount the noble Sardonyx (bought by her father in America), and trot off down Oxford Street, the family coachman riding behind on a less glamorous steed.

All this lasted until 1908, when the Colebrookes in turn began to feel that the house was too much of an undertaking for them, and sold out to the 17th Earl of Derby. With his arrival the last and in some ways the most spectacular phase in the history of Stratford House as a private residence began.

To Lord Derby, as I have already indicated, it appeared decidedly on the small side. He was living at the time in Derby House, on the Charles II street corner of St. James's Square, with the Bishop of London hemming him in to the south; Stratford House was at least partially free-standing, and therefore capable of expansion. Derby, a much more nimble-minded character than his public image suggested, knew exactly what he wanted to do. He needed room for political entertaining and, with the coming of the motor-car, he did not need stables. Therefore the latter could be abolished and a state dining room, with a ballroom above, could be fitted into the site. We shall see in the next chapter how this worked out in practice, and what has happened to those large constructions since. Then he demanded better living and sleeping space for his wife and himself, and far more up-to-date accommodation for their staff. No amount of juggling with the existing structure would secure this—extension, and on a big scale, was the only remedy. Next, room had to be found for the various relics of the past such as chimney-pieces, to be brought from Derby House, St. James's Square, but originating in the far more famous Derby House, Grosvenor Square, built by Robert Adam for the 11th Earl in 1774.

Finally, there had to be alterations to meet the 17th Earl's personal taste—at least that is the only way one can account for his decision to destroy Lord Aldborough's original staircase and substitute one of his own.

All this work was placed in the hands of the then very fashionable architectural partnership of Romaine-Walker and Besant, but they do not seem to have been Lord Derby's original choice. As a result of a conversation about Stratford House, Mrs. Margaret Richardson, of the Royal Institute of British Architects' Prints Department, unearthed—much to my surprise—a set of drawings signed by MacVicar Anderson[1] and dated 1908, the very year in which Romaine-Walker and Besant started work. It is possible of course that Lord Derby asked two architectural firms to submit ideas simultaneously, but MacVicar Anderson's designs seem rather too detailed for that. It is more likely that Lord Derby commissioned them, turned them down, and called in Romaine-Walker and Besant as an alternative. If so, one must applaud his decision, certainly so far as the façade is concerned. A glance at *Plate 20* will show that had the MacVicar Anderson scheme gone through, Stratford Place would have been dominated by a piece of heavy Edwardianism, instead of a pastiche which comes near to genius.

In spite of his costly alterations and his efforts to make the old mansion more 'liveable', Lord Derby never regarded Stratford House, now rechristened Derby House, as his home. A Lancashire man to the core, he used it, as Mr. Randolph Churchill points out[2], 'mostly for entertainment, either of a political or social character'. Like Mr. Lloyd George, under whom he served in Coalition days, Lord Derby was a great one for political breakfasts, eaten no doubt in what he called the 'small dining room' (now the Garden Room). One of these repasts has its place in English history. On Tuesday

[1] J. MacVicar Anderson prepared one of the many abortive schemes for enlarging the old Oriental Clubhouse (1889).

[2] His *Lord Derby, King of Lancashire* (London, Heinemann, 1959) has been my principal source for this period.

5 December 1916, Lloyd George, Bonar Law and Edward Carson breakfasted at Derby House; later in the day Lloyd George, followed by Lord Derby, resigned from the Cabinet and Mr. Asquith's fate was sealed.

On the social side Derby House had perhaps reached its peak some five years before, when, on 27 June 1911, Lady Derby gave the grandest ball of the coronation season. The supper list, printed by Mr. Churchill, includes eight Imperial Highnesses, 32 Royal Highnesses and only one plain Mr., the American Ambassador (Whitelaw Reid). The fact that the number of Ambassadors present was six (those of France, Russia, Austria, United States, Spain and Japan) out of a possible nine[1] reminds us that even in 1911 ambassadorial rank was still almost as exclusive as in the days of Esterhazy and Lieven; in 1968 there are some 72 Ambassadors accredited to the Court of St. James's.

To a man with Lord Derby's teeming interests, his study was the real heart of the house. For this he chose the old dining room on the ground floor, now the Bar. No doubt this was mainly because of its convenience for political and business callers, but there was another reason. Mr. Churchill gives us a vivid and indeed intimidating picture of the Derby correspondence—an average of 40 letters a day received, and an equal number dispatched, and a total archive (since everything was kept) of one and a half million items. Lord Derby fairly devoured his mail and was much upset if it was late, so one of the charms of the 'ground floor front' was that he could sit in the window seat nearest the hall door and (as a tradition of the house relates) could give the postman a cheery greeting and take in the letters himself.

After World War I Lord Derby decided to consolidate his position as 'King of Lancashire' and to spend less and less time in London. Nevertheless, in 1930 he negotiated with the City of London to buy the freehold of the Derby House site.

The terms agreed were '75 years purchase' of the ground rents then being paid, as follows: No. 11 Stratford Place, £8; Stables,

[1] The absentees were Italy, Turkey and the German Empire. The very last of all the balls held in Stratford House as a private dwelling was given by Lord Derby shortly before World War II. Sir John Leslie's great-grandson, Jack Leslie, Irish Guards, was among the dancers.

Coach House, etc., £2; part of 12, Stratford Place, £5—total £15. So the purchase price at 75 years was £1,125, and in this way Lord Derby became the undisputed owner of the historic piece of ground on which Stratford House and its appurtenances stood. A modest outlay, but the figures line up more or less with the £3 15s. od. ground rent which to this day the Oriental Club pays the Corporation for its Tenterden Street backyard, though the charge is now borne by the lessees of the building on the site.

The transaction, along with others involved in the partial liquidation of the City Mead Estate, attracted a good deal of criticism. Two years elapsed between the proposal coming before the City Lands Committee of the Corporation and the final offer being accepted by the Common Council (17 March 1932). Nos. 3 and 4 Stratford Place were disposed of at the same time.

The final comment on Derby House can only be in its owner's words. Asked some time in the thirties why he continued to keep up a large house which he used so little, his unchallengable answer was —'Well, Lady Derby must have *somewhere* to change when she comes up from Coworth to go to the play'.

And now we are approaching the moment when, for the first time in its long history, the front door of No. 11 Stratford Place was opened to all comers. This seemed bound to occur, eventually, but it was precipitated by World War II. The first stage was that Lord Derby at length made up his mind to sell Derby House. He then consulted his art adviser, Sir Alec Martin, Managing Director of Christies, about emptying the house and finding somewhere to store its art treasures and furniture, at a time when all warehouse space was under pressure. Sir Alec was able to arrange for the works of art to go to a friend's house near Ross-on-Wye, Herefordshire, and here, on the night of their arrival, they were greeted by the only bomb dropped in the neighbourhood during the whole war, but no damage was done. The rest of the Derby House furniture and effects had been taken to Druce's Depository, Baker Street, while other storage was sought for them, and they were all lost when enemy action sent the Depository up in a stupendous bonfire.

Christies itself was destroyed in April 1941. Sir Alec Martin was due to conduct a stamp auction for the Red Cross, and telegraphed Lord Derby asking whether he could hold it at Derby House. The reply came back, 'Certainly, and if any use afterwards to Christies, go there'. Sir Alec would have liked to get a lease, but Lord Derby wanted to sell; however, he generously undertook to let Christies stay on, rent free, for the duration of the war and six months after. Meanwhile—oh, indignity!—a great 'To be sold' board was hoisted on the front of the old house, but there was no queue of would-be purchasers while the threat of bombing remained.

And so Christies' sales got under way once more, among the stripped-down splendours of the Derby House ballroom. One of the famous pictures which came up was Lord Swaythling's Constable, 'The Young Waltonians', sold to Mr. Walter Hutchinson for £41,000.

The war ended and so did the 'six months after' period, without, of course, a licence for the rebuilding of Christies getting appreciably nearer. Sir Alec Martin hoped to stay on in Stratford Place, but he woke up one morning to find that Derby House had been sold over his head, so to speak, to a financial syndicate. He tried to obtain a lease from them, to tide him over, and thought he had succeeded, but in the end the house was resold—to the owner of 'The Young Waltonians'! Mr. Hutchinson let Christies stay on a little longer, but in the end they had to go. It was lucky that Sir Alec had another friend among the picture-owning aristocracy—Lord Spencer immediately offered him Spencer House, St. James's. Here sales continued until Christies could resume on their original site, which they did in 1953.

And now our story takes a truly surprising twist. Like Christies, Hutchinson & Co. had been made homeless by war—they were one of the many publishing firms which lost their headquarters when Paternoster Row was virtually wiped out in the great air raid on the City in December 1940. From then onwards the Hutchinson companies carried on at various addresses as best they could.

Directly Derby House was put on the market by the syndicate in 1946, Walter Hutchinson, Chairman and Managing Director of the Group, saw in it the chance of fulfilling a secret ambition he had long cherished, and began negotiations at once. Art connoisseur and sportsman as well as publisher, his dream was to open his collection of sporting pictures (suitably extended) to the public as a 'National Gallery of British Sports and Pastimes'. The fine rooms of Derby House seemed ideal for this purpose and at the same time there would be enough space for the executives and staffs of his many businesses.

Mr. Hutchinson set to work with characteristic energy. He re-christened the house after himself; out of a stock of 3,000 paintings he selected some 560 for hanging; and he brought in Mr. John Wheatley, A.R.A. (formerly of Sheffield Art Gallery) as Curator. The Gallery was opened to the public in February 1949.

To some readers of this book—I wonder how many?—*Pl. 24* may bring back curious memories. The National Gallery of British Sports and Pastimes, as I recall it, was unlike any other which had existed in London for 100 years at least. Wandering from room to room one was confronted with a mass of pictures which covered the entire walls, as it might be in Zoffany's famous painting 'The Florentine Gallery'. Race-horses, cricketers, partridge-shooters, skaters jostled each other, and while only a small number of the works may have been important, the effect was strangely charming. Whether Mr. Wheatley or his employer chose the method of display is a moot point, but as Walter Hutchinson was one who always 'knew better', whatever the subject, he probably called this tune too.

The only moment of repose was at the end of the ballroom, where the pride of the collection, 'The Young Waltonians'[1], was given a special setting with a rope and a row of chairs in front of it.

With the untimely death of Walter Hutchinson in 1950, the venture came to an end, having lasted a bare two years. Without his energy and enthusiasm it could not succeed, though *Country Life* in an article of 1 June 1951 said it failed through being 'too ambitious and on insufficiently selective lines'. The gallery was closed, and the whole vast heap of pictures dispersed, with Sir Alec Martin's help. Three sales were held at Christies, covering altogether nearly 600 paintings and engravings.

The first of these sales, on 20 July 1951, contained the 'plums'. 'The Young Waltonians', on the block once more, went to Captain

[1] This is of course one of Constable's great river-pieces, and was known in the

(now Sir Reginald) MacDonald-Buchanan for £2,000 more than Walter Hutchinson had paid for it. Other big prices (they would be eclipsed today!) were 12,000 guineas for Stubbs's 'Gimcrack,' which had been bought at Derby House out of Lord Bolingbroke's collection for 4,200 guineas, and over 5,000 guineas each for two Morlands.

After the removal of the collection, Hutchinson & Co. remained in Stratford Place for a further four years. The staff were able to 'spread themselves' a little, but the State rooms were let from time to time for wedding receptions and debutante parties; in fact many people's recollections of Hutchinson House date from that phase. However, by 1955 it was felt that the heavy overheads could be saved by a move to more convenient modern premises. Hutchinson House (quickly reconverted to Stratford House) was sold to the industrial group of Birfield Ltd.

Following World War II there had been quite a vogue for the use of large private houses as offices. But the results were seldom happy, and this was probably the least satisfactory purpose to which Lord Aldborough's legacy has been put. How well one knows the effect in numberless 'adapted' mansions, town or country—the big rooms awkwardly partitioned, the small ones lacking light and air; departments split up or out of sequence; supervision at a low ebb!

Aesthetically, too, is there anything more wretched than an eighteenth-century drawing-room with a row of green filing cabinets jostling the Adam chimney piece and strip lights hanging from the stuccoed ceiling? Better concrete, steel, and fitness for purpose!

Messrs. Birfield in fact did their best to avoid such solecisms and to preserve the atmosphere of Stratford House, but I think it was with relief that they once more put it on the market, with the felicitous results which we have already seen.

Hutchinson Collection by its alternative and perhaps more authentic title of 'Stratford Mill by the Stour'. It only qualified for the Gallery because it includes a group of boys fishing.

11 *One More Metamorphosis*

The best Clubhouse in London.
Charles Graves, Leather Armchairs

When, in the early months of 1961, the Committee of the Oriental Club and its various Sub-Committees sat down to plan their new Clubhouse in detail, they were faced with a double task—to rehouse the members as conveniently, comfortably and economically as possible[1], and to do their duty by one of the last of the 'private palaces of London'. Thanks largely, it must be said, to the bold and sometimes ruthless aggrandisement already carried out by Lord Derby, it was found that these aims could be reconciled without further outrage upon what was left of the eighteenth-century fabric of Stratford House.

Many of the pieces, of course, fell neatly enough into place. The state dining room—that was a 'natural' for the members' Dining Room; Lord Derby's small dining room—just right for mixed luncheons; Lord Colebrooke's library would be the Club's Library, the original ballroom its Drawing Room, and so on. Other requirements needed more thought. There was the innovation of a Bar to be fitted in, and what about a Private Dining Room, and above all where was space to be found for an adequate array of bedrooms?

In this chapter I propose to look at Stratford House as inherited by the Club and as adapted for its own needs, and also to show it as part

[1] Also to cater for an increased number of them. A recruitment drive, given impetus by the Stratford House project, resulted in 252 elections in 1961, 288 in 1962 and 221 in 1963. The total at the end of 1967 was 1650, plus 740 Associate Members.

of a historic environment. My next and final chapter will describe the living organism which has fitted itself so cosily into this tough, enduring shell.

For those fond of exercise, the tour might well begin at the corner of Davies Street and Berkeley Square! It is always a surprise to get a glimpse of Stratford House from that distance. The eighteenth century delighted in these long 'vistoes', but this particular alignment is in fact imperfect and fortuitous; Davies Street was there first, and the placing of Stratford House was dictated by the narrow confines of the Banqueting House grounds.

As we move forward, more and more of the mansion comes into view, but before reaching it we must pause at the feature of Stratford Place on which every past writer has commented. This was the entrance from Oxford Street, with its lion-topped 'sentry-boxes' and the gates between. At least, they all mention the sentry-boxes, but I do not recall reading much about the gates. *Were there any?* Versions of them appear in *Pls. 17* and *18* and they are even described on page 171 of this book! But the plates are 'artists' impressions', not topographical views, and the few and unsatisfactory glimpses we get in old prints of the Stratford Place entrance as actually built do not show or suggest gates, or indicate how they could have been hung. Perhaps we had better leave them floating in the air!

The lions were solid enough, and they sat placidly on their elegant Adamesque plinths for nearly a century and a half. The westward one was the first to be disturbed. In a letter to Sir Shane Leslie, Lord Derby described the circumstances:

> Whilst still on the outside I may tell you of a thing which has always very much distressed me. At the entrance to Oxford Street you will see on the one side opposite the Bank [*he means, 'on the same side as the Bank'*] some sort of sentry box. There was one on the other side, and when there were some alterations going on I begged Lilley & Skinner, who were the holders of the property, not to remove it. I got a charming letter back saying they realised what an attraction it was and they were not going to alter it. However, some years later, when the Managing Head had passed away, they did do away with it, and built the hideous erection which is now their shop. I have never forgiven them for that.

So the eastward lion was left solitary, though strangely enough the house to which he was originally attached—No. 1 Stratford Place—had been the first piece of Edward Stratford's original composition to disappear. And here we find a very satisfying link between the Oriental Club and Stratford Place, long before 'the move' was dreamt of. When the Club was launched, the Committee—keeping things 'in the family' as usual—opened a banking account with the firm of Sir William P. Call & Co., of 25 Old Bond Street. The founder of the Call fortunes, you see, was a 'nabob', Colonel Sir John Call, Bt., M.P. (1732–1801) and at least two later Calls were members of the Oriental. The connection lasted until 1848, when it was decided to transfer to a joint stock bank on the grounds that

> No private bank allowed interest on deposits, and that in consequence the Club was driven to resort for security and for the employment of its balances to the purchase of Exchequer Bonds, which were continually fluctuating and therefore objectionable.

The joint stock bank chosen was a branch of the London and Westminster, then installed at No. 4 Stratford Place. And this branch (now, of course, of the National Westminster) holds the account still, together with the signatures of the Club Trustees who originally opened it. However, in 1890 the branch moved, buying No. 1 from the Portland Club, which had been there since 1816. The sequel, alas, was that the fine old house was almost immediately pulled down and there was substituted a totally incongruous structure of granite and plate glass. The best that can be said is that the Bank *did* preserve their lion, whereas Messrs. Lilley & Skinner, while trying hard to conform architecturally, let theirs go.

Then in 1961 a fresh threat developed. The eastward lion was now in danger! Messrs. R. Seifert and Partners applied for permission to pull down the 1890 bank, and to rear a modern office block on the site. The issue was keenly fought, and Messrs. Seifert only got their permission subject to certain conditions—including the reinstatement of the lion and his plinth!

But the affair was also memorable for invoking the best and most detailed account of Stratford Place and its architecture that is ever likely to be compiled. This was presented to the public enquiry on behalf of the then London County Council (see note 2, page 166). I cannot attempt to reproduce it, even in the most summarised form. All that can be said is that in Stratford Place today we see the unchanged ground-plan of a beautiful fabric, but only the ghost of its elevation. The actual score is this: on the east and north there is an unbroken sequence of houses from No. 3 to No. 11 which maintain a semblance of their eighteenth-century appearance, whereas on the west side demolitions and bombings have left only No. 12 (the old Dower House), No. 13 and No. 16 more or less intact. No. 16 occupies a key position, standing as it does at the angle of one of the two confronting terraces and the little 'square' to which they lead. Strange to think that if the offer mentioned on page 15 had been accepted, Nos. 17–19, next door, might now be the Oriental Club!

The original houses varied greatly in the elaboration of their interiors, though all had naturally to conform to that basic plan which the London terrace imposes, whether in Bermondsey, Campden Hill or Regent's Park. One of the best must always have been No. 3; it was elaborately 'written up' when Lady Mayo lived there in the thirties and we are lucky that it is being zealously safeguarded by its present occupants, Messrs. Coty.

One gets the impression that, in contrast to other London enclaves, Stratford Place actually became slightly more aristocratic with the passing of time, until our cataclysmic age made a virtual clean sweep of residential Mayfair and its off-shoots—aristocratic or otherwise. Occupancy in the early nineteenth century was pleasantly mixed. For instance, we have already met artists like Pickersgill and Cosway—the latter lived next to the westward lion until a rather silly pasquinade about lions and monkeys is said to have driven him a door or two away.

This is perhaps the moment to protest that Stratford Place has been strangely unlucky in the matter of 'blue plaques'. Some of its celebrities are perhaps of the second rank, but so are many of those honoured by the Greater London Council! Whom to suggest? Perhaps not the worthy academicians Sir George Hayter (c. 1847) at No. 9, or Sir Robert Smirke (c. 1842), father of the architect, at No. 5? Nor Charles Lamb's stage idol Robert Elliston (c. 1815) at No. 8? Nor Quintin Hogg (c. 1903), grandfather of the present Quintin and founder of the Polytechnics, at No. 10?

But three residents for whom I do stake a claim are Richard Cosway, Sir William Vernon-Harcourt, the heavyweight Victorian statesman, who occupied No. 14 for a whole decade (1868–78)[1], and above all Edward Lear.

Lear's was a wandering and lonely, though gregarious, life, and much of it was spent abroad. All he needed in England was a studio base, where he could 'work up' his material and hold a periodical Private View. Stratford Place suited him very well[2]. His first choice was No. 17, where he lodged in 1850–1. But the front room ceiling fell down and then, just when he had returned from a foreign trip, the back room ceiling fell down too. Nothing to be done but to pack up the debris of his possessions and to retreat to Hastings, where at least there were 'fresh air and muffins'. Surely a Nonsense Verse has been lost:

There was an old person called Lear,
Whose lodgings were humble, though dear,
When the ceilings fell down
He rushed out of Town
Crying 'Fresh air and muffins for Lear!'

A few years later, however, he was back in Stratford Place, this time at No. 15 (1861–9). Here he entertained the Prince of Wales (who bought 10 sketches), and had for housemate none other than the Oriental's card-playing parson, the Rev. J. O. Oldham!

Finally, what about Stratford House itself, with its galaxy of distinguished if somewhat ephemeral owners and tenants? Surely a strong case could be made out at least for the well-loved politician and sportsman who re-christened it Derby House and made it his London headquarters for over thirty years?

I explored all this with Miss E. D. Mercer, Head Archivist to the Greater London Council. Miss Mercer accounted for the bareness of Stratford Place walls by explaining that the Council nowadays prefers to attach plaques to original houses rather than to sites, and where a celebrity may have had two or more homes to give prece-

[1] Three of his predecessors in the house were Sir William Knighton, the dubious Court physician (see page 46), W. H. Pickersgill and a lesser artist, the Chevalier Louis Desanges. They would make a fine collection on a plaque.

[2] For Lear in Stratford Place see Angus Davidson, *Edward Lear* (London, John Murray, 1938).

dence to the one least altered. Unfortunately, the Cosway, Harcourt, and Lear houses we have been discussing are among those which have been completely rebuilt. Lear has been given a plaque at 30 Seymour Street, but as he only lived there for a brief period in 1857–8, I still think a point should have been stretched in favour of No. 17 Stratford Place!

Over Stratford House itself no such problem arises, and as a result of this correspondence the Oriental Club put in a formal application for a plaque commemorating the 17th Earl of Derby. At the time of writing the Council's decision was not known.

By the turn of the century, there were fewer artists in Stratford Place and more fashionable residents—a spot check for the year 1902 reveals, in addition to the Mayos at No. 3, Captain the Hon. A. E. Somerset at No. 8, Sir Rennell and Lady Rodd[1] at No. 17, and Lord and Lady Ampthill at No. 19—the last-named house became a German club and was visited by the Kaiser.

One other tendency must be noted. As early as the 1880s, Stratford Place had begun to serve as an overflow area for Harley Street. Soon Nos. 14, 15, 18 and 20 bore doctors' or dentists' name plates, and it was a dentist who in 1896 made the first and much criticised break in the classic skyline by adding a storey (still detectable) at No. 6. After 1900 Nos. 2 and 7 also became consulting rooms.

Today medical men and titled residents alike have vanished. But though commerce has virtually swallowed up Stratford Place, it is pleasant that the arts are still represented by the Folio Society at No. 6, and the Royal Society of Musicians at No. 10.

And so up the famous little cul-de-sac past the ranks of parked cars (Lord Derby believed he had the right to exclude them, but the police did not encourage him to try) and into 'the Square'. Missing from the centre of it is a feature which the Oriental Club would no doubt cherish today. This was a pillar erected towards the end of his life by the 2nd Lord Aldborough, though the impulse may have been supplied by General Strode, who had promoted something

[1] Sister of Walter Murray Guthrie, the then owner of the 'big house'—our last glimpse of Stratford Place as a *dépendance du manoir*, to borrow a phrase from Mr. Seymour Leslie.

similar in neighbouring Cavendish Square. It seems to have been a poor thing—his Lordship's finances were under strain at the time—and within two years it showed fearful signs of wear and tear. For a description of it in 1804 we are indebted (surprisingly enough) to Richard Phillips's *Street Cries of Modern London* (1804). Attached to his plate of 'Baking and Boiling Apples' is this paragraph:

Stratford House is now occupied by the Duchess of St. Albans. The late Lord Aldborough erected a pillar in the form of a candlestick surmounted by a most despicable statue of His Majesty in a composition resembling stone. It is already almost destroyed, two sides of the railing being pulled down and the inscription almost defaced. Barren as London is of the classical design of statues and public monuments, we cannot wish to see the Stratford Place pillar repaired on the same inelegant and puerile design in which it was originally executed. The object, however, was good.

The sad thing is that among the pompous inscriptions in English and Latin with which Lord Aldborough bedizened his monument was one which the Club would have valued as yet another link with its members' ancient antagonist, Tippoo Sahib:

In this memorable year, on the 4th of May, 1799, Seringapatam was taken by storm, and the perfidious Teppoo Sahib slain in his capital, by the English forces under General Harris; the territory of Mysore, and Port of Mangalore, annexed to the Eastern dominion of Great Britain; and quiet and security restored to that quarter of the Globe.

In front of us now (*Pl. 21*) is the façade of Stratford House. The first thing to keep in mind is that most of what we see is the work of Romaine-Walker in 1908. We have already noted how he carried up the wings to a height uniform with the centre, but Lord Derby reveals that much more than this was necessary. After explaining how he had had to abolish the 'little colonnade' so as to get more light into his sitting-room (i.e. the present Bar), he goes on:

Some years ago the vibration of the Tube[1] brought down part of the house, and it was found then that the stonework was really only veneer. It had to be replaced entirely by stone, and the balustrading which was

[1] Hard to believe, since it passes well to the south of Stratford House. But Mr. Leslie reminds me that the heavy electric locomotives being used by the Central Line when he lived within range of it in the early 1900s set up vibrations of seismic proportions, and led to many threats of legal action.

crumbling away had to be replaced. But what was more curious, and much more expensive, was that the foundations had to be put in again for the old part of the house, as we found they were built on wooden piles.

Lord Derby's word 'veneer' is no exaggeration; it is said that the Portland stone façade was only an inch thick, secured to brickwork behind with dowel pins. One presumes that the Ionic pillars and the pediment which form the frontispiece of the house were solid stone and have always remained intact.

Granted that the enlargement of Stratford House was necessary at all, a dexterous job was made of it by Romaine-Walker. Perhaps it is appropriate that a man who, though articled as an architect, spent most of his early life in the theatrical company of Sir Herbert Tree, should have been a master of eighteenth-century pastiche[1]. The curious thing is that, according to a note by Sir John Summerson of a conversation with Romaine-Walker's partner Herbert Jenkins (who died only a few years ago), the former was really only interested in Gothic; Jenkins and the other members of the practice must therefore get the main credit for the firm's classical exercises.

Certainly, nothing could be more tactful and harmonious than their treatment of the Stratford House façade, with its simple lines, fine stonework and reticent touches of Adamesque decoration. The urns along the skyline, by the way, are a nice little puzzle. Early prints and pre-Derby photographs (*Pl. 15*) show that originally there were four tall urns on the top parapet and eight squatter ones along the arcade[2]; now there are eight altogether, uniformly tall it would seem (though three have had their tops knocked off), and uniformly weathered. Another Romaine-Walker conjuring trick?

Inside, the 1908 innovations are more questionable. We do not meet them until we reach the Staircase Hall. The Entrance Hall (including the front-door with its fine original metal-work) appears to be very much as Lord Aldborough left it, except that, when the

[1] For a somewhat similar example of his skill I would quote Buckland House near Faringdon in Berkshire, where, once again, low wings have been brought up level with a tall and narrow centre. The results are completely convincing.

[2] Lord Aldborough was greatly addicted to urns and imported them into Ireland almost by the shipload, along with the lions and the sphinxes visible in Fig. 4. These creatures, like their confrères the Stratford Place lions, were probably made of the composition 'Coade stone'.

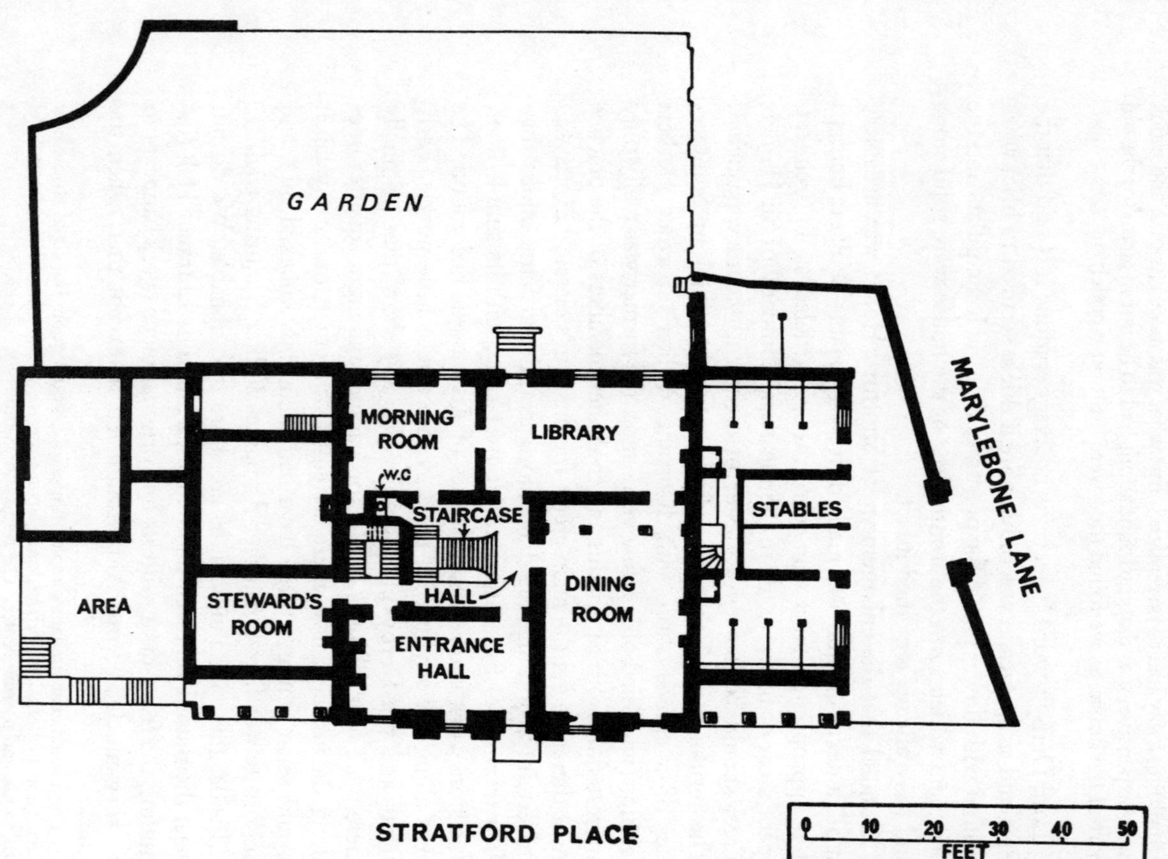

Fig 5 Ground-plan of Stratford House before enlargement

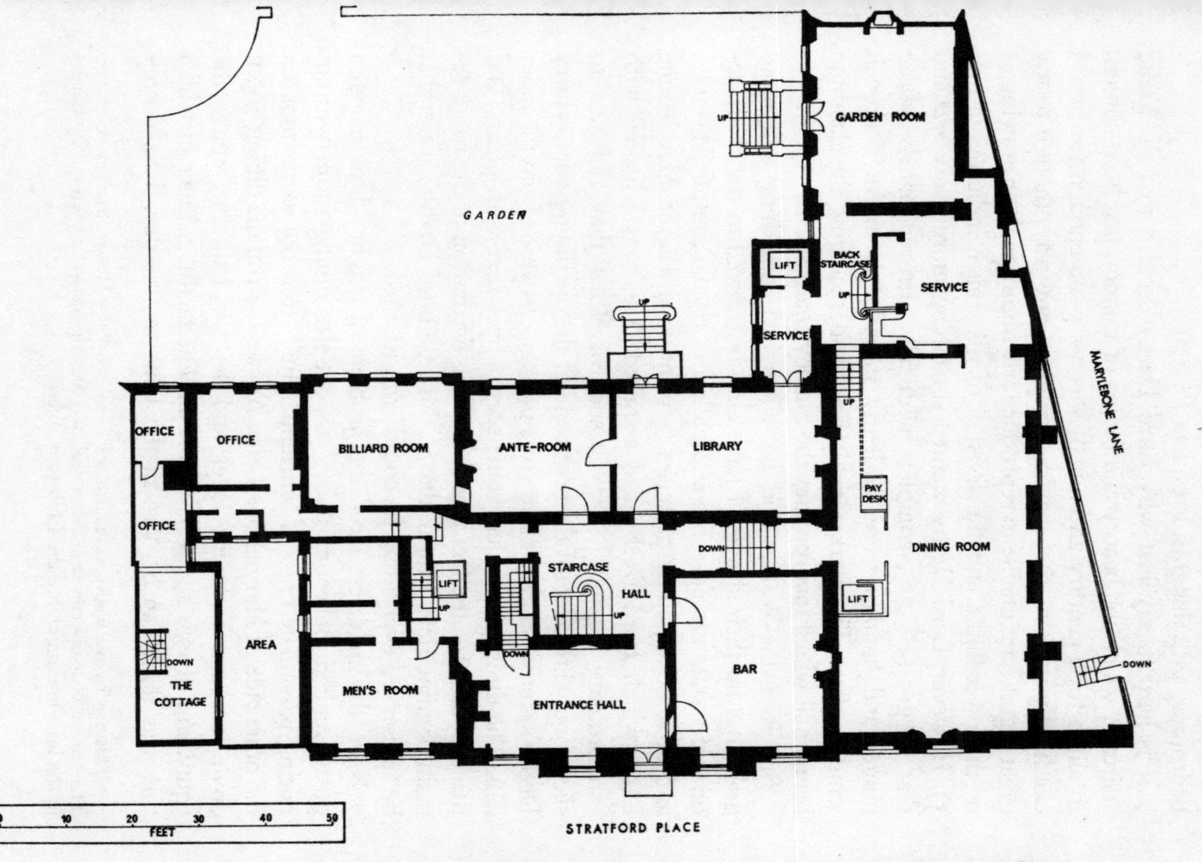

Fig 6 Ground-plan of Stratford House as now in use by the Oriental Club

Club took over, the fireplace was a plain, box-like affair, so an elegant chimney-piece (either a Stratford House original or more probably a Derby importation) was brought down from one of the bedrooms, with delightful results (*Pl. 27*).

It is hard to say just why Lord Derby decided that the grand staircase, which the beauty and brains of London had been content to climb for a century and a half, was not good enough for him. I can hardly imagine that it was decrepit in any way, though to my great regret I am unable to reproduce any photograph or drawing of it (the lower flight, and the division of the arms is indicated in Fig. 5). However, Lord Derby wanted something more *beaux arts* and that he got (*Pl. 22*), complete with tall mirrored panels whose hinges and handles were evidently intended to make a French window effect. The workmanship was good, including the elaborate balustrade which incorporates the Stanley coat-of-arms[1].

But Romaine-Walker and his client had something still more grandiose up their sleeves. I have already referred to the construction of a state dining-room and ballroom on the site of the stables and of some adjoining premises (a printing works) in Marylebone Lane, which Lord Derby had acquired. This was achieved with extraordinary ingenuity (Figs. 5 and 6). What they did was to slice about eight feet off the north end of the old dining-room (Lord Derby's study) so as to allow for a passage eastwards from the inner hall. The dining-room had some sort of apse here with pillars, and this accounts for the fact that the ceiling decoration of the room remains symmetrical. I think that in this case Lord Derby's claim that he 'preserved everything he could' was justified.

Next, the architects faced the problem of height—how to put a great vaulted ballroom above an out-size dining-room without raising passionate cries of 'ancient lights' from the workshops on the other side of Marylebone Lane. Answer—drop the dining-room down to semi-basement level and let the ballroom enjoy the equivalent of two and a half storeys. The tactful manner in which this was done can be seen in the Lane to this day. I have only

[1] This was by the well-known firm of metal-workers, Messrs. Starkey, Gardner. The present coat-of-arms is in fact a replica—the original was ripped out by thieves in the brief interim before the Club took over.

dim recollections of that ballroom in the Hutchinson era, but *Pl. 25* conveys the massive grandeur of its marble pillars, minstrels' gallery and heavily Kauffmann-esque ceiling designed by Sir Charles Allom. The ceiling, by the way, still exists, though rather knocked about, and can be seen in alarming close-up by those who know which door to open on the top floor of Stratford House.

Elderly people who have family links with the mansion as it was before the Derby alterations, are unanimous in condemning them—*vulgarity* is their key word. Yet it is a striking example of the never-ceasing evolution of taste that, in 'preservationist' circles, I have heard much more concern expressed recently over the loss of this formidable ballroom than over Lord Aldborough's staircase.

For the state dining-room (*Pl. 26*), Lord Derby and Romaine-Walker reverted to pseudo-Adam, and it is a work of most curious provenance. The idea was to reproduce as closely as possible the banqueting hall from the fantastically elaborate temporary building erected—as we might put up a marquee—in the grounds of The Oaks, Epsom[1], for the wedding of the 10th Earl of Derby with Lady Elizabeth Hamilton in 1774. This building was designed by Robert Adam and it remains famous because Angelica Kauffmann's husband, Antonio Zucchi, did two paintings of it which are still at Knowsley and which were engraved for *The Works of James and Robert Adam*.

The Oaks banqueting hall had pillared apses at both ends and these were duly reproduced at Derby House, but when the Club moved in the pillars had to be eliminated to make room for an adequate number of tables; at the same time the symmetry of the room was disturbed by a rectangular bay built into the west side to accommodate a cash desk and a passenger lift. The 1908 and 1962 'repro-Adam' plaster reliefs are of fine quality and indistinguishable, both being derived from eighteenth-century moulds, and just to complete an architectural booby-trap of the first order, the ceiling paintings are over 100 years older than anything else in Stratford House! Lord Derby told Sir Shane Leslie that they were brought from The Oaks and were 'by a painter named Romanelli (I know nothing

[1] The house after which the race, founded by the same Lord Derby, was named. It was only demolished fairly recently.

about him)'. However, Mr. Croft-Murray (see below) has identified this artist with Giovanni Francesco Romanelli (?1610–62), a pupil of Pietro da Cortona. These panels, which have a touch of Poussin's neo-classicism, are very dark, but it is possible to distinguish the subjects: Hercules and Omphale; The Triumph of Amphitrite (or a similar marine fancy); and Orpheus being stoned by the Bacchantes.

Those with less modish tastes than the amateurs of Edwardiana are grateful that so much still remains of the house as originally conceived. I have already mentioned the Entrance Hall, and we can resume our tour from there. Puzzles abound—in fact we meet one immediately in the old dining-room (now Bar).

In her *Journal*[1] for 1873 Anne Thackeray records:

March 15th. Walk in the rain with Carlyle. Splash! Splash! Dined with the Leslies at Stratford Place. Eventful dinner. Sir John told me about Angelica Kauffmann and showed me her ceiling—thought of writing her story.

Later the *Journal* notes, 'Began to write Angelica Kauffmann, January 30th, 1874' and *Miss Angel* duly appeared the following year.

All later writers on the famous woman artist mention this incident[2], adding that the ceiling roundel at which Thackeray's daughter and Sir John Leslie gazed from the dinner table below represented 'The Nymph Aglaia Tied to a Tree by Cupid', a favourite Kauffmann subject. Now it had never seemed to me that the nymph, whatever her name, is the least tied to a tree—in fact she appears to be leaning comfortably against it, being toasted by a young gentleman. So I sent a photograph of the roundel to Mr. Edward Croft-Murray, Keeper of Prints and Drawings at the British Museum, and an authority on eighteenth-century decorative painting. Back came the reply—*not* Aglaia tied to a tree, but Ariadne being comforted by

[1] Quoted in *The Letters of Anne Thackeray Ritchie*, ed. Hester Ritchie (London, John Murray, 1924).

[2] Cf. Frances A. Gerard, *Angelica Kauffmann* (London, Ward and Downey, 1893); also Lady Victoria Manners and Dr. G. C. Williamson, *Angelica Kauffmann R.A., Her Life and Work* (London, John Lane, The Bodley Head, 1924). Both books attribute the Stratford House decorations generally to Angelica, but without critical commentary or proof.

Bacchus in the island of Naxos, and *not* by Angelica Kauffmann, but more probably by Zucchi. So much for literary legend!

This room retains a fine original chimney-piece, as do Lord Colebrooke's library (already described) and its adjoining ante-room, which also has a pretty eighteenth-century ceiling. The Library itself, though Edwardian, preserves what must have been a very early fitment, since it is suggested in Fig. 5. This is a tall sash window with half-door below, which gives access to the garden steps.

The other important rooms are on the first floor and we might as well ascend to them by the back-stairs which (unusually) are much more interesting than the front! But on the way we need to peep into the Garden Room (successor to the old Strangers' Room in Hanover Square). This was Lord Derby's 'small dining room' or breakfast room, where we have already heard the downfall of Mr. Asquith being plotted over the kidneys and bacon. Its main decorative feature is a graceful wooden overmantel, imported from goodness knows where, but probably French.

The back-stairs were built by Lord Derby to connect with what he called his 'winter garden' (a domed conservatory) above. Their importance lies in the fact that they are lined with a miscellany of Italian landscapes and *capricci* (*Pl. 28*) of the type which English travellers used to bring home in quantity from the Grand Tour. Only one of the painters has so far been identified. This is Antonio Jolli (1700–77); an artist of Modenese origin, and a follower of Panini. Mr. Croft-Murray has a special interest in Jolli, because sometime in 1740–50, when he was resident in London, he did wall-paintings in the house in Maids of Honour Row, Richmond, where Mr. Croft-Murray himself now lives. The Club's picture, near the top of the stairs, represents the so-called Temple of Neptune at Paestum; it appears as Plate 4 in the series of engravings, *Antica famosa Città di Pesto*, issued in 1765.

And now we arrive at the great Drawing Room (or ballroom, as it was usually called before Lord Derby constructed his own brontosaurus). Its serene proportions, fine decoration and tall windows looking down Stratford Place, make it one of the most satisfying rooms of its kind in London. But even here Angelica Kauffmann, to whom unquestioning obeisance has been done by a whole succession of Stratford House owners, has had to be dethroned. Mr. Croft-Murray confidently attributes the ceiling paintings, depicting the story of Cupid and Psyche, to another painter of the same school, Biagio Rebecca (1735–1808).

The chimney-piece (*Pl. 24*) is quite different from any we have met so far—big and bold with three-quarter-size figures of Fame and Mars, supporters of the Stratford coat-of-arms. It was therefore beyond doubt designed for the house, and has been attributed to Thomas Banks. The whole room, in fact, appears at first sight as an untouched relic of the eighteenth century. I must confess that I accepted it as such myself until Lady Packe suddenly remarked, recalling the far past—'Something has happened to the doors—they were not as high as this.' I looked again, and realised that the door cases, now reaching almost to the ceiling, must have been reconstructed by Romaine-Walker so that, outside, they should be symmetrical with the looking-glass panels on the stairs[1]!

Pure 1774, and justly considered by Lord Derby as the 'prettiest' room in the house, is the Writing Room (former small drawing-room). Its elegant barrel roof is adorned with some rather mixed mythologies, again by Rebecca.

The most tiresome problem I have left to the last. One of the high Drawing Room doors leads into another 'Adamish' room looking out on the garden. In order to provide an adequate Smoking Room, it has been combined with a somewhat larger apartment on the same axis. This is the real puzzler. The woodwork is of oak discreetly gilded; painted canvas panels of pastoral scenes are inserted into it (they have recently been cleaned with most delightful effect); and there are nice rococo flourishes along the ceiling cove (*Pl. 1*). What is all this about? Mr. Croft-Murray's guess is a complete importation from South Germany or Austria, but if someone were to prove that the thing had been put together in London for Lord Derby, or Lord Colebrooke (it seems somehow in his taste) or even Murray Guthrie, I for one would be equally convinced! Lady Packe is fairly, but not quite, sure that this was her mother's bedroom,

[1] *Pl. 23* confirms. A door on the east side was definitely a Derby insertion, giving access to his ballroom. It is ponderously carved.

though she does not recognise the wall treatment. Sir Shane Leslie thinks Guthrie kept his stamp collection there!

A few objects of art or curiosity are to be met with when one walks round Stratford House in its latest incarnation. I have already mentioned Mr. Tarbett Fleming's elephant in the Entrance Hall, at the other end of which the fine bronze Buddha, presented in 1909 by Mr. J. A. Anderson, looks down from the overmantel. The Staircase Hall houses a particularly suitable Oriental Club relic—an elaborately carved chair once owned by Tippoo Sahib. This was given to the Club in 1955 by Miss Margaret Bellasis, and the inscription states that her ancestor, General John Bellasis (1743–1808), received it 'from the Queen of Cannore' in return for his help in liberating her territory[1]. Nearby stands the water pipe which ushered in Part II of this book, and Mr. Dickson Wright has matched it with an old engraving showing how such pipes were bored and fitted together.

At the top of the Grand Staircase we encounter the Weighing Machine. This sounds prosaic enough, yet it is a piece of Club history in its way. If ever there were a Society of Friends of the Weighing Machine, its President would certainly have been Colonel John Smith (e. 1827). It was he who began to agitate for one in 1845, but the then Committee thought the purchase unjustifiable. Three years later Major William Drake came to his support with the news that the United Service Club had just bought a machine from Messrs. Young & Sons of Bear Street, Leicester Square, for £12 12s., and he thought this might be just the job. The Committee still wavered—felt it would be better to wait and see how the apparatus was 'found to answer' at the Senior. Finally, the plunge was taken, but the selected machine caused nothing but trouble. Colonel Smith opined that it might work better with weights instead of springs, and on 26 November 1849 the following tell-tale notice was posted:

> Gentlemen are requested to sit down and rise from the weighing machine as gently as possible, the needle being liable to be put out of order by any sudden jerk.

The poor thing was just not hardy enough, and after the Club had

[1] But see M. Bellasis, *Honourable Company* (London, Hollis and Carter, 1952) (O.C.L.) for a fuller description of Tippoo's ejection from the Malabar coast in 1790. The name of the Queen's territory is there correctly given as *Cannanore*.

had it only two years we find Colonel Smith moving that a new machine be purchased 'on the plan to be hereafter approved'—whatever that may mean.

What I suspect is that (as in some of the older Clubs and at Berry's wineshop in St. James's Street) the weighing machine was used as a primitive substitute for the one-armed bandit—as a betting medium in fact. This would account for a furious complaint round about Christmas 1858 that a riotous party had 'spent a quarter of an hour weighing themselves', to the disturbance of members dozing in the Library.

Every few years the report on the weighing machine continued to be 'out of order' and a suggestion was made in 1866 that a Mark III version 'would contribute much to the convenience of members'. This was left in suspense, and I do not know whether the present charming apparatus with its shining rail and plush seat dates from 1866 or 1851. The makers were certainly Young of Leicester Square. The weighing machine always attracts the eye of visitors and I can readily believe that Alice 'sat down and cried' when she came in one morning in 1967 and found that two of its beautiful brass weights, which she has been polishing for 50 years, had been stolen.

An ornament of the Smoking Room is a very splendid ram's head snuff mull, for which the Club is indebted to the late Mr. Robert Thorburn, and which had originally been given by his father to the Byculla Club. This is a reminder that over the years the Oriental has fallen heir to a number of sporting trophies (ponderous silver cups, in the main) and other objects belonging to overseas clubs, regiments and associations which have ceased to exist or have lost their European character. Unfortunately some of these were stolen in rather mysterious circumstances shortly before the move to Stratford Place.

Also in the Smoking Room is a remarkable collection of Campaign medals presented by Lady Leetham in memory of Sir Arthur Leetham, and two precious framed documents—an original prospectus of 1824 sent to '—Arbuthnot Esq., 25 Upper Wimpole Street'[1]

[1] This was given to the Club in October 1894 by Mr. Keith Douglas 'on the part of Mr. Hugh Gough Arbuthnot'.

and the list of 1825 Debenture subscribers referred to on page 41 (note 3).

Dealing with the rooms I have so far described was no great problem for the Committee and Mr. Daydon Griffiths, their architect—it was largely a matter of sympathetic redecoration, and furnishing either with the best of the old Hanover Square pieces or with appropriate additions. The question of a Private Dining Room was settled by assigning the Library and its ante-room to this purpose when necessary; the Club Christmas card for 1967 showed how handsomely this works out.

The Library, however, continues to function as a depository and disseminator of books! And here, as in the case of the Club portraits, a difficult policy decision had to be made at the time of the move. The old Hanover Square Library had no doubt become a somewhat inert collection, and it was felt that there ought to be a fresh start. Messrs. Knight, Frank and Rutley were therefore asked to sell the greater part of the books by auction, and on 18 December 1961 this was done in 227 lots. Apart from one or two outstanding items—a run of 219 volumes of the Hakluyt Society publications fetched £2,000—the prices were modest and the total of £5,846 5s. 0d. obtained was hardly vital at a time when (for once!) the Club was not pressed for cash.

On the debit side, several books written or presented, or both, by famous early members such as Sir John Malcolm, Sir Henry Pottinger and James Fergusson, passed into the dealers' hands. The result is that the present Honorary Librarian has had to fill some unnecessary gaps, as well as acquiring new works, but the Committee's aim of building up a really significant collection (especially for the British-Indian period) is being steadily achieved.

The real challenge to the architect's ingenuity lay with the problem of bedrooms. Even after the Guthrie and Derby extensions, Stratford House had not been lavishly equipped in this respect. Now the target was some 14 double bedrooms mostly with private bathrooms, 17 single bedrooms (three with private bathrooms) and all the additional bathrooms and service quarters required. No amount of juggling with the existing bedroom space could provide the necessary cubic footage. There was only Lord Derby's ballroom left.

Accordingly, with the decorative features dismantled but with the Marylebone Lane façade and even the great bay window still intact, it suffered the strange fate of having two floors of extremely neat and functional bedrooms built into it. It is above the upper tier, of course, that Sir Charles Allom's ceiling already referred to survives.

For the rest, the bringing-up-to-date of Stratford House might be called a plumbing job, on the noblest scale. Lord Derby left no mean legacy in the way of basement kitchens and servants' quarters, but everything had to be scrambled and re-equipped, to meet modern needs. There were to be no more relays of runners between kitchens and dining room lifts! And above the basement level there were Men's Rooms[1] and Powder Rooms, Pantries and Serveries to be jig-sawed in as unobtrusively as possible. And though 'living in' has been greatly reduced, there is still quite a lot of staff accommodation tucked away here and there either in the main building or the 'cottage' which nestles in the angle of Stratford House and No. 12, and which may well date from a remote past.

In fact, Stratford House has at last reached a standard of comfort and efficiency, a balance of domestic snugness and public *panache*, adequate to the needs of its lordliest occupants—of the Esterhazys and Lievens, the Archdukes and Grand Dukes, who pigged it in such insanitary splendour under this same roof a century and a half ago!

[1] The main Men's Room, facing Stratford Place to the west of the Entrance Hall, occupies one of the original apartments of the house, once used by the Steward, but labelled 'Lord Stanley's Room' on a Derby House plan. Lord Stanley (the Earl of Derby's eldest son) later occupied the old Dower House, No. 12.

12 *Change, no Decay*

We still retain our old characteristics—a sort of oasis of peace and comfort in the midst of a rather bewildered world.

Thomas McMorran, at the Annual General Meeting, 1931

A member of the Oriental was lunching with a friend at an eminent club in Pall Mall. During their preliminary drink, his host looked round the bar with quiet satisfaction. 'I like this place', he said. 'I don't know any of the members, and I don't want to.'

One brand of English clubmanship carried to extremes! Its opposite may be represented by that establishment in Brook Street, thinly disguised by Evelyn Waugh as the Greville, where the taste for general conversation in the dining room was so strong that service was made almost impossible by members at the centre table leaning back to chat with those along the sides.

The Oriental, in its Stratford House phase, seems to follow a *via media*. In the Bar, under the genial influence of Ramm[1], members who have not met before will positively converse, especially if the place is not full, while pleasant 'Good mornings' and remarks about the weather are freely exchanged elsewhere. On the other hand, attempts to establish a centre table in the Dining Room on Greville lines have not caught on. This may be in part a legacy from Hanover Square where, though communal tables existed, the traditional favourites were those placed side by side along the wall[2], whereby talking to one's neighbour was strictly optional.

Whether the Club is less sociable, because less cohesive, than in its strictly 'oriental' days, or more so because there are fewer in-

[1] G. E. G. Ramm, Barman, in the service of the Club since 1936.

[2] The row under the Hanover Square windows was known as the Flying Nine, and used to be laid up two or three times a night in 'the old days'.

flamed livers about, is an arguable question. But its atmosphere has been definitely changed by its altered membership and by the easier manners of today, coupled with a third influence, the pervasive presence of ladies.

It is many years now since the non-Eastern element, once allowed in on sufferance, began to be actively encouraged. As long ago as 1931 Sir Alfred Pickford was reminding members that the rules 'nowhere lay down that past or present overseas residence is an essential qualification for membership' and that there were already plenty of exceptions. An analysis made during the 1951 crisis showed that out of 817 men elected during the previous 17 years (while numbers had remained more or less static at just under 900), 439 were or had been resident in India; 79 were or had been resident in other Eastern countries; 65, though generally resident in the U.K., had Eastern connections. This made a total of 583 from 'traditional' sources, against 234 'non-traditional'.

I have not worked out a comparable analysis for our own time but a run-through of the 120 candidates elected in 1967 gives the striking result that almost exactly two-thirds of them could claim close ties with the territories East of Suez—or at least of Table Bay!

It is the Eastern element which has naturally provided those 'family' memberships which are always prized by a club. I have already mentioned the ancient dynasties of the Colvins, the Stracheys and the Arbuthnots. One hardly less remarkable link with the earliest days is still unbroken. This may be described as the 'Dirom/Crawford connection'.

The story begins with Lieut.-General Alexander Dirom, the veteran of Seringapatam (see page 117). He had 10 children, including two sons William and Thomas, both of the Bengal Establishment, who were elected to the Club in 1855 and 1859 respectively. A third son, Alexander, had a daughter Christina who married James Alexander Crawford, East India merchant and son of a Bombay Civil Servant. James Alexander, like his cousin Robert Wigram (e. 1843), was an enthusiastic Oriental man. Having been elected in 1860, he was thrice Chairman in the eighties (a rare distinction) and no problem or proposal was too small for his attention—he may even have been the 'Mr. Crawford' who persuaded the Committee to try an anti-cockroach specific which yielded a harvest of three bushels!

More memorably, J. A. Crawford proposed in the year 1888 the simultaneous election of three of his sons, Dirom, James Muir and Malcolm. All three survived to be entertained by the Club to a Jubilee Lunch in 1938, and to receive a congratulatory message from the King. The line is continued today with Malcolm's son Mr. K. M. Crawford (now in Australia) and less directly with his wife's nephew, Mr. Etienne Verniquet, while Miss Diana Crawford, daughter of a fourth brother, Alexander, is Secretary to the Royal Asiatic Society, birthplace of the Oriental[1].

As far as I know there is nothing else to compare with this, but a few father-to-son memberships extending through three generations and covering a wide span of years may be mentioned. I have in mind, for example, the Cumberleges—the late Francis Henry Cumberlege (e. 1891)[2], Mr. C. F. Cumberlege (e. 1930) and Mr. F. M. Cumberlege (e. 1948); the Chettles—the late E. A. Chettle (e. 1908), Mr. J. E. Chettle (e. 1931) and Messrs A. R. and J. M. Chettle (e. 1968); and the Findlays. The latter have so far comprised three brothers—Charles (e. 1904, Chairman 1934), Henry (e. 1914) and James (e. 1921); James's three sons James and John (both e. 1934) and Charles (e. 1952), together with John's son Dr. John (e. 1967) and Charles' son Peter (e. 1961).

In spite of such dynastic bonds with the 'oriental' world, there were those in 1951, and again in 1961, who felt that the old name was itself a discouragement to recruiting, and that if the Club was to restart elsewhere it had better do so under a less restrictive title. An additional argument brought forward by Mr. C. F. Maxwell (A.G.M. 1961) was that 'Oriental' suggested to taxi-drivers and others 'a

[1] Lieut.-Colonel Dirom Crawford died in 1942 and Lieut.-Colonel Muir Crawford and Mr. Malcolm Crawford in 1947. The Club possesses an inscribed photograph showing them together at the Jubilee gathering. I am grateful to Miss Crawford and Mr. Verniquet for their help with this Dirom/Crawford pedigree.

[2] Mr. Cumberlege can, I think, be acclaimed as the Club's second oldest member ever. He reached his hundredth birthday on 1 May 1955, when the Committee sent him a message of congratulation, and he died on 1 July following; he therefore fell short of the celebrated Mr. Macauley's span (pp. 122–3) by exactly two months.

shady dive in Soho'[1]; he offered 'Stratford Club' as an alternative. But the general sentiment was against him. And though one still hears plenty of Calcutta gossip round the Bar, the current admixture of London business and professional men—including a contingent from Harley Street, linked so indissolubly with the Oriental's fortunes!—makes Club life and conversation less 'shoppy' than of old.

There is one direction, by the way, in which the Club would seem, superficially, to have become *more* 'in-grown' since the move to Stratford House. I refer to the marked decline in invitations to distinguished men from overseas to become Honorary Members. We saw the custom originate as far back as 1831, and in the present century it assumed rather grandiose dimensions. The names are impressive enough—practically all the great Maharajahs in 1902; Borden and Laurier of Canada, Botha of South Africa, Deakin of Australia and Ward of New Zealand in 1907; Maharajahs and Premiers again, with lesser fry to a total of 70, in 1911; followed by Smuts and other War leaders in 1917, Mackenzie King and Stanley Bruce in 1923, 44 variegated names in 1937, and a strong Indian contingent (including 'Ranji') in 1942.

But as one or two of the dates will have hinted, these were for the most part mass invitations to Coronation or Imperial Conference delegates, who were no doubt offered a similar compliment by other clubs. Nor do more isolated elections, such as those of 'Maréchal de France Lyautey' in 1928 or 'Lieut.-General D. Eisenhower' in 1942, necessarily indicate a strong personal link with the Oriental. Nowadays, with V.I.P.s flying in and out every week, and even Commonwealth Conferences being far from cheery family gatherings, the tradition has become somewhat pointless, and I doubt whether many members are even conscious of its decline.

Reverting to the main tides of change, I do not think there is any question but that our modern manners are more genial. The alleged 'moroseness' of the nabob has several times been mentioned, and assuredly the Oriental has had its quota, equal maybe to the Service

[1] This actually happened to a friend of mine. Arriving all innocent from the East, he was invited by his Chairman to a state lunch at the Oriental. He took a cab, but his driver slightly misheard, and in no time the unfortunate young man found himself up two flights of stairs and through a bead curtain. He was very late for lunch.

clubs'[1], of gruff old bears with whom one passed the time of day at one's peril. Perhaps we have at last grown out of those trivial yet bad-blooded disputes over the opening or shutting of windows and doors which, according to a note by Francis Mathewson, still made the Inner Library a scene of acrimony during the early 1900s; and since there are now no rooms where silence is enjoined, there is nothing to provoke black looks or poker-rattling by the Mr. Havisides of 1968.

However, the greatest social change has undoubtedly been the conversion of the Oriental into a *mixed* club—since that is what it now is in practice. Associate membership for the female relatives of members dates of course from the 1951 reforms, and after that desegregation progressed until in Hanover Square's last days ladies walked boldly in through the front door and up the main staircase to the Smoking Room, where they had already been long accustomed to take their drinks and coffee with the men (by a freak of nomenclature, the Drawing Room remained 'men only' till the end).

Yet the psychological difference at Stratford House is great. It goes back to the days of the 2nd Earl of Aldborough! He was an illusionist, and in the modest-sized house which he contrived to make so impressive, he put everything he had got into the staircase and the first-floor reception rooms behind the stately south façade. It is in these rooms that mixed parties assemble, or Associate Members entertain their friends, and though of course the men use them too, and with appreciation, they do so in a distinctively feminine ambience. For their own domain they have the north-facing Smoking Room, where by chance or genius, the old Hanover Square atmosphere has been wonderfully re-created, and the Dining Room, to which no ray of sun penetrates either! Only in the Bar do they have a bit of eighteenth-century gaiety and sunshine all to themselves.

'Does this mean that when I am walking down the corridor in my dressing gown *I might meet a woman*?', asked a horrified member when the idea of married couples using the Club bedrooms was first broached. It did indeed, and the peril is one to which the men are

[1] There are some fearful examples in Major-General Sir Louis Jackson, *History of the United Service Club* (London, 1937).

exposed almost anywhere in Stratford House. But they are hardened to it now, and neither the Club as an organism nor the graceful old building which shelters it is imaginable today as the exclusive haunt of celibates or of married men on the run.

I have said that our modern manners are more genial. They are also much less *ceremonious*, and that I think goes to the heart of things when we take a last look at what the Oriental Club means to its members in 1968. Few of them, I fancy, regret the more formal past—in fact a keener sense of 'what's what', or rather 'what *was* what' is probably retained by a handful of the older servants. Parsons remembers when there were three valets and two or three boys in attendance on fewer bedrooms than he manages with one assistant today. This is of course because valeting as such is virtually extinct. 'Why', he says, 'those old members would never have thought of unpacking their own suitcases; they relied on me to do that, *and* to lay out their evening clothes, put studs in their shirts, see that the boys ran their baths, and practically dress some of them.' It is an odd reflection that those who are still used to this sort of personal service in the East take for granted its disappearance when they get home, even in nooks and crannies like the Oriental where the ideal still lingers.

In the same way, the majority of members take far less trouble over what they eat and drink. Perhaps *too* little—they are almost too aware of what is and is not possible in modern Club catering, and are pleased enough to be assured by 'lodgers' that the Oriental menus are superior to their own. The wine cellar, though zealously maintained, has fewer devotees. Hand in hand with drinking less discriminatingly goes simply drinking *less*. Whereas it was a common thing 30 years ago for Alice to find herself opening nine or 10 bottles of whisky in the course of a busy evening in the Drawing Room and Card-Room, today the evening staff make do with two or three. How much of this is a true social change and how much purely a matter of *tax* (on the drinker and the drink) I would hesitate to guess.

Yet, compared with the immediate past, the Club presents a more animated scene, even in the evenings, when West End clubs are, by definition, 'dead'. One certainly got that impression towards the end in Hanover Square. I wonder how many readers have shared the eerie experience of dining *absolutely alone* in the Coffee Room? Of sitting securely planted against one of the end walls, with no other mental resource than to gaze down the great shining vista and count the empty chairs?[1] Nowadays the number of diners has increased quite substantially and they 'dress the house' (if not themselves!) much better; moreover as often as not there is a cocktail party or private dinner in the Library to give a sense of *va-et-vient*. Particularly is this so in summer, when the garden is also brought into requisition and the guests assemble under the great *shamiana* or ceremonial awning, recently presented by Lord Inchcape.

Except on such occasions, it must be confessed, the garden is more looked down into than used. Perhaps the very word 'garden' should be put into inverted commas; apart from the immortal fig-tree, it has had more the nature of a courtyard since Messrs. Birfield, needing a car park, substituted a rather charming pattern of cobbles and tiles for the bedraggled grass which they inherited. But walk down the steps from the Library and look back. You get a really uproarious comment on Lord Aldborough as illusionist. Though there has been endless pulling-about since his time, it is patent that even the 'veneer' with which he dressed up the public face of Stratford House was never carried round the back. There is simply *nothing there*, except a plain flat wall of London stock brick. What the garden does provide for the members and their guests is a sense of quiet and enclosure miraculous at this point in time and space.

GAME OF POOL

Great injury having been done to the cloths by gentlemen throwing their money on the tables, it is requested that the practice be discontinued.

Notice, September 1851

It is naturally tempting, in a book of this kind, to linger over customs, traditions, mere habits, which have long passed out of view. There is so little billiards today that a whole mystique connected with the game has been lost and it is many a year since the Club last 'entertained' a marker. Card-playing too has dwindled. No modern

[1] Finally, the Coffee Room was closed, and all dinners were normally served in the Strangers' Room. The main Dining Room is used in the same way in the new Clubhouse.

waiter is likely to grow fat on a racket in the disposal of used cards such as arose in the last century; the tightening up which followed, reveals, incidentally, that the 1966 'innovation' of producing cards with the Club badge was no novelty at all:

> Colonel Metcalfe having asked whether he can buy Club cards with the Elephant from Messrs. Whittingham & Co., to be told that by waiting his turn he can have second-hand Club cards at 6d. a pack.
>
> Minute, January 1886

Debasement of the coinage has abolished a whole range of antique notions. We shall never return to the day when the Head Waiter haughtily declined to accept gold sovereigns unless he was allowed to weigh them first; when even the silver was 'rubbed or polished with a leather' before being given as change; and when nothing was charged at less than 6d. so as to avoid the necessity of gentlemen carrying nasty coppers about with them.

In the Dining Room, no member is given even a chance of 'hacking about the joints and disfiguring them' while carving for himself. On the other hand, he can reserve a table without going through the ritual of turning a plate upside down. This custom caused a fracas in 1828 between Lieut.-Colonel Barker and the Head Waiter, who had accidentally 'turned his plate back again' while changing the cloth. The curious thing is that within a few years the rule of 'first come, first served' in the Coffee Room had become rigidly established and the reservation of tables was frowned upon right up until the move from Hanover Square.

One old-fashioned rite which survived there and charmed many a guest was the removal of the cloth before dessert; there was a certain grandeur in consuming one's banana behind a square of shining mahogany....

It is possible, of course, that the next generation of members, queueing up at the self-service counter or buying their drinks from an automatic machine, will look back on 1968 with nostalgia. They may even come to regard the present membership as a delicious set of old oddities. When I first discussed this book with Mr. Samuel Carr of Batsfords he remarked 'Plenty of *eccentrics*, I hope', and I would like to think that his wishes have been met. We can hardly expect to see another Lytton Strachey, leaving his trousers with the Invisible Mending people in Piccadilly Circus and lunching at the Oriental with an ulster wrapped round those long, long legs of his. But at the moment the Club does not seem even to be producing successors to Mr. X, who not long ago used to scuttle round the rooms pulling out all the light and power plugs, or Mr. Y who insisted on sleeping in an all-black bed in an all-black bedroom, or Mr. Z, who regularly descended to the Drawing Room in his nightie and sat by the fire until coaxed back to bed in the early hours by Alice. . . .

Mention of that famous name brings me to my final word, which will be about the Oriental Club staff. We have seen them pass through the phases of rather sordid *laissez-faire* and of vigorous community life based largely on sport. Both have vanished—the former mainly by the intervention of the State, the latter because of 'living out' and the increase in part-time employment. The Recreation Fund exists no longer and, in accordance with modern needs, the old Provident Fund has been 'frozen' and a Pensions Scheme has taken its place.

It is commonly said that when the present small group of long-service employees passes away they will have no successors. We need not be too sure of that. The 'stayers' never were more than a minority, and though the proportion of 'floaters' today is high, there are several among the later comers, of various nationalities, to whom Oriental Club life seems specially congenial, and who may ripen into the 'old stagers' of tomorrow. If they do not, it will be almost entirely on economic grounds—the familiar story of higher wages (plus tips!) beckoning from the commercial world; if they do, the Oriental Club will continue to be 'an assembly of good fellows' in a wider sense than even Dr. Johnson dreamed.

APPENDIX I

Founders of the Oriental Club

The signatures of the following appear on the original prospectus of the Club and they constituted the first Committee:

His Grace the Duke of Wellington, K.G., President.
The Rt. Hon. Lord William C. Bentinck, G.C.B.
The Rt. Hon. Charles Williams-Wynn.
Vice-Admiral Sir Richard King, Bt., K.C.B.
Vice-Admiral Sir Pulteney Malcolm, K.C.B.
Major-General Sir John Malcolm, G.C.B., K.L.S.
General Sir Alured Clarke, G.C.B.
General Sir George Nugent, Bt., G.C.B.
Lieut.-General Sir Thomas Hislop, G.C.B.
Lieut.-General Sir Miles Nightingall, K.C.B.
Major-General Robert Haldane, C.B., Colonel 26th Bengal N.I.
Rear-Admiral Lambert.
Major-General Rumley.
Colonel Baron Tuyll.
Colonel Alston.
Colonel Baillie, M.P.
Alexander Boswell, Esq.
David Colvin, Esq.
Major Carnac.
N. B. Edmonstone, Esq.
John Elphinstone, Esq.
Major Harding.
James Hallett, Esq.
D. Hemming, Esq.
Major-General Sir Patrick Ross.
Sir George Staunton, Bt., M.P.
Sir Charles Forbes, Bt., M.P.
Sir Robert Farquhar, Bt.
Sir Christopher Cole, K.C.B., M.P.
Major-General Malcolm Grant.
Colonel Robert Houstoun, C.B., 6th Bengal Light Cavalry.
Colonel Hull.
A. Macklew, Esq.
Colonel Nugent.
C. E. Pigou, Esq.
Colonel Ranken.
Colonel George Raban, C.B.
J. G. Remington, Esq.
Thomas Snodgrass, Esq.
William Sotheby, Esq.
William H. Trant, Esq.
Henry Saint George Tucker, Esq.
J. Ruddell Todd, Esq.
Colonel Weguelin.

APPENDIX II

The Picture Collection

The following is a list of the Club's collection of portraits and other oil paintings. The portraits are listed in alphabetical order of subjects. The position where the pictures were hanging at the time of going to press is also indicated.

'ALICE' (Miss E. E. Moore). In the service of the Oriental Club since 1916.
By Margaret Aldridge.
Presented by Mr. James McFarlane, 1958. (*Bar*)

BARNEWALL, Colonel Robert. Born (?). Served in Bombay Army. Retired 1833. Member of the Oriental Club (e. 1829). Died 1848.
By Robert Home 'Historical Painter to the King of Oudh', well known for his many Indian subjects.
Presented by two members, Messrs. Warden and Williamson Ramsay, 1850. (*Writing Room*)

BRUCE, Sir Arthur. Chairman, Oriental Club, 1954–5, 1958–62.
By Charles Eastman.
Bought by the Club, 1962. (*Grand Staircase*)

CARNAC, Sir James Rivett, 1st Bt. Born 1785 as James Rivett, but took the name of Carnac in honour of his great-uncle, Clive's second-in-command. Soldier, East India Company Chairman and Governor of Bombay (1838–9). Original Committee Member of Oriental Club. Died 1878.
By H. W. Pickersgill, R.A. He produced an enormous number of portraits during his long life (1782–1875 and had his studio at No. 14 Stratford Place from 1851 to 1866. The handling is free and fresh—no suggestion of hackwork. In the Royal Academy ('painted for the Oriental Club'), 1840.
Bought by subscription. (*Drawing Room*).

CHURCHILL, Sir Winston ('Mr. Bullfinch'). Born 1874. Prime Minister 1940–5, 1951–5. Died, 1967.

By L. Burrell, 1943. Painted soon after Mr. Churchill (as he then was) had visited the Middle East under the *nom de guerre* of 'Mr. Bullfinch'.

Presented by Brigadier-General H. A. Jones. *(Bar)*

CLIVE, Robert, 1st Lord. Born 1725. Died 1774. No further biographical details are needed here!

One of several very similar portraits of Clive (but not less fine and moving for that) produced by Nathaniel Dance, son of the architect George Dance the Younger, who was Surveyor to the City of London in connection with the building of Stratford House.

The provenance is curious. As early as 29 June 1829, the Committee had thought of asking Clive's son, the Earl of Powis, to present the Club with a portrait of his great father. It was decided to postpone this for the time being, but five years later the gift was made—whether unsolicited or otherwise does not appear. The 'Senior' was allowed to have a copy taken of this picture in 1851. *(Bar)*

CLOSE, Major-General Sir Barry, 1st Bt. Born 1756. Saw service at Seringapatam (1792 and 1799). First British Resident at Mysore. Baronet 1812, but died the following year.

From a family portrait. The copyist was called Moore, but the name of the original artist is unknown.

Presented by Colonel Robert Close, nephew of Sir Barry and himself an Original Member. *(Bar)*

COMPTON, Sir Herbert. Born 1770. Chief Justice of Bombay. Member of the Oriental (e. 1830). Died 1846.

By R. R. Reinagle, R.A., another very long-lived artist (1775–1862). Member of an interesting family—his father was Philip Reinagle, eighteenth-century Court painter. This picture was in the Royal Academy of 1832.

Presented by Compton's daughter, Mrs. Skirrow. *(Writing Room)*

COOTE, Lieut.-General Sir Eyre. Born 1726. Went to India with the old 39th Regiment—'*Primus in Indis*'. Won fame against the French and Hyder Ali in the Carnatic. Died 1783.

Artist unknown, but a portrait of strong character.

Given to the Club by the executors of Thomas Snodgrass in 1835. *(Drawing Room)*

CORNWALLIS, Charles, 1st Marquess. Born 1738. Governor-General of India, 1786–93 and again in 1805. Died the same year.

By Samuel Lane, a pupil of Lawrence. In this three-quarter-length portrait, Cornwallis is wearing the Blue Ribbon of the Garter. Background shows the City of Seringapatam, with the British flag flying. Lord Cornwallis figures also, of course, in Mather Brown's big picture (see page 114).

Bought by subscription. *(Bar)*

CURZON of KEDLESTON, George Nathaniel, 1st Marquess. Born 1859. Viceroy and Governor-General of India, 1899–1905. Died 1925.

By Alfred Hayward, after John Singer Sargent, R.A.

Bought out of the J. A. Apcar Bequest, 1921. *(Ante-Room)*

EDWARD VII, H.M. King. Born 1841. King-Emperor, 1901–10. Died 1910.

By Sir Luke Fildes, R.A. (replica).

Bought by subscription, 1911. *(Writing Room)*

ELPHINSTONE, The Rt. Hon. Mountstuart. Born 1778. Made his name in the Wellesley era. Governor of Bombay, 1819. Said to have refused the Governor-Generalship three times. Original Member of the Oriental Club. Died 1859.

By Pickersgill—fine and thoughtful, like its subject[1]. In the Royal Academy, 1839.

Bought by subscription during Elphinstone's lifetime (1839). Copied for Mr. Richard Strachey (1841) and used as a model for the Elphinstone monument in St. Paul's Cathedral. *(Smoking Room)*

FRASER, Captain John Small Henry, of the East India Company's Navy (1803–29).

By James Sant.

Given, together with the following, by their great-niece, Mrs. Saunders, in 1908.

FRASER, General William Charles. Madras Army (1798–1839). Served at the Battle of Assaye.

By James Sant.

Presented as above. *(Drawing Room)*

GOUGH, Field-Marshal Hugh, 1st Viscount. Born 1779. Served under Wellington in the Peninsula; Commander-in-Chief, India, 1842; the hero of Chilianwallah. Honoured by the Oriental Club at a dinner, 1850. Died 1869.

[1] He must have been a handsome boy when, in the post-Bastille epoch (not unlike our own), 'the hair which he wore down his back was intended to be the outward sign of his revolutionary sentiments'—Sir John Kaye, *Lives of the Indian Officers, Mountstuart Elphinstone* (London, Strahan, 1867).

By Lowes Dickinson (1819–1908).
Bought by subscription at the auction of Lowes Dickinson's Gallery, New Bond Street, 1864. Copied in 1907 for Lord Kitchener's house at Simla. *(Smoking Room)*

HASTINGS, Francis, 1st Marquess of. Born 1753. Served in America and Holland. Governor-General of India (1813–20). Died 1825.
By Samuel Lane.
Presented by Sir Charles Forbes, Bt. (Original Member), 1836.

HASTINGS, The Rt. Hon. Warren. Born 1753. Died 1818. As with Clive, a 'potted biography' would be an impertinence. The Club has two portraits:

1 By John James Masquerier, an artist of French parentage, who had mysterious adventures in Paris during the Revolution and the Directory. It is not a great work of art, but strikes one as a carefully achieved likeness. In the Royal Academy, 1809. *(Drawing Room)*

Also given by Sir Charles Forbes[1].

2 By Bright Morris, after Sir Thomas Lawrence. Presented by Mr. A. Murray-Smith in 1929. *(Ante-Room)*

JEJEEBHOY, Sir Jamsetjee, 1st Bt. Born 1783. Parsee philanthropist, much esteemed by Queen Victoria. Died 1859.
By John Smart. No fewer than three artists of this name worked in India during the late eighteenth and early nineteenth centuries. The two best known (father and son) were miniaturists. The third, who painted this picture, seems to have specialised in portraits.
Presented by Lady Isabella Fitzgibbon in 1852. See page 112 and *Pl. 8.* *(Writing Room)*

The Club also possesses a small marble bust of the famous Parsee, presented by Mr. R. W. Crawford in 1878. *(Library)*

KITCHENER of KHARTOUM, Field-Marshal Herbert, 1st Earl. Born 1850. Commander-in-Chief, India, 1902–9. Secretary of State for War, 1914–16. Drowned at sea, 1916.
By the Hon. John Collier (replica).
Bought by subscription, 1916. *(Smoking Room)*

[1] The first Minutes of the Committee record a different but no less welcome gift from Sir Charles—'a fine Turtle'. For a comparable gesture we have to wait until the early 1920s, when Mr. A. Mair formed the pleasant habit of sending the members an annual Tay salmon, usually about 22 lbs. in weight.

LAKE, Gerard, 1st Viscount. Born 1744. One of the great military figures of India; Commander-in-Chief, 1800. Died 1808.

This somewhat primitive rendering of a strong, wise face is by an unknown artist. It was used as the model for a bust of Lake, a replica of which was presented to the Club by the Rajah of Khetri in 1897. (*Pl. 13*)

Painting acquired by subscription[1].

(*Painting in Smoking Room, Bust in Ante-Room*)

LANSDOWNE, Henry, 5th Marquess of. Born 1845. Viceroy and Governor-General of India, 1888–1894. Died 1927.

By Sydney P. Kenrick, after John Singer Sargent, R.A.

Bought out of the J. A. Apcar Bequest, 1921. (*Dining Room*)

LAWRENCE, Major-General Stringer. Born 1697. First British Commander-in-Chief in India. Died 1775.

Artist unknown, but attributed to Sir Joshua Reynolds. The National Portrait Gallery has a painting of Lawrence by Gainsborough.

It is appropriate that 'the father of the Indian Army' should have been the subject of the Club's first picture; it was presented by Thomas Snodgrass in 1824. (*Dining Room*)

LINLITHGOW, John, 1st Marquess of. Born 1860. First Governor-General of Australia, 1900–2. Died 1908.

By J. Quin, after Brough.

Bought by subscription, 1916. (*Smoking Room*)

MALCOLM, Major-General Sir John. Born 1769. First Chairman of the Oriental Club. Died 1833.

For his career and connection with the Club see page 24 *et seq.*; for the acquisition of this portrait, see page 109. (*Pl. 3.*)

By Samuel Lane.

Bought by subscription. (*Grand Staircase*)

MAYO, Richard, 6th Earl of. Born 1822. Viceroy and Governor-General of India, 1868–1872. Assassinated 1872.

By the Hon. John Collier. Painted from 'a very large photograph in the possession of Captain Lockwood'.

Bought by subscription. (*Writing Room*)

MEHEMET ALI. Born 1769. Viceroy of Egypt. Died 1849. For his

[1] It was this picture which, in its massive original state, might well have caused casualties when it fell from the wall of the Strangers' Room not long before the move to Stratford House. Fortunately it missed those having dinner just below, and landed upright.

connection with the Club, see page 66; for the acquisition of this portrait, see page 110.
By Thomas Brigstocke.
Acquired by a 'deal' with the artist. (*Smoking Room*)

METCALFE, Charles, 1st Lord. Born 1785. Died 1846. For his career and honours paid him by the Club, see page 65. For the story of this portrait see page 113.
By F. R. Say, 1843.
Bought by subscription. (*Writing Room*)

MUNRO, Major-General Sir Thomas, 1st Bt. One of the great 'makers of India' along with Malcolm, Metcalfe and Elphinstone. Governor of Madras, 1819–1826. Died of cholera in 1827. 'Sir Thomas joined the Club in 1824, but he could never have entered it' (Baillie). (*Pl. 9.*)
By R. R. Reinagle.
Bought by subscription about 1834. (*Drawing Room*)

NOTT, Major-General Sir William. Born 1782. Won fame as commander of the Army of Kandahar in the Afghan War. Died 1845.
By Brigstocke. See page 111.
Apparently painted for the Club soon after Nott returned from India in 1844 and was made an Honorary Member. (*Writing Room*)

OCHTERLONY, Major-General Sir David, 1st Bt. Born 1758. After service in the Mahratta Wars was resident at Delhi. His victories in Nepal were rewarded with the K.C.B., the first ever conferred on a Company's officer. Ochterlony was a legendary figure in the old East Indian style—hence a fine piece of folklore from his Delhi days about 'the gallant soldier's thirteen wives taking the air on thirteen elephants'. Died 1825.
By Reinagle—a posthumous portrait, which was in the 1837 Royal Academy. Originally it was a dashing piece of work—the artist got the best of all worlds by portraying his subject on the field of battle, but in full levee dress. Of these accoutrements only his wind-blown cocked hat remains. A loss.
Bought by subscription. (*Drawing Room*)

OUTRAM, Lieut.-General Sir James, 1st Bt. Born 1803. Died 1863. The only Mutiny hero to figure in the Oriental portrait gallery. For his other links with the Club, see page 83.
By Brigstocke.
Bought by subscription. In the Royal Academy ('painted for the Oriental Club'), 1863. Like the portraits of Barnewall, Gough, Lake and

Pollock, it was thus acquired well within the period of 70 years before 1910, referred to by the Committee in that year (see page 108).
(*Dining Room*)

POLLOCK, Field-Marshal Sir George, 1st Bt. Born 1786. Shared the honours of the Afghan War with Sir William Nott, and one would like to see their portraits hung side by side. Died 1872.
By Lane.
Bought by subscription. (*Drawing Room*)

POTTINGER, Lieut.-General Sir Henry, 1st Bt. Born in Ulster 1789. Soldier, traveller and diplomat. Envoy to China 1841–3. Governor of Madras, 1847–54. Member of Oriental Club (e. 1830).
By Sir Francis Grant, P.R.A., an artist essentially of the Victorian age. Pottinger is in civilian clothes, and the picture causes one to speculate: If he had been painted by Reinagle or Pickersgill, would he have looked quite so like the Prince Consort?
Bought by subscription. (*Writing Room*)

ROBERTS of Kandahar, V.C., Field-Marshal, 1st Earl. Born 1832. Commander-in-Chief, India, 1885–1893. Died 1914.
By F. M. Shipworth, after John Singer Sargent, R.A.
Acquired by subscription. (*Smoking Room*)

SNODGRASS, Thomas. Born 1759. The famous Collector of Ganjam (see page 25), and benefactor of the Oriental Club. Died 1834.
Painted in India by an unknown artist and acquired by the Marine Society after the death of Snodgrass, who had been on their Committee since 1819. The Society (owners of the training ship *Warspite*) gave it to the Oriental in 1957. See *Memories of Madras* by Sir Charles Lawson (London, Swan Sonnenschein, 1905). (*Pl. 4*). (*Ante-Room*)

STRACHEY, Lieut.-General Sir Richard. Born 1817.
By Lowes Dickinson (painted 1889).
Bequest of Jane Maria, Lady Strachey, 1929. (*Drawing Room*)

TIPPOO SAHIB. Born 1753. The warlike Sultan of Mysore, with whom the Club has so many links. Killed at Seringapatam, 1799.
By an Indian artist. Clearly copied, but with simplified background, from the picture by G. F. Cherry, once in the possession of Lord Wellesley and now in the India Office Library. An engraving of that original forms the frontispiece to Lieut.-Colonel Alexander Beatson's *A View of the Origin and Conduct of the War with Tippoo Sultaun*

(London, G. and W. Nichol, 1800) (O.C.L.), and the comparison is highly interesting.

Presented by Mr. G. W. Gent in 1848. (*Ante-Room*)

WELLESLEY, Richard, 1st Marquess. Born 1760. Governor-General of India, 1798–1805; later Secretary of State for Foreign Affairs and Lord-Lieutenant of Ireland. Died 1842.

The Club has two portraits, both the gifts of members, but neither is outstanding:

1 After Sir Thomas Lawrence.

Presented by Mr. John Wilton in 1833. (*Drawing Room*)

2 By Robert Home, painted in India, probably in 1805.

Presented by Benjamin Sydenham, to whom it was given by Wellesley himself. (*Ante-Room*)

WELLINGTON, Arthur, 1st Duke of. Born 1769. First and only President of the Oriental Club. Died 1852.

By Pickersgill. See page 110 and *Pl. 2*.

Bought by subscription. (*Library*)

Also in the Library is a small bust of Wellington, given by Mr. William Harwood in 1912.

Addendum. In 1968 the Club acquired a portrait of Edward Stratford, 2nd Earl of Aldborough, builder of Stratford House. It is unsigned, but is attributed to Mather Brown. (*Pl. 14*.) (*Grand Staircase*)

In addition to portraits, the Club owns the following:

BROWN, Mather. 'Earl Cornwallis receiving the Sons of Tippoo Sahib as Hostages'. For Brown's career and the history of this picture see pages 114–17. (*Pl. 12*.) (*Bar*)

HERRING, J. F., Senior. 'Horse and Dog'. Presented to the Club by Dr. Lindley Scott. The late Secretary, Brigadier Callaghan, discovered this picture hidden away in the Hanover Square cellars, and had it cleaned and identified. (*Dining Room*)

KETTLE, Tilly. 'Hindu Woman Preparing for Suttee'. Believed to be identical with the 'Ceremony of a Gentoo woman taking leave of her Relations and distributing her Jewels prior to her ascending the Funeral Pile of her deceased Husband', which Tilly Kettle (1735–86) exhibited at the Free Society in 1776. The picture is said to have been brought home by Colonel Hugh Grant, who retired from the service of the East India Company in 1774. Presented by his kinsman, Mr. John Grant, in 1957. (*Dining Room*)

APPENDIX III

The team which managed the move

The members of the General Committee of the Oriental Club, who held office during the period of the move to Stratford House (1960–2), were:

Sir Arthur Bruce, K.B.E., M.C. (Chairman)
The Rt. Hon. The Earl of Inchcape (Vice-Chairman)

G. S. Bozman, C.S.I., C.I.E.
W. E. Catto
G. Fellowes
E. L. C. Gwilt
F. M. Innes, C.I.E., C.B.E.
Sir George Mackinlay
H. T. B. Morison
G. H. J. Richmond
Sir Alexander Sim
H. C. Waters, O.B.E.

The Secretary of the Club was Brigadier R. G. W. Callaghan, O.B.E.

The architect responsible for the conversion of Stratford House was Mr. Daydon Griffiths, and the contractors were Messrs. Humphreys.

The Committee were advised throughout by Sir Aynsley Bridgland, C.B.E.

Supplement 1969–78

In the past decade, there have been events or developments of one kind or another affecting almost every aspect of the Oriental Club's life. Some have been substantial, others no more than slight, if entertaining. Such material hardly lends itself to narrative, so it is offered here in the form of self-contained notes under appropriate headings with, in conclusion, a brief look at some new facts about the past history of the Stratford Place estate.

General Review of the Period. When they asked Talleyrand what he did in the French Revolution, he replied 'I survived'. If the Oriental had achieved no more than that during the ten years since the first edition of this book appeared, it could still have claimed ten years of success. The casualties in Clubland have been truly alarming, with such great names as the United Service ('The Senior'), the St. James', the Guards, the Devonshire, the Junior Carlton either disappearing altogether or being engulfed in mergers. The situation can perhaps be symbolised by the present full title of that fine old establishment in St. James's Square with which the Oriental was more than once involved in earlier times (see pp. 75–6, 79–80). Originally known as the East India United Service Club, it is now compendiously described as 'The East India, Devonshire, Sports and Public Schools Club Ltd.', and is understood to be in a flourishing condition.

What has kept the Oriental afloat and independent during this unpropitious decade? Apart from its intrinsic excellence—which members do not need to be told about and which others will have to take on trust!—it has had two assets peculiar to itself. These are: the far-sighted financial arrangements made when the Club moved from Hanover Square, and described in Chapter I; and the unhoped-for persistence and even extension of its appeal to the very people for whom it was originally founded—namely, British folk working overseas, particularly in Asian countries. To them are being added quite a number of nationals of such countries, mainly of course those who have close links with, or pay regular visits to, the United Kingdom.

I will return to finance later, but the question of membership can be pursued a little further here. The healthy state of affairs at the time of writing (Summer 1978) has not come about by accident. Membership of the Club reached its peak so far in the year 1972, when there were 1,930 full members, plus 870 Associates. Anxiety having been expressed about overcrowding, the Club's election procedures were reviewed, and to some extent tightened up, with a view to containing if not reducing numbers. However, (as has happened before) at that very moment a decline set in, mainly due to higher subscriptions and general financial stringency. By early 1975 the roll had dropped to well below the 1,800 mark, and looked like falling further.

It was at this point that an excellent decision was made—to get into touch with senior members in likely overseas territories, encouraging them to undertake recruitment and also to lighten the Election Committee's labours by doing a bit of preliminary 'vetting'. This has worked well, and has contributed to the fact that between 1975 and 1977 the membership graph rose steadily once again and the latest returns are more than encouraging.

One recalls that a rough analysis (p. 216) of elections in 1967 showed a good two-thirds with eastern or East African affiliations. 1977–8 revealed much the same pattern, Hong Kong being the No. 1 contributor. Admittedly, overseas recruitment is subject to wastage; a man may sign on more or less light-heartedly 'out East', then repent at leisure when he gets home and the demand for a much heftier subscription comes through the letter box, but only a very small minority actually vanish in this way.

One of the Committee's rightful preoccupations is to ensure that, with a large overseas business element, Stratford House is not just used as a convenient staging-post. It is with this in mind that they have been discouraging when approached about 'corporate membership', and are always cautious in the matter of 'reciprocal arrangements'.

And what about the *Pinjrapole* image? (The *what*? Perhaps you have skipped p. 122.) An analysis made in January 1978 showed that 551 members, or close on 29%, would attain the age of 65 years or over during the year; only 12½% would be under 40. The oldest member would be 98 and the youngest 18. This does not sound too good, but as Clubland goes—and even as the general population is going—it is hardly cause for serious alarm.

Incidentally, the Club's 98-year-old, Mr. E. C. Danby, elected in 1918, is also its senior member since the death in 1977 of Mr. Kenneth Warren, whose marvellous span commenced as long ago as 1912. Kenneth Warren was the quintessence of the Oriental man, with his Assam background, his wide family connections in the tea trade and his life-long devotion to the Club. 'He loved life, loved fun, loved work, loved play', said G. A. Rainey at his memorial service. It was a good epitaph[1].

Finance. It was remarked in an earlier chapter that no historian of the Oriental could avoid writing a good deal about money since the Club, throughout its long history, had never been 'in the black' for more than a few years together. The tradition persists. The Oriental is in no way exempt from the terrifying inflationary pressures which have forced so many of its contemporaries into unwilling liquidation or merger. Consider just the following figures:

	1968 £	1972 £	1977 £
Rates and Insurance	7,195	10,350	18,690
Light and Heat	5,052	6,129	17,116
Salaries, Wages, etc.	50,955	72,799	123,923

It is easy to deduce a series of operating losses. As an example, even after allowing for the Club's invaluable ground rent and investment income, which in such a year as 1972 was £13,678 after tax, this meant that for that year a deficit of £4,506 had to be debited to General Reserve.

The next conclusion is easier still. Uniquely in Clubland, Oriental subscriptions had remained unchanged since 1951. Now they had to go up. I need not enter into the various permutations considered,

[1] Kenneth Warren's own very readable little book, *Tea Tales of Assam*, incorporates family memories of the London as well as the Assam tea trade going back to the middle of the 19th century.

and in some cases put into force, for tempering the impact at the top and bottom of the age scale, but the end result was that, as from January 1975 the basic subscription for Town members was raised from £29 (inc. VAT) to £50, in January 1976 to £75 and two years later to £100. The entrance fee, too, has been involved. This is an item which, over a period of a century and a half, has provided a sort of barometer of the Club's prosperity—kept stable during uneventful periods, raised at moments of euphoria, then rapidly reduced again or even suspended when candidatures consequently slumped. One such period of suspension lasted from 1952 until 1963. The fee was then cautiously reintroduced at £26.50 and upped to £55 in 1971. For once, this did no permanent harm to recruitment, and judging by heartening lists of candidatures posted since January 1978, when there was a further rise to £75, it looks as though that particular hoodoo has been broken.

In spite of all these measures and the strictest economy in the Club's day-to-day housekeeping, the operating losses continue, but at least in 1976 and 1977 there was a comfortable net surplus instead of a deficit to go to General Reserve.

Meanwhile, there has been good husbandry, too, of that ground rent and investment income which has provided such a fortunate cushion to the Club's finances since the move from Hanover Square. The problem is that since the ground rent element is a fixed figure, any hedge against inflation can only be provided by careful management on the investment side. An alternative way of dealing with the Club's residual interest in the old site at the north-west corner of Hanover Square—namely, to sell the freehold of No. 18 and the leasehold of 1a Tenterden Street for cash down and to reinvest the proceeds—was put before an Extraordinary General Meeting in April 1973, but after an adjournment it was decided not to take any further action for the time being.

Stratford House and its Neighbours. The neighbour that really counts at this moment is the one lurking 101 ft. 9 ins. below the foundations—namely the Fleet (now Jubilee) Line of London Underground. Though this was a long-planned project, it had had scarcely a mention in public when the original edition of *The Oriental* came out. It makes, in fact, its first appearance in Club records on November 27 1968, but not until October 20 1971 does the Committee take note of the proposal to use the 'Debenham Car Park' as a works site. Since this might well involve interference with the Club's courtyard access, to say nothing of damage to the house itself, a sub-committee was prudently set up to monitor the whole operation, which it did with care and zeal.

On the whole, the consequences have not been too bad. They were rather worse, in fact, in front of Stratford House than at the back, since a miserable mess was made of the entrance to Stratford Place and even by the end of 1978 this had not been totally cleared up. The 'works site' was a rather noisy neighbour, and uncertainty still remains about its future, apart from the fact that a permanent silo-like structure has been erected more or less in the middle of it; this is understood to be a ventilation shaft for the new line.

It was mentioned on p. 202 that when the Central Line was opened in the early 1900s, its clumsy old electric locomotives set up shock waves which did damage over a wide area and even, according to Lord Derby, 'brought down' part of Stratford House! So how much worse might be the consequences of tunnelling exactly beneath the foundations of the venerable mansion? However, all that has happened so far is that during construction minor cracks and displacements appeared in various places, notably in the Clerk's office and the Ante-room. Compensation was paid to the modest tune of £1,620, and the Club was entitled to claim for any further damage up to two years after the opening of the line. The latest bulletin is merely that a few sharp ears or sensitive nervous systems are alleged to have detected faint vibrations, especially in the stillness of the night.

Modest again was the transaction whereby the Club sold to G.L.C. the freehold of its sub-soil—not, one may add, as far as the centre of the earth, but to cover the relevant zone involved in their burrowings. Asking price £1,000, bargain struck at £520. The Club, by a fascinating historical quirk, also owns the sub-soil under the Stratford Place roadway as far as Oxford Street; rights over this have likewise been transferred to the G.L.C., but here the relevant Act of Parliament does not allow for compensation.

Members of the Oriental have long valued their direct link with the City by Central, and though the Jubilee Line has been a bit of a nuisance in various ways, they will no doubt find cause to bless it too.

The recent story of surface communication is not so happy. It was in June 1972 that the G.L.C. announced its intention of closing Oxford Street to all traffic except buses and taxis. The leaflet issued at the time (with smiling pedestrian shopper and attendant child) called the scheme 'experimental', but since it involved pavement-widening and even tree-planting, on a quite extensive scale, it was obviously going to be a case of *c'est la provisoire qui dure.*

Whether the traffic congestion caused in all the much narrower adjacent thoroughfares outweighs the improvement to Oxford Street it is not my province to judge, but from the point of view of the Oriental Club and every other denizen of Stratford Place the scheme is an unmitigated pest. Access by car is not wholly denied, but is made as tortuous as possible; westwards along Wigmore Street, southwards into James Street, dog-leg into Bird Street, and a final eastward lap along Oxford Street. Repeated pleas, with Westminster City Council endorsement, for permission to cross the latter direct from Davies Street, have been haughtily rejected by the G.L.C.

Even this may not be the ultimate ordeal, since it has been recently argued that in the supposed interests of bus passengers, taxis as well as private cars ought to be banned from Oxford Street.

Stratford Place itself looks, externally, much as it did ten years ago—the surviving fragments of the 18th century untouched and with a general air of restrained and elegant spruceness, which ought always to be the keynote. There have been changes of tenancy, of course, and these have led to more internal alterations than meet the eye. For example, No. 12, the old 'dower house', has been taken over by the Chrysalis and Air Groups of record companies and linked with its neighbour, and while the resultant extensive premises are full of the most modern electronic gear, the fine ceilings and other original features have been carefully preserved. No. 12 also continues to exhibit the two or three splendid chimney-pieces which, from their resemblance to those known to have been brought into Stratford House by Lord Derby (p. 190), may have been similarly installed at No. 12 when it was the home of his son, Lord Stanley.

An extra touch of panache has been given to Stratford Place by the cleaning of the Clubhouse façade. In November 1972 an estimate was accepted of £1,758.30, plus £250 for minor repairs. The immediate result was a rather chalky whiteness, which has now toned down nicely. At the rear, almost unnoticed, pressure on the Club's sleeping accommodation has been relieved by the building of four new bedrooms on the flat roof at the north-east corner of the building. This was carried out in 1970 at a cost of £18,476.

It has to be added, though, that this most necessary construction left an unlucky legacy in the shape of a lump of concrete wedged into a waste pipe. In due course this caused a flood which, among other things, did quite serious damage to one or two of the Romanelli ceiling paintings in the Dining Room. Expert repairs were of course carried out, but the traces remain.

A similar job, though not enforced by a flood, later attracted some publicity. Readers of *The Times*, *The Field* and possibly other journals were made aware that the interesting operation of cleaning Biagio Rebecca's ceiling paintings in the Drawing Room and Writing Room was completed during the 1978 summer recess. At the same time a good deal of redecoration was carried out in colour schemes as faithful as possible to the 'Adam period' origins of Stratford House, and a number of the Club's portraits were cleaned and rehung. The latter process has converted the Bar into a 'Tipu Room' unique perhaps in London, with the fine Indian portrait of Tipu Sultan[1] himself confronting the enormous 'Hostages' painting and an excellent selection of prints ranged in support.

Early in the decade, the then Chairman referred to 'money well spent in beautifying, maintaining and improving our delightful Clubhouse', and it will be seen that the good work goes on, year after year; not the least expensive item, incidentally, has been the application of gold leaf to the enrichments in the state rooms.

One work of art has disappeared from the walls. This is the painting 'Horse and Dog', by J. F. Herring, senr. Disinterred from the cellars of Hanover Square by the late Secretary (p. 232), it had no particular relevance to the Oriental, and even though the

[1] The designation more generally accepted today, though he is 'Tippoo Sahib' in most of the Club references and in the main text of this book.

hunting subjects of this artist are in far greater demand, 'Horse and Dog' fetched a satisfactory £3,000 at Christies in 1970.

The Club's collection of portraits, on the other hand, has had an interesting addition. This is 'Sir Stewart Pears', by Oswald Birley—a documentary piece, since it shows Sir Stewart in the long-since obsolete uniform of a Commissioner of the Indian Civil Service (1931). The portrait was the gift of Mr. Etherington-Smith.

In spite of the security and insurance problems which arise nowadays, loan exhibitions seem to struggle on, and the Oriental continues its courteous custom of contributing in suitable cases; one such was certainly the Royal Asiatic Society's 150th anniversary show at the V. & A. in 1973, when the Club was represented by 'Sir John Malcolm' and 'Sir Mountstuart Elphinstone'.

Permanent departures, alas, have been a group of minor but cherished works of art, the loss of which was the cause of great disquiet. Within a short space of time no fewer than six of the Club's clocks disappeared, an epidemic of thieving which claimed among its victims the pretty French example in the Garden Room (9 September 1972) and others in the Drawing Room and Bar.

The perpetrator of one particularly regrettable theft was no doubt a specialist, since a casual burglar would hardly have selected the fine series of campaign medals, presented by Lady Leetham and kept in a glass case in the Smoking Room. This outrage, however, has had something of a happy ending. At the May 1978 A.G.M. a new series of medals, collected on behalf of the Club by Messrs I. M. Hanson and R. B. Magor, was exhibited in a setting with a map of the Indian Sub-Continent as its centre-piece. It covers the whole period of the Club's existence.

Social Life and Catering. The present generation of Oriental clubmen does not seem to go in for the grumbling and dissension which arose so frequently in the past. I asked the Secretary whether anything in particular had ruffled the members' feelings during the past decade. 'Parking fees in the Courtyard and the removal of the Elephant from the Front Hall to the Back', was his prompt reply. Both, it will be perceived, arose from much the same sense of proprietorship and tradition.

The decision to allow the parking of members' cars in the Courtyard (repaved for that very purpose by the previous occupants, Messrs Birfields) was taken in 1973, partly to keep in good repair the Club's right of access from the rear. In January 1974 a scale of parking fees was worked out, ranging from £1.50 for 24 hours down to 25p for a meal. This was, however, regarded as a niggling imposition when the members were already paying increased subscriptions, and the plan was gracefully dropped. Parking, incidentally, only operates in the winter. It is rightly felt that nothing should be allowed to interfere with enjoyment of this rare oasis, either for sitting in the sun (if any) after lunch, or for open-air cocktail parties and receptions.

The Elephant, after a brief exile, duly returned to his former place of honour in the Front Hall[1].

Apart from these more general discontents, the venerable practice of 'backing' bills continues, though very intermittently. Mild remonstrances with regard to the sardine salad ('only *one* sardine') or alleged margarine in the sandwiches take one musingly back to the days of Colonel Campbell and his outsize apple dumpling (p. 54).

The pattern of usage of the Club and its facilities has only slightly changed in recent years. There tend to be rather fewer big cocktail parties in the Library and Ante-Room, and though a corresponding increase in the number of private dinner parties may have compensated for this financially, it has given a lot more trouble to the kitchen!

Propaganda in favour of a 'mixed' bar has so far been resisted, as have proposals for a snack-bar as an alternative to the Dining Room. The arguments *against*—that it would mean the loss of the Garden Room and the certainty of reduced takings for full meals—seem to have substance.

An amenity of a quite different sort has also been canvassed. Why not a squash court? Answer: there simply isn't room, short of a devastating encroachment on the Courtyard. There would also be problems of control, changing facilities and so on.

The Oriental has never been lavishly addicted to formal Club

[1] The ancient water pipe featured on pp. 154 and 211 has now been moved upstairs.

dinners, and there have been only two during the past ten years. The first was that given to Earl Mountbatten on 19 May 1969, the other the 150th Anniversary Dinner on 29 October 1974. The latter represented a considerable whittling down of the celebrations as originally planned, when it was hoped to attract the attendance of a Great Personage. However, the dinner went off very happily, with a menu which, though excellent, was equally a whittling down from that enjoyed on the 100th Anniversary (p. 144). As a permanent memento, the Club acquired the fine long-case clock which now stands in the Inner Hall.

An initiative which had a modest success was a short programme of evening events of a social or cultural kind in late 1975 and early 1976. The more traditional summer and Christmas cocktail parties have been invariably well supported.

One sign of the times was the suspension in 1975 of the long series of Christmas cards issued by the Club. It had been reported in January of that year that half the stock of 1974 cards remained unsold, this being mainly attributed to the enormous growth in charity cards.

It is perhaps inevitable that attempts should have been made to involve a mansion of such architectural importance in the current mania for group tours of 'stately homes'. However, the Committee evidently feels that such visits would be disruptive of the family life of the inmates, and all approaches have up till now been turned down.

As in most families, the present age has seen some divergence between those who tend towards the free-and-easy and the defenders of traditional ways. As Carlyle perceived, clothes provide the surest clue. By-law 5 in the Oriental's Rule Book consists of a single sentence:

> Members and their guests are expected to wear conventional dress at all times in the Club.

Wisely unspecific! In practice, the word 'conventional' is taken to mean collar and tie, even though the latter may have been borrowed from the emergency stock in Hall Porter Harris's cupboard. Recently, after grave deliberation, the Committee decided that a roll-neck sweater might qualify—but only at breakfast-time and week-ends.

One observes that By-law F.8 is followed immediately by another reminding members that while they may bring their children in to meals, they are expected to make sure that the 'age, dress and behaviour of such children should not cause inconvenience to other members'. This rule was no doubt invoked when an allegation of 'Carnaby Street or beatnik-style attire' in the Drawing Room reached the Committee. Let it be recorded that the upshot was a charmingly phrased letter of apology by the ring-leader, dated from his public school.

A further instalment of this sartorial saga can be expected in the Third Edition (circa 1989).

Browsing through Club reports and Committee minutes in search of comfort for the nostalgic, I picked up the remarkable fact that in the year 1977 the Club spent no less than £22,000 on the purchase of '1975 and 1976 clarets. Also red burgundies and a pipe of Taylor's '75 vintage port'. Did this mean that members, against every modern trend, were regressing to that community of topers—not to say intoxicated swells—whom we glimpsed in Chapter 5? The facts are more prosaic; the Club does an excellent retail business in 'wines by the case', and these purchases were mainly to lay down stocks for the future.

The Library. The long and (in the past) not always happy story of the Club's book collection has been brought up to date in a pamphlet by Mr. Fergus Innes, Hon. Librarian, who has given the collection his loving care since 1962. It will be recalled that the sale of a large proportion of the books at the time of the move to Stratford Place turned out to have been rather too drastic and indiscriminate, with the result that the shelves in the new Library were by no means filled and many books which should have been retained were missing from them.

The process of recuperation has gone steadily forward. At least one volume which ought not to have been parted with, Beale's *Oriental Biographical Dictionary*, was discovered by Mr. Innes in a dealer's hands, still complete with its Oriental Club binding, and was somewhat expensively redeemed; other losses have been made good with duplicates. There have been fresh purchases, of course. Mr. Innes points out that the literature of the 'Raj' is so vast that any collection such as this must inevitably be 'somewhat haphazard', but it is strong in respect of certain key points in history—the trial of Warren Hastings, the wars with Tipu Sultan and his father Haidar Ali, the conquest and administration of Scinde, and the Indian Mutiny. Holdings in topography and natural history have been much strengthened and Eastern countries other than India have been given their due space.

At the time of writing the shelves (including new provision for books of what the original authors would *not* have described as 'coffee-table size') still have their gaps; however, these are rapidly diminishing, thanks to Hon. Librarian's no doubt enjoyable safaris in Charing Cross Road and elsewhere and the generous gifts of many members, notably Messrs D. A. Hackman and the late J. E. J. Taylor.

One conspicuous feature of the Library which ought to be recorded is the ever-growing array of contemporary books about the 'old days' in the East. Not long ago an Indian visitor to the Club expressed incredulity that there could be a public for this kind of thing; it had to be explained to him that in modern Britain the loss of former imperial grandeur seems to provoke nostalgia rather than resentment!

The Staff. The problems of manning a London club today remain much as they were in 1968, nor do they seem to have been lessened by the existence of a 'pool' of a million and a half unemployed. Wages in the catering industry have received a good deal of adverse publicity over the years, yet there are obviously severe limits on what it is possible for an institution like the Oriental to pay. When a vacancy for a Head Chef occurred a few years ago, exactly three applications were received.

Nevertheless the Club appears to be in a somewhat happier condition than many of its contemporaries. In the last paragraph of the original edition I expressed the hope that successors might yet be found to the little group of long-time employees who have been such a wonderful mainstay up till now. This hope has not been altogether disappointed. More than ten years' service has been notched up by such as Harry Cawley, Drawing Room Waiter (part-time from 1958, full-time 1963), Pilar Mirabent, Chambermaid

(1963), Bill Parsons, Basement Porter (1965), D. Plant, House Manager (1966), H. Giorgiou, Head-waiter (part-time 1964, full-time 1968), G. Bomba, Valet (1967), Joan Smith and Nellie Moran, Stillroom Maids (1967) and Peter Faventi, 2nd Chef (1968).

So far, of course, these are modest spells compared with those of the real 'old stagers', only one of whom has been lost to the Club since I last wrote. This is Jack Parsons, Head Valet, who retired in 1970. What the members thought about his long and most faithful service, going back to the year 1917, was shown by the £1,336.14 subscribed to his testimonial fund.

Among the others, first place, as ever, must be taken by 'Alice'. As time has gone on, she has become something of a celebrity beyond the confines of the Oriental Club, a subject for articles and interviews—*Woman's Realm* ('Women in a Man's World', 8 May 1968), features in *The Observer* (13 July 1975) and *Sunday Times* (7 March 1976) and so on. Finally she reached the apotheosis of a 'television personality' when on 29 October 1978 B.B.C. 2 gave peak time to a most engaging interview with her in the setting of the Oriental Club.

The Club itself was delighted to mark her completion of sixty years' service by the appropriate presentation of a gold Elephant brooch. And letters of gold, too, one feels, ought to be used for a passing reference in the Committee Minutes for 21 January 1976, where it is stated that one of the stolen clocks was '*missed by Alice at 6 a.m. on Friday*'.

The other veterans remain as in our first edition—Harris as Head Porter, Ramm[1] in the Bar and Kathleen King in the Cash Desk. Their years of service are (1978) 43, 42 and 38 respectively. The whole Club's debt to them is incalculable.

Reference to the older Club servants is a reminder of another modern problem—that of pensions. They are always difficult to organise for small groups, and though the senior staff will benefit from the scheme mentioned on p. 223, it has been decided that it

[1] A tremor ran through Stratford House in January 1975, when it was learned that Ramm had been knocked off the bike which has carried him between his home and the Club for so long. It was a nasty experience, but after not too great an interval, he came up smiling!

would be useless to contract out of the State system so far as the others are concerned.

The Stratford Place Estate. I took advantage of this 2nd edition to find out whether the research which goes on continuously into London's past had shed further light on the rather obscure early history of Stratford House and Stratford Place, and the conversion of the 'Banqueting House site' into Lord Aldborough's aristocratic building estate. I was not totally unrewarded. There is still no proof positive as to who was his Lordship's designer; however, Mr Howard Colvin, in the latest edition of his great work the *Biographical Dictionary of English Architects*, now devotes an entry to Richard Edwin (see p. 165 *et seq.*), and establishes him sufficiently as an architect in his own right to make it unnecessary for us to look beyond him[1].

Meanwhile the Record Office of the City of London has been cataloguing and indexing some of the Comptroller's Deeds, and in doing so has brought to the surface a series of documents relating to the Stratford Place development. The earliest, a building lease dating from 1772, the very year of the original grant of the Banqueting House lands, is chiefly memorable for a marginal sketch plan. This displays, a little west of the serpentine line which always indicates the course of the 'Aye Brook' (River Tyburn), another pencilled-in double line, straight as a ruler, and marked 'Course of the Aye Brook as altered by Mr. Stratford'. In the text, moreover, the western boundary of the estate is defined as 'formerly the centre or middle of the ancient course of the Aybrook, several times altered'. This is something quite new—the idea that, before 1772 even, the bed of the Tyburn had become strictly notional and the poor little stream had been moved hither and thither as though it was a mere sewer.

Skipping now to a renewal of the Banqueting House Grounds lease, granted to John Wingfield-Stratford as late as the year 1842, we find some most remarkable stipulations.

[1] Following an article on Stratford House in *The Antique Collector* (Feb.–March 1972) it was suggested that the architect might have been Richard Jupp, who later designed East India House, Leadenhall Street. The argument is purely stylistic, and does not seem very strong.

'Reserved out of the present Demise', says the document, 'is the ancient aqueduct running through the grounds hereby devised, belonging to the said Mayor and Commonalty and Citizens, and the reservoir to be made upon the said ground'. Even more specifically, an attached plan marks out an area now occupied by the rear portion of Lilley & Skinner's premises, including No. 19 Stratford Place, together with a strip south-westwards, and reserves the right to enter upon it,

> to dig and make a reservoir of reasonable dimensions for the reception of water instead of the conduits now or lately standing upon the ground hereby devised, and to place and lay pipes or other things necessary underground for conveying of water from the said reservoir and any of the springs and water works belonging to the said Mayor and Commonalty and Citizens and to repair and amend the same.

Well! Could it be that in Victoria's reign and seventy years after Lord Aldborough had built over the said ground, the City seriously contemplated reopening the mediaeval works which had ceased to supply the City long before his Lordship was born? It seems utterly impossible. And yet, looking back through some of the earlier leases now brought to light, while the reference to the 'ancient aqueduct' and to the 'reservoir to be constructed in place of the conduits' had become common form, re-copied from document to document, the 1842 demise is far more specific than its predecessors, making detailed reference to 'access along a covered way at the rear of the area on the West Side of Stratford Place, occupied by the Earl of Wemyss and March'. Now the Wemyss family did not assume the additional title of Earls of March (in somewhat disputable circumstances) until 1810, so this reference cannot be something left over from the old 18th century leases. On the other hand, they *did* succeed the Pouletts at No. 19 Stratford Place in about 1820 and were still in possession long after 1842. And there, I am afraid, a very intriguing mystery must be left for the present.

The renewal of the lease to Mr. Wingfield-Stratford was for a period of 61 years at £147 ground rent per annum and comprehended of course the whole Stratford Place complex, stretching right back to the end of the Mews which stood on what we currently call the 'Debenham Car Park site'. This renewal would have taken him up to the year 1900, but we know how in the early 1880s the Wingfield-Stratford interest was disposed of (pp. 185–6). Thereafter the various occupiers became responsible for paying their own ground rents. The Leslies and their successors at Stratford House and No. 12 must have had a further renewal or renewals from the City, since it was not until 1930 that Lord Derby finally acquired the freehold of the historic ground on which his mansion stood.

Unfortunately the suggestion to the Greater London Council that his Lordship should be commemorated with a 'blue plaque' (p. 201) was eventually turned down.

Index

Members of the Oriental Club are in italics; 'Oriental Club' is abbreviated to 'O.C.'.